al Settlements in Pennsylvania, North America

COUNT ZINZENDORF

Count Zinzendorf

by

JOHN R. WEINLICK

Illustrations drawn by Fred Bees

ABINGDON PRESS
New York — Nashville

COUNT ZINZENDORF

SET UP, PRINTED, AND BOUND BY THE
PARTHENON PRESS, AT NASHVILLE,
TENNESSEE, UNITED STATES OF AMERICA

CONTENTS

1

THE ERA INTO WHICH
ZINZENDORF WAS BORN

A man destined to be great becomes so irrespective of the time in which he lives. But the time does determine the line along which his gifts express themselves. Count Nicolaus Ludwig von Zinzendorf had the genius to achieve in any generation. Because he happened to be born in Germany in the dawn of the eighteenth century, he became the apostle of Moravian Pietism, a way of life which that century needed as one of its several ingredients. The Protestant Reformation of the sixteenth century had struck Europe with terrific impact. Yet within a relatively short time, about a half century, it was stalemated. Lines between Roman Catholics and Protestants were more or less permanently drawn. Each of the emerging Protestant groups, Lutheran, Calvinist, Anglican, and Radical, became absorbed in its organizational and theological problems. In Lutheranism especially, a scholasticism developed which was not much different in spirit from medieval scholasticism. The wars of religion absorbed much of the latter half of the sixteenth and the first half of the seventeenth centuries. A fuller development of Protestantism was to be that of a delayed reaction which did not gain momentum until the eighteenth century. It was then that the full implications of the Protestant revolt—rationalism, individualism, freedom of worship, political freedoms, separation of church and state—came to vigorous expression in the Western world. The eighteenth century, consequently, from the modern point of view remains a fruitful one with a galaxy of brilliant figures.

One of the great forces of the era was Pietism, a spiritual renewal arising within German Lutheranism in the late seventeenth century and spreading to other nations. Though in a narrow sense the term "Pietism" is associated with Germany, it is a type of Christianity not confined to any place or period; for it means a Christianity of experience as opposed to emphasis upon creed and outer conformity. Another name for it is "enthusiasm." Germany, prostrated by the Thirty Years' War, was in need of religious revival. Luther's revolt had arisen out of an experience of a vital relationship between the individual believer and his God. Following that there arose the problem of defining this experience and the task of organizing a church. Theologians and territorial rulers were not long in bringing to a halt what Luther had begun. The authority of the state and a body of dogmatic theology told the people of what Christianity consisted. Emphasis was upon pure doctrine and the Sacraments as the constituent elements of the Christian life. The layman's role was the entirely passive one of accepting the dogmas which he heard expounded from the pulpit, of partaking faithfully of the Sacraments, of sharing in the ordinances of the church. That kind of religion could not satisfy a crushed and poverty-stricken people.

Reaction came in the form of Pietism, a return to the inwardness of the original Lutheran revolt. It took various forms as time went on, but it had at least three general characteristics common to all its manifestations. There was the mystical element in it, with its emphasis upon emotional experience. People turned to a simpler and more heartfelt expression of religion, not dependent upon intellectual formulation. Growing out of this experiential emphasis was the practical emphasis of religion in terms of purity of life and active benevolence. The underprivileged at home and the heathen overseas were equally the concern of Pietism. There was, finally, a rediscovery of the doctrine of the priesthood of all believers. Laymen, under its impetus, began to take an active part in the church, to read the Bible, to pray, to share their religion with like-minded friends in extra-church meetings.

Whatever the various springs of Pietism were—Anabaptist influence, Roman Catholic mystical piety, Puritanism, the mysticism of Jacob Böhme—its immediate father was Philip Jacob Spener, Lutheran clergyman, born in Alsace in 1635. His early reading of Arndt's *True Christianity* roused him, as did treatises of English Puritans. His student years at Strassburg impressed him with the greater attention to biblical exegesis and church discipline in the Reformed Church as compared to his own. Further studies in Geneva, Basel, and Tübingen deepened these impressions. Yet he was not estranged from Lutheranism.

Following an assistant pastorate in Strassburg, Spener assumed his first full pastorate in 1661 at Frankfort, where he began to carry out some of his wished-for reforms. He avoided dogmatic dissertations in his sermons, setting forth, instead, simply the saving power of the gospel. He improved catechetical instruction which had fallen into the indifferent hands of schoolmasters. Most far-reaching of all, in 1670 he began holding private meetings at his home for Bible reading, prayer, and discussion of the Sunday sermons, the object being to deepen the spiritual life of individuals. It was these conventicles from which the name derives, for they were called *collegia pietatis,* literally "associations of piety," hence the term "Pietist."

Spener was soon attracting wide attention, particularly after the publication of his *Pia Desideria* or *True Evangelical Churches,* in which he called attention to the evils of his time and set forth his plans for improving the situation. He attacked government interference in the church, theological controversy, and the unworthy lives of both clergy and laity. Among his proposed reforms he included his conventicles, which he called *ecclesiolae in ecclesia,* little churches within the church. He insisted that Christianity was more than intellectual knowledge. Better training of the clergy should include more attention to the practical aspects of the Christian life. He called for sermons less learned and more devotional. Basic in his thought was that the Christian life begins with a conscious new birth. He espoused an asceticism similar to that of the English Puritans, for he rejected the theater, dances, and cards, and called for moderation in food, drink, and dress.

The favorable response he received was matched by equally wide disapproval. Lutheranism was soon divided into opposing sides. The fact that some overzealous followers, despite his protests, withdrew from the church played into the hands of those who feared the separatism inherent in his program. As the movement spread, legal measures were passed here and there, restricting conventicles. The city of Frankfort itself took such action. Spener was happy to accept a call, in 1686, to Dresden as court preacher. There his experience was similar. The Saxon clergy looked upon him as an intruder. The two Saxon universities, Leipzig and Wittenberg, opposed him. He incurred the displeasure of the elector by his pastoral rebuke of the ruler's drunkenness. He became involved in a lively literary controversy over the merits of Pietism.

Spener's last post was that of provost at the Nicolaus Church in

Berlin, where he went, in 1691, at the invitation of Frederick, elector of Brandenburg. The court at Brandenburg adhered to the Reformed Church but was seeking to establish peace between Lutherans and Reformed within its realm. Because Frederick saw in the unionism and practical tendencies of Pietism an aid to his efforts, he heartily supported Spener. The years in Berlin were for the father of Pietism, up to his death in 1705, the happiest years of his life.

The real center of Pietist development was the University of Halle, founded in 1691. There, under August Hermann Francke, the movement became efficiently organized, and there its benevolent enterprises reached their height. Francke did more for the development of Pietism than even Spener himself. The son of an official in the service of Duke Ernst the Pious, Francke was born in Lübeck in 1663. Even as a child he was under the influence of the religious spirit of the court at Gotha. Following his theological education at Erfurt and Leipzig, he became an instructor in the latter institution. Prior to this Pietism had made its way into Leipzig, and Francke was one of those drawn into its circle. The injection of this spirit into his lectures and his organization of a *collegium philobiblicum* for Bible study and devotional purposes created serious tension within the university. Measures were taken to restrict his activities. Forced to leave Leipzig in 1699, Francke went to Erfurt, where he spent another uncomfortable year and a half. Through Spener he obtained a professorship in the new university at Halle and a pastorate in the suburb of Glaucha, where he went in 1692. From the first Francke dominated the theological scene in Halle, and until his death in 1727 kept the institution the center of Pietism.

Francke was more than a professor of theology. His charity school, established in 1695, was so successful that it led in 1698 to the founding of his famous paedagogium. Soon were added an orphan asylum, a home for the poor, a foreign-mission society, a seminary for teachers, a printing office and bookstore, an apothecary shop, and an infirmary. His friend Baron Carl von Canstein established a Bible house which was renowned for its publication and circulation of the Scriptures in inexpensive editions. The influence of this cluster of institutions centering around the university was tremendous. Gifts flowed in from all over Germany. A remarkable number of nobles were Francke's patrons, and many of them sent their sons to his paedagogium and, from there, to the university.

A notable feature of Halle was its interest in foreign missions, then unknown among Protestants except for the efforts of a few scattered individuals residing in European colonial possessions. When Frederick IV of Denmark wished to send missionaries to his possession in India, he turned to Halle to find them. It was from here that Bartholomew Ziegenbalg and Henry Plütschau went to Tranquebar in 1706. They were the first of a line of missionaries sent out from this center, long before the beginning in 1793 of the foreign-mission movement associated with William Carey.

Apart from Halle the Pietist awakening had its strongest following in Württemberg, where from the first it had less official opposition than in other parts of Germany. Württemberg Pietism developed along its own lines, and, in general, was of a more tolerant spirit than that of Halle. Depending less upon the sponsorship of the nobility than in central and northern Germany, it was more a people's movement. Nor did it tend to divide church people into converted and unconverted as rigidly as in the case of Halle Pietism. It shared some of the gentler qualities of the South German temperament as compared to that of the North. The University of Tübingen became a stronghold of Württemberg Pietism.

Spener meant simply to be an orthodox Lutheran in harmony with the doctrinal standards of his church. But the reformation he sought involved a far deeper revolution than he had anticipated. Pietism was to become a mighty stream accomplishing more than it hoped, but at the same time attracting a host of fanatics and obscurantists. A higher quality clergy, better preaching, better Christian training of the young, were among its fruits. It brought the laity into a more active share in church life. It spread the use of the Scriptures and the practice of the devotional life. It did not escape the censoriousness for which it had originally attacked the theologians. It became narrow in its insistence on conscious conversion as the only entrance to the Christian life. It produced few intellectual leaders. But the assets far outweigh the liabilities. Statistics are of little value in trying to appraise the extent of its influence, so subtly was its leavening character diffused throughout Europe.

All of this is basic to an understanding of Zinzendorf. The Moravian Church, a renewal of the Bohemian Brethren, for which he was so largely responsible, is to a large degree another phase of Pietism, beside those of Halle and Württemberg. The career of the Saxon count must be viewed in the light of the fact that he was one of the thousands in the grip of this revival of spiritual life within German Protestantism. Had it not been for the coming of the surviving remnant of the Bohemian Brethren into his life, almost by accident, no separate church body would have grown out of his religious activities. In all probability he would have carried on his program within the framework of the state church. As a matter of fact, part of the Moravian movement through the years to this day has maintained that status.

Zinzendorf was a seminal mind who brought much that was original and fresh to the church life of his day. At the same time we must not ignore what was happening all around him and what had been happening before his career began. The spiritual awakening which had taken hold of many of the nobility, of which his family was a part, helped to shape his development. Much in the life of Zinzendorf, both good and bad, that impresses the modern mind was not exclusively Zinzendorfian at all but typical of a phase of the age in which he lived. The count, with his native gifts, winsome personality, and driving energy, brought to Pietism a vigor unmatched by that of any of its other leaders. Also, the organization of the Moravian Church, the only denomination growing out of the movement, gave a direction, a permanence, and an international spread to Herrnhut Pietism not possible in the case of that Pietism which lacked such an organization.

2

FAMILY BACKGROUND

Shortly following the birth of Count Nicolaus Ludwig von Zinzendorf his mother wrote in the family Bible:

On May 26, in the year 1700, on Wednesday evening about six o'clock, Almighty God blessed me in Dresden with the gift of my first-born son, Nicolaus Ludwig. The Father of mercy govern the heart of this child that he may walk blamelessly in the path of virtue. May he allow no evil to have control over him, and may his path be fortified in his Word. Thus that which is good will not fail toward him, neither in this temporal world nor beyond in eternity.[1]

Only six weeks later the infant's father lay fatally ill of tuberculosis. Among his final words was a blessing spoken over the sleeping child: "My dear son, I should bless you who are already more blessed than I who am about to stand before the throne of Jesus." He died on July 9, 1700, at the age of thirty-eight. His widow was twenty-five.

Both piety on the part of his immediate family and a distinguished ancestry were the count's heritage. The house of Zinzendorf was of remote antiquity in the duchy of Austria. Already in the eleventh century it was numbered among the twelve noble houses supporting the Austrian dynasty. Nicolaus Ludwig was of the twenty-second generation from the time of Ehrenhold, its founder. In 1662 Emperor Leopold conferred upon its head the dignity of count of the Holy Roman Empire. When Protestantism came, part of the family embraced it, the first being John who died in 1552. Some of his descendants distinguished themselves by their adherence to the Protestant faith in a land where being a Protestant was a handicap. In 1661 Maximilian Erasmus von Zinzendorf, grandfather of Nicolaus Ludwig, seeking greater freedom

[1] Gneomar Ernst von Natzmer, *Die Jugend Zinzendorfs,* p. 1.

of conscience during the Counter Reformation, sold his Austrian estates and removed to Oberbürg in Franconia. There he died in 1672, leaving three daughters and two sons. The daughters married into the Franconian families of Ortenburg, Polheim, and Castell. The two sons entered the service of the elector of Saxony. The older, Otto Christian, a Saxon field marshal, died childless in 1718. The younger, George Ludwig, privy councilor at Dresden, was the father of Nicolaus Ludwig by a second marriage. Surviving children of the first marriage were Frederick Christian and a daughter, Susanne Louise, who subsequently married a Count Ortenburg.

From his mother's side of the family the count was equally well born. The house of Gersdorf was outstanding both for talent and piety. The Gersdorfs, like the Zinzendorfs, were under the sway of Spener's Pietism. Baroness Charlotte Justine, daughter of Nicolaus von Gersdorf, prefect of Upper Lusatia, shared the devotion of George Ludwig von Zinzendorf to the things of the spirit. Philip Jacob Spener himself was one of the godparents at the baptism of their son.

From the paternal family seems to have come a delicate constitution. The same illness which took his father prematurely threatened the son for his first twenty years. The Zinzendorfs were not conspicuous for longevity. Maximilian Erasmus, the grandfather who transferred the one branch of the family from Austria to Germany, died at thirty-nine; and George Ludwig, the count's father, as noted, died at thirty-eight. A glance at the Zinzendorf genealogical table betrays that the line shared in the excessively high infant-mortality rate of premodern days.

The record on the Gersdorf side is better. His maternal grandparents lived into their seventies. His mother survived him by three years, dying at the age of eighty-nine. The evidence suggests also that more of the genius of the count came through his mother than through his father.

The grandmother, Baroness Henrietta Catherine von Gersdorf, had both talent and the natural drive to use it. In cultured society she drew recognition as a poetess in German and Latin, as an artist in oils, and as a musician. In 1729, three years after her death, Professor Paul Anton of Halle did her the honor of publishing a collection of her hymns and poems. She was as much at home in Latin dogmatic theology as in managing a household on a baronial scale. She read the Scriptures in the original Hebrew and Greek. Her influence in court circles was extended through her extensive correspondence. Her doors were always open to the meetings of Pietists, the *ecclesiola in ecclesia*. Spener,

Francke, Anton were her frequent guests. She contributed liberally to their projects. She assumed a sense of responsibility toward the widowed, the orphaned, and the underprivileged in her community. Following the death of her husband in 1702, she proved herself fully capable of directing the affairs of a family whose obligations involved all that goes with nobility. If the death of the infant count's father was a tragedy, its compensation was that it brought Zinzendorf under the direct care of this remarkable woman. The fruitful environment with which she surrounded him was thus to be added to what he got from her by way of heredity.

THE BARONESS GERSDORF

Her daughter, Charlotte Justine, who became the count's mother, was not of the same caliber but still superior enough to merit attention. She, too, was conversant in theology and learned in Greek and Latin, which book learning in the case of the Gersdorfs was more than the polite finish of cultured society. She had, along with a trained intellect, a knowledge of the ways of the world, sound judgment, poise, and a systematic way of procedure in whatever she did. Having the count with her only during his first four years, she nevertheless had considerable influence upon him, even during the years when she was the head of a home with children by her second marriage. Though personal contacts with her first-born son were infrequent, she shared through correspondence in the important decisions pertaining to his training. He sought her advice on many matters as long as he lived. Her place in his life seems to have been underemphasized in most treatments of the count's life.

3

LIFE IN A COUNTRY CASTLE

George Ludwig von Zinzendorf had appointed as guardian of his children Otto Christian, his brother the field marshal, who took the two older ones into his home. Nicolaus Ludwig went with his mother to her parents, living in Dresden where the baron occupied his position with the government.

Bereavement was aggravated by financial stringency for the widow. Means there were in the Zinzendorf family, but not immediately available. The count was not to receive his full inheritance until he came of age. Meanwhile there was only a limited income, doled out by the guardian, for the son. Though her parents were generous, the young baroness was a woman of pride, sensitive about her predicament.

Nicolaus von Gersdorf, his wife's senior by nineteen years, died in 1702. The following year the widow took possession of her ancestral home, the castle of Gross-Hennersdorf in Upper Lusatia, some sixty miles to the east of Dresden. With her to this former hunting lodge of Bohemian kings went her daughter with the three-year-old count, and another daughter, eighteen-year-old Henrietta Sophie. Here in the remote fastness of a country castle were to be spent the most formative years of Count Zinzendorf.

The mother did not remain there long, for in December of 1704 she married the Prussian field marshal Dubislaw Gneomar von Natzmer, a childless widower of fifty. Thereafter her permanent residence was in Berlin. Spiritually the count's mother was as much one with her second husband as she was with her first. Von Natzmer, too, was a Pietist, an intimate friend of Baron Canstein, an associate of Francke at Halle. It was a happy marriage of thirty-five years, blessed with two sons, born in 1705 and 1709 respectively. Both preceded their parents in death in the year 1738. A year later the mother became a widow for the second time.

THE CASTLE AT GROSS-HENNERSDORF

One of the striking aspects of Zinzendorf's references to his childhood

THE COUNT AS A BOY OF THREE

is the omission of references to other children in his grandmother's castle. His biographers, following his lead, give us the impression that his was a lonely childhood. It obviously was, but not entirely because there were no other children around. Hennersdorf, though remotely situated, bustled with activity. Friends and relatives visited frequently, as did others connected with the grandmother's far-flung benevolent activities. In the case of the relatives, at least, children were often along with them.

The older of the two von Natzmer boys, the count's half brother, was born at Hennersdorf in 1705. Four years later, before Lutz (the young count's nickname) left for school at Halle, this half brother spent considerable time there while his mother was accompanying her husband on a tour of duty. It was during the period when the third son was born to her. Zinzendorf speaks much of his close relations with his aunt Henrietta. He ignores the presence of an uncle, Nicolaus, only twelve years his senior, who did not leave Hennersdorf for the university until 1706. There must have been other children there for considerable periods of time.

Nevertheless, the picture we have of the count is that of a delicate, precocious boy, either surrounded with pious adults or alone with his imagination. Tutors were there to do for him what teachers do for less privileged children in classrooms in company with other children. At least such was the case until after his tenth birthday. The truth of the matter is, no doubt, that much of his loneliness was due to his own inclinations. Apparently caring little for normal play life, he was attracted to older people and hence lived in an adult world.

Let Zinzendorf speak for himself in describing his early inner life and experience:

Up to my tenth year there was more care bestowed upon me by way of shielding me from evil influences, and fostering in my heart the work of God's grace than would have been possible anywhere except in a well-ordered church of Jesus Christ. I can say with truth that my heart was religiously inclined as far back as I can recollect; and even at such times when refractory, proud, and peevish humors seized upon me, and vain and foolish pride of rank beset me, my heart's affections never departed from my Saviour, and there always remained within me a deep and tender interest in his cause on earth. I dearly loved the good old church hymns and vastly enjoyed hearing them sung in the churches. . . .

During my stay with my revered grandmother two circumstances occurred which decided my whole career. When I was six years old, my preceptor, Herr Christian Ludwig Edeling, after a service of three years, took leave of me. In doing so he spoke a few words to me about the Saviour and his merits; and in what sense I belonged to him and to him only. These words made so deep and lively an impression on me that I fell into a long protracted paroxysm of tears, during which I firmly resolved to live for him alone, who had laid down his life for me. My very dear Aunt Henrietta endeavored to keep me in this frame of mind by often speaking to me loving and evangelical words. I opened all my heart to hear, and we then spread my case before the Lord in prayer. I was not in the least afraid of her. I freely told her all about myself, both bad and good. My open and candid intercourse with her was of so great benefit to me that I could never forget it. This confidential interchange of thought and feeling prompted all my endeavors in later years to establish bands or societies for mutual conference and edification.

In my eighth year an old hymn, which my grandmother sang on retiring to rest, led me into a long train of thought as I lay sleepless on my couch. The most subtle and refined speculations that atheists have ever invented, spontaneously arose in my mind and threw me into no little perplexity. This temptation, however, had the good effect that, when in later years these selfsame cavils and speculations were again thrust upon me, they seemed to me to be very shallow and superficial, and made no impression whatever on my mind.[1]

One of the significant references in this autobiographical excerpt is that concerning Henrietta. It was she perhaps more than any other who compensated for a void in the boy's life. Fifteen years his senior,

[1] *Büdingische Sammlungen,* translated by F. F. Hagen, *Old Landmarks,* p. 120.

she was old enough to guide him but young enough to understand him. She was part mother and part older sister to him. She must have been a great help to a boy whose intellectual grasp of things seemed so much ahead of his capacity to adjust emotionally.

Various other items fill in the portrait of religious precocity. At age four he had a remarkable grasp of Christian teaching. Very early also he came to treasure Luther's *Smaller Catechism* second only to the Bible itself. This high regard for Luther continued throughout his life. At church he was often present for the Lord's Supper, even before he himself was old enough to partake. His thoughts were entirely directed to it, and he felt a reverence toward those whom he saw approaching the altar. He early believed that in partaking of the Sacrament the individual became united with God himself. He was attentive to public prayers to the point of being able to repeat them at home. He not only loved to hear of the Saviour but also to speak of him. Failing an audience he would speak alone to an imaginary one. Illustrative of his early environment is a visit of Spener, in the course of which the man laid his hands in blessing upon the boy, then only four, in the hope that he would further the kingdom of Jesus Christ. The incident remained indelibly impressed upon him.

In 1706 the Swedes under Charles XII overran Saxony. A detachment of their army came to Hennersdorf to commandeer supplies. Entering the castle, they burst into the room where the six-year-old count happened to be at his customary devotions. They almost forgot their mission, so awed were they as they heard the boy speak and pray. The incident was prophetic of the way the count was to move others with the depth of his religious experience the rest of his sixty years.

It was more than intense Christian training to which the boy was exposed at Hennersdorf. After all, the tradition on both sides of the family was to rule. Feudalism in eighteenth-century Germany had still some generations left before its course was run. The houses of the nobility which fostered the conventicles of the Pietists did not cast aside their hereditary role in society. If anything, Pietism deepened their devotion to their calling as rulers. Lutz was not allowed to forget that he was a count, and it was as such that he was expected to serve when his turn came. His tutors were under direction to teach him the niceties of court circles. This included mastery of manners, proper dress, proper conversation, a variety of social skills. It carried with it the obligation to become an educated person. For the count it meant long hours of study in basic subjects preparatory to further schooling. In an account of his boyhood, written by himself twenty years later, he says that between the ages of eight and nine he studied history and languages diligently in order that some day he might administer a land worthily. Nor was Lady Gersdorf one to allow affection to express itself in the form of indulgence. Those who rule must prepare for it early through self-discipline. This self-discipline came hard for her grandson. His mother once remarked of him, "He is like tinder."

The union of piety and nobility is one of the keys to an appreciation of the career of Zinzendorf. His name carried prestige and gained him entry wherever his zeal drove him. Yet the two elements frequently clashed, within the count himself and in the reactions of others. A full-time religious vocation was not socially acceptable for men of rank. Throughout his life this fact caused many, including his most pious relatives, to regard his enterprises as an intrusion into a realm reserved for the regular clergy. His earliest vocational choice was that of a clergyman, but family pressure kept him from carrying out this resolve for many years. Not until he was thirty-four did he take this bold step. An innovator, he was at the same time loyally conformist to the state church. He constantly sought to keep his religious activities within the status of legality. Despite obviously sincere efforts to be one with the humble Moravian Brethren, he succeeded only on the purely religious level. In whatever he did Zinzendorf could not escape being a count.

The years in Hennersdorf deprived the boy of a normal childhood, but that is what made them years of destiny. Unwittingly, the grandmother, Aunt Henrietta, pious tutors, visiting Pietists, diverted the count from becoming just another member of Germany's ruling class. He often declared in later life that it was owing to this careful education under his grandmother's direction that in his mature years he could relish nothing but the doctrine of Jesus Christ and his death and merits. The piety that his superiors intended to be part of his equipment as a devoted public official was to become his vocation. The culture which was intended to grace court circles was to be deflected into the society of refugee peasants from Moravia and Bohemia.

Hennersdorf laid the foundation for a conception of Christianity which was to be his contribution to Protestantism. His precocious attachment to Christ, deepened by his loneliness, was to become part of his philosophy of Christian nurture. The child is to know Christ from earliest infancy, a deviation from the Pietism of Francke, with its emphasis upon a sense of sin and the struggle preceding conversion. Christ as the daily companion, Christ the elder brother, became the motivating force of Moravianism at its best. A certain inwardness and tenderness which Zinzendorf detected in himself, he ascribed to his training under women's direction. Perhaps this is part of the explanation for the gentleness of Moravian Pietism. Already in these preschool years he imbibed catholicity in the religious life of the castle. The baroness was on cordial terms with others besides Halle Pietists. She welcomed orthodox Lutherans as well. She had respect for Calvinists and Roman Catholics. There could be differing intellectual formulations of Christianity but only one religion of the heart.

Spangenberg, who knew the count better than anyone else, finds three pillars in his Christianity, which, established in childhood, grew in strength up to the very time of his death: ". . . his deep impressions of the suffering and merits of Jesus; his firm determination to be wholly his who died for him; and in consequence thereof, his unreserved and plain conversation with his nearest friends." Concerning the last, Spangenberg says further that one of his own first impressions of the count at Herrnhut was the freedom with which he could converse with individuals on intimate matters pertaining to the soul. The serious conversations of the boy in a country castle with Henrietta had borne fruit.

4

SCHOOL DAYS AT HALLE

Early childhood at Hennersdorf was decisive for the career which Zinzendorf eventually chose for himself. It hardly provided the kind of training to fit a boy for life at a boarding school. Physically frail, sheltered, and without adequate experience in the give-and-take of contact with other children, he was totally unfit for what lay ahead when he was sent off to Halle in August of 1710. The first five of his six years there were among the most trying days of his life. He fared badly alike at the hands of instructors and fellow pupils. Fortunately what he lacked in the way of physical stamina and the right kind of social experience, he made up for in inner resource. Halle taught him how to get along with others, without destroying his faith in the continuing presence of Christ. His stay there advanced him far toward the goal ahead.

The decision to send Lutz to Halle was one in which grandmother, mother, and stepfather heartily concurred. Francke's paedagogium would give him contact with many sons of other nobles of pietistic inclinations. Only his anti-Pietist guardian demurred. Lady von Natzmer in person escorted her son, accompanied by a tutor named Christian Homann, to Halle. Following the accepted custom for sons of the nobility, he was to have his own tutor who also rendered service to the school as a whole. Both this tutor and the one who succeeded him two years later made the problem of the boy's adjustment still more difficult.

His mother's parting advice to Francke added an additional handicap. She described her son as a youth of great abilities, but one who would have to be kept in check, lest he become proud and presume upon his talents. It took Francke more than three years to overcome his low opinion of the character of his young charge. Consequently, in any subsequent difficulty which the boy got into, the head of the school himself was usually against him. Little did the mother realize how her advice played into the hands of Francke's concept of man's natural state as depraved. Beneath the count's zeal to bear witness to his Christian faith, Francke saw only corrupt human nature in need of conversion.

Truth there was in Lady von Natzmer's description of him. Zinzendorf himself says: "I was not free of pride. But it was a pride with reference to my rank as one of the nobility. It did not carry over into things pertaining to the affairs of Christ." He admits that his mother's good intentions had the opposite effect with reference to this pride. Having heard the description given of himself, he had all the more reason to believe that he was an unusual person.

The effort to humble him began immediately with his being put into classes lower than his previous preparation warranted. He was assigned menial tasks and punished for trivial offenses. To physical punishment was added ridicule, such as hanging imitation donkey ears upon him and making him stand in front of the room. Taunted on one such occasion, the count replied in Latin: "This shame shall not crush me. On the contrary, it shall raise me up." When fellow students through their badgering would prevent him from getting to class on time, he would be punished for his tardiness. He says that he had to endure daily the torture of the heartless horseplay of his fellows. It is easy to understand why such should have been the case. The conceit of a precocious child is not palatable to his peers, particularly if accompanied by sweet piety, genuine as such piety may be, and if the child, in addition, be frail and sheltered.

Limited facilities in the paedagogium made it necessary for some of the pupils to find accommodation in private homes. For the first two years Zinzendorf and his tutor were lodged in the home of a tailor. Along with others he took his noon meal with Francke himself, where the boys were seated according to their rank as sons of the nobility. This close contact with Francke at the dinner table, as we shall see, proved decisive for the future. It probably did not improve his relationship with the student body.

Homann left Halle rather abruptly after two years with Zinzendorf, leaving the boy for some weeks without tutorial supervision. At this same time Francke's orphanage moved into its new quarters, and the old quarters were turned over to the paedagogium. Zinzendorf was lodged in this old dormitory for a year, until the fall of 1713, when he moved into a newly completed one.

A considerable correspondence involving the family, Francke, and

Canstein ensued in the process of finding a successor to Homann. Canstein was consulted because of his close friendship with von Natzmer. Eventually Daniel Crisenius, already employed at Halle, was engaged. Not a Pietist at heart, he had, nevertheless, won his way into the confidence of Francke and others. Grandmother Gersdorf herself took part in the exchange of letters and expressed her distrust of Crisenius. She was personally unacquainted with him but had reports about him. In a letter to Francke she relates what she had heard concerning his conduct in the home of one who had befriended him. He had been arrogant as a guest and rude to and demanding of the servants. After a lengthy stay he had left without ever thanking his host.

Such was the grandmother's report of the tutor to be engaged for the count. It is doubtful whether she, with her gracious tact, would ordinarily have written such a letter. But it appears that her grandson was being blamed for the family's doubts about the man, through his carrying tales home from school by letter and by what he had told a relative who visited him. She wished it known that this was not the source of her information. At any rate Crisenius was chosen despite her doubts.

This was at the beginning of Zinzendorf's third year and about the time that the school authorities' estimate of him was at its lowest. In an exchange of letters Canstein and Francke seriously entertained the thought of returning him to his family because they were having such difficulty with him. They mention disobedience, lying, hypocrisy, vanity, troublemaking. They reveal that von Natzmer had raised the question of whether his education should not be turned over to his guardian, the elder Count Zinzendorf, since he had opposed his nephew's going to Halle in the first place and was refusing to contribute to the cost of his schooling. In the discussion over the matter Canstein expresses his low opinion of the guardian: "Though he amounts to nothing, he does hate vanity and lying, and would try to break the young count of it. At least he would use force in his attempt, the authority for which does not exist at Halle." Canstein's estimate of the uncle was not shared by others. It appears to have been the prejudice of a Pietist toward one who had no sympathy for Pietism.

Toward the end of the year 1712 Zinzendorf's mother and grandmother planned for him to visit Hennersdorf for a few weeks. The anxiety over his trouble at school seemed to deepen Lady Gersdorf's affection for him. More serious, his health was a matter of continuing concern. However, Francke and Canstein, who consulted each other frequently in matters pertaining to the count, decided against the visit at that time. Perhaps they feared that too close a contact with the family at the moment would not be for the best interests either of the boy or of the school. Their problem was not only to deal wisely with their pupil but also to maintain the good will of such influential patrons.

The visit did take place the following summer and turned out to be a prolonged one, due to the boy's ill health. In the company of Crisenius the count arrived at Hennersdorf in late June of 1713 and returned to Halle in late September. Under his grandmother's watchful eye he continued his studies with Crisenius. She wrote to Francke about his physical condition, mentioning her concern over his inherited weakness of the lungs and reporting that he had had several hemorrhages. She also spoke about his further instruction in French, asking for more advanced work as his class seemed too elementary for him. Included was advice concerning his living quarters in view of his physical condition. Upon the count's return to school, Francke saw to it that the suggestion pertaining to his French lessons was carried out.

His return from Hennersdorf seemed to be the beginning of better days for him at Halle, but the way was still rough. His mother and stepfather visited him over the Christmas season of the year 1713. Other relatives and friends came together, and the occasion took on the nature of a family reunion. This visit further improved the boy's situation, for there was from this point on a change in Francke's attitude. Zinzendorf was given more liberties than he had hitherto. In the new quarters he had a roommate for the remainder of his school days.

However, Crisenius was still difficult to get along with. He even stooped to contemptible trickery to get his charge into trouble. Having advised the boy to write to his guardian about his severe treatment, he intercepted the letter and carried it to Inspector Freyer, who became further prejudiced against the count. Crisenius then threatened him with severe discipline if he told or wrote to anyone about what had happened. When later Zinzendorf was assigned a personal servant, Crisenius saw to it that the attendant should do nothing without first consulting Crisenius. He went out of his way to countermand the count's instructions to his servant.

Francke's changing attitude was helpful. On one occasion when Crisenius lodged a complaint against his charge, Francke told him not always to complain but to help himself. Even Inspector Freyer was beginning to doubt the methods of the tutor and advised him to deal with Zinzendorf not only with "sharpness and accuracy" but always with the "proper caution" in the best interests of his pupil.

Much has been said concerning Zinzendorf's personal problems at school. What about his academic progress? The evidence is clear that he was a student far above average in ability, though not so in application. According to Spangenberg he studied out of a sense of duty rather than ardor. His preoccupation with things religious kept him from putting academic work on a level of highest importance. Yet his progress was quite acceptable in most of his subjects. He did well in Greek, learning to read the New Testament and Greek classics with ease. In his sixteenth year he had advanced to the point of being able to give an oration in Greek. His progress in Latin was even better. Given any subject to speak on by way of exercise, he was able to extemporize fluently in Latin. French was as natural to him as his native German. He did poorly in three years of Hebrew study. Poetry was a field in which he excelled. Having a genius for poetic composition, he was often able to compose faster than he could put his thoughts on paper, a gift he retained for life.

That Zinzendorf did well in his studies as a whole is revealed in the fact that in his last year at Halle he and a Hungarian nobleman, Johann von Jony, were together put into a class called the *selecta classa,* a sort of postgraduate group for those who had completed the program which the school had to offer but who were considered still too young for the university. In this class he studied in a cursory manner academic theology, jurisprudence, philosophy, and science.

The count's own version of what once happened to him at age fifteen tells much about the youth's aptitudes:

In the year 1715 it pleased God for the first time to cross my natural pride. I had often pronounced public orations in Latin, German, French, and Greek languages, but from a certain kind of presumption at solemn examination, I had not learned by heart my oration, consisting of three hundred verses, but confided in my having composed them; and in the presence of the marquis of Bayreuth, the University of Halle, and many other persons of distinction, toward the end of the oration I found myself at a nonplus, although the auditory did not observe it, yet I perceived a divine caution therein. Since that time I have lost my passion to excel and have begun to satisfy myself with doing my duty.[1]

[1] Augustus Gottlieb Spangenberg, *Leben Zinzendorfs,* tr. Nyberg, I, 66.

Seen in perspective, the years in Halle were not as unhappy as some of the count's own appraisals and those of his biographers would lead us to believe. The negative side had its positive counterpart, much of the evidence for which comes from Zinzendorf himself. He was long in becoming adjusted to the school, but in the process he did develop some intimate associations of lifelong duration. As expected, it was with those to whom he was drawn through a mutual sharing of Christian experience. At a Pietist school it would have been strange had there not been other boys who had his religious outlook. At the same time we cannot help inferring that there must have been many who reacted against the intense religious atmosphere of the institution. Piety had its detractors within the very walls of the place which specialized in it.

The genuineness of the boy's religious life could not help breaking down barriers in the course of time. In line with the prevailing pattern of what Pietists were doing everywhere, he took the initiative in gathering small groups of boys for prayer and testimony. If the modern man smiles at that, knowing that Zinzendorf left Halle before he was sixteen, he is unaware of the nature of Pietism. The count says that before leaving the school he handed over to Francke a list of seven such associations. These little prayer groups would meet frequently at various secluded places or in students' rooms, wherever they could carry out their purpose unmolested. To meet in Zinzendorf's room itself was difficult because of the ridicule of Crisenius. Through these gatherings the count became especially attached to four friends, George von Söhlenthal, Anton von Wallbaum, a von Tanz, and Frederick von Watteville, all of whom helped him in later years.

Zinzendorf with his active imagination projected these religious activities into a much larger sphere. With these four friends, and others from among the prayer circles, he often discussed the formation of a society of those pledged to serve Christ in a special way. In later years he gave the impression that this society actually came into being at Halle, and Spangenberg so states in his life of the count. However, it is one of the several instances in which Zinzendorf is mistaken about dates in relating his own experiences. Even so, tentative rules and regulations must have been discussed at Halle. Out of these schoolboy plans there emerged in the course of a few years, after the group had already scattered, a Christian fraternity successively called "Slaves of Virtue," "Confessors of Christ," and finally the "Order of the Grain of Mustard Seed." Lady Gersdorf was one of those whom the count took into his confidence regarding this society. Along with giving other good advice, she counseled the boys to keep it a quiet affair. One of the main reasons for the lack of data on this society is that it had the nature of a secret order through the years.

A few weeks after Zinzendorf's departure from Halle he records in his diary that he discussed his society with his aunt Henrietta. In the course of this same visit at Hennersdorf his grandmother presented him with a gold medallion, on one side of which was an *ecce homo* with the inscription *vulnera Christi* (the wounds of Christ). On the other side was an angel with the symbols of martyrdom and the inscription *nostra medela* (our healing.) This type of emblem is probably what Zinzendorf had in mind for the society in discussing the plans with his colleagues and which led Spangenberg to record mistakenly that the boys wore it already in school.

The young baron Frederick von Watteville of Switzerland was particularly close to Zinzendorf at Halle. The two made a vow to work for the conversion of the heathen. Being of the conviction that they themselves could not become missionaries because they felt themselves called to serve the world in other ways, they prayed that God would eventually raise up people who would become the instruments to carry out their plans. It was this schoolmate's adopted son John who later married the count's daughter Benigna.

Halle was a likely place for something like missionary ambitions to take rise in idealistic youths. There they lived daily in an atmosphere of zealous Christian activity, as Zinzendorf himself testifies:

The daily meetings in professor Francke's house, the edifying accounts concerning the kingdom of Christ, the conversation with witnesses of the truth in distant regions, the acquaintances with several missionaries, the flight of divers exiles and prisoners, the regulations of the orphan houses, which at that time were in a very prosperous state, the cheerfulness of that man of God in the work of the Lord, together with various heavy trials attending it, increased my zeal for the cause of the Lord in a powerful manner, and laid the foundation of the knowledge of such things as tend either to the furtherance or hindrance of true Christianity.[2]

Among the missionaries referred to was Ziegenbalg, home on furlough from his mission field in Tranquebar. The count came to know him well at Francke's dinner table. The links were being forged

---

[2] *Ibid.,* p. 69.

in the chain of events leading to the launching of Moravian missions in 1732.

An important event in Zinzendorf's life was his first Communion in the St. Ulrich's Church in Halle on the first Sunday after Trinity. He writes twenty years later concerning it:

As the time came for me to go to Communion, I experienced an unusual stirring in my soul and promised my Saviour to be eternally true and to follow him. . . . Twenty years later it is as fresh to me as if it had happened today. I have not lost what I found there then.[3]

Three years after the event he wrote a lengthy hymn about it, a hymn which found wide use in the Moravian Church. The first stanza is:

> Happy, thrice happy hour of grace!
> I've seen, by faith, my Saviour's face:
> He did himself to me impart,
> And made a cov'nant with my heart.

A much more mature and adjusted youth left Halle in April of 1716 than had entered in August of 1710. From Gavernitz, where, before returning to Hennersdorf, he had stopped to visit his uncle, he wrote under date of April 8: "Now I am gone from dear Halle! I shall never forget it as long as I live, for there I learned that which can make me happy for time and eternity." Here is the resilience of youth ignoring the unpleasant side of his training in favor of the affection for the place which had taken root in him. Halle had been in effect a proving ground where the count passed through the kind of experiences he was to encounter throughout his career. In this center of Pietism he made intimate contacts which were both to aid him and to hinder him in the future direction of the program of the Moravian Brethren. He acquired lifelong friendships but also lifelong opposition. As the Halle schoolboys made their mark in the church world of Europe, some of them were to be for the count, others against him. Among the latter was to be the younger Francke, Theophil August (1696-1769), the confidence of whose father Zinzendorf had eventually succeeded in winning. The elder Francke died in 1727, just when the Moravian venture was beginning to get well under way. The new regime at Halle was no friend of Zinzendorf and the Moravians.

[3] *Ibid.*, p. 78.

5

AT THE UNIVERSITY
OF WITTENBERG

The sixteen-year-old youth left the paedagogium fully hoping to return to Halle for his university training. This time, however, the decision was not made by the Pietist side of the family but by his guardian uncle, Otto Christian. He let it be known during the count's two-week visit with him at Gavernitz, on the way home to Hennersdorf in April, that he was not to continue at Halle. Both mother and grand-mother from this point on allowed the guardian a larger voice in his training. Sympathetic as his mother's family was with Halle, they were realistic enough to see that Zinzendorf needed training more specifically aimed toward his future career in state service. Even they were be-ginning to be concerned over his lack of interest in such a calling. It was, therefore, with only mild reluctance that they acceded to the guardian's plans. Wittenberg was, after all, a Saxon university, an advantage to those who intended to serve in Saxon territory.

The elder count, to his nephew's discomfiture, saw in Crisenius qualities which he felt would be good for the boy. He correctly analyzed the tutor as a man shrewd in the ways of the world, a trait he wanted the boy to acquire. There was no doubt about the man's ability as a scholar and his skill as a teacher. Therefore, Crisenius was not only continued as tutor but was given added authority in the position.

Zinzendorf, having progressed far in taking disappointments philo-sophically, bowed to the decision unwillingly but gracefully. The next three months at Hennersdorf, as reflected in the pages of his diary which he began to keep about this time, strike one as a happy, relaxed inter-lude in his crowded life. He spent his days reading books in Lady Gers-dorf's excellent library, writing numerous letters, dashing off poems, listening to lectures read by his tutor, conversing with his aunt Henri-etta, riding through the countryside by carriage or on horseback. He became better acquainted with Luther, Spener, Francke, and the Bible. In his diary he notes that a whole afternoon was spent in reading a medical book by a distinguished authority of Amsterdam. Of his letters over twenty were written to friends in Halle. Sometimes his discussions with Henrietta turned into sharp clashes of opinion. He participated wholeheartedly in the warm devotional life of Hennersdorf.

The middle of July found him with Crisenius visiting his brother Frederick Christian in Dresden and his uncle in Gavernitz. He spent the next month in their company. On August 17 the uncle confronted him with detailed written instructions for his future course of study and behavior at Wittenberg under the supervision of his tutor. The intent of the instructions was clearly to wean him away from pietistic inclinations and to prepare him for statecraft. To say that his guardian was anti-Pietist is by no means to say that he was indifferent or opposed to religion. He was a devout, orthodox Lutheran, as can be seen from an excerpt from the rules he laid down:

It must be the chief care of the tutor that the good foundation of godliness, which has been laid down in the young count at Halle, remain firm and undisturbed; and that the true knowledge of saving faith, and a sincere love to God and our neighbor be built thereon.

The public church service must not be neglected, but he is to attend the prayers and singing of the Christian congregation, hear the word preached, and pay due regard to the doctrine and wholesome admonitions proceeding out of the preacher's mouth, without any prejudice whatever.[1]

In the order to attend public church services is to be seen the orthodox Lutheran aversion to conventicles. Elsewhere in the regulations there is the strongly implied warning against the kind of extra-church religious activity engaged in by young Zinzendorf at Halle. He is specifically directed to take expert instruction in fencing and dancing, social skills against which he was developing scruples.

On the whole the uncle's instructions were sound advice in line with what any father or guardian might give to a youth leaving for college. They include advice on money matters, amusements, habits of eating and sleeping, exercise, choice of companions. They are quite detailed concerning curriculum and reveal that the uncle himself was an intelligent and well-educated man. From the modern point of view

[1] Spangenberg, *Leben Zinzendorfs*, tr., Nyberg, I, 86.

their error was, of course, in trying to mold the count to fit the pattern of the family's plan for his life. Also hard to agree with is the extent of the authority given to Crisenius, which left little room to the young student for independent decision. Yet within that restricted sphere Zinzendorf made the most of his situation, and the years in Wittenberg were to be as fruitful as had been the years in Halle. He was to look back upon them as part of God's plan for him.

It was on August 25, 1716, that Count Zinzendorf arrived in the university town where, just short of two hundred years earlier, Martin Luther had struck out upon his world-shaking course. Anticipation of the coming Reformation bicentennial the following year was attracting special attention to this respected seat of learning and orthodoxy. The current controversy with the Pietists further helped to keep Wittenberg in the limelight. Enrollment, including considerable numbers of the same social class as the count, was at a high level. Though in the eyes of Halle vital religion was dead in this birthplace of Protestantism, in the eyes of many others Wittenberg was the custodian of pure doctrine and the bulwark against error. The true state of affairs was a matter of opinion. Scholarship seems to have been on a high level.

The count and his tutor took lodging in the home of Burgomaster Keil, on a scale of elegance in accord with his rank. There with quarters consisting of a well-furnished drawing room and a combination study and bedroom, attended by a servant, and dining at a large table with other students, he cut an important figure at the university. Had he been so inclined, his might have been a dazzling social life in an era and in a place where being highborn still carried prestige.

The pictures he displayed in his drawing room show that he did not take his nobility lightly. Among them were portraits of the kings of Prussia and Poland, the czar, Louis XIV, and Baron von Söhlenthal. In his study, where were also two field cots to serve as beds, were portraits of the elector John George of Saxony, the Holy Roman emperor, the king and queen of England, the kings of Spain, genealogical tables of the Polish and Swedish kings and of the house of Prussia, a historical painting of the popes, his grandfather Gersdorf, his great-grandfather von Teufel, and a Lady von Schweinitz.

Two weeks after his arrival in Wittenberg, on September 7, he was formally matriculated by his tutor's reading the academic oath in his name to Dr. Schröer, the prorector. One departure from the normal pattern was his statement—in Latin—"I, Nicolaus Ludwig, Count von

Zinzendorf, do not swear, but promise. . . ." Thereupon the academic statutes were presented to him, and he added of his own volition, "So help me God." He lost little time in settling down to serious academic work.

Majoring in jurisprudence, he heard Dr. Spener, the son of the father of Pietism, lecture on the history of the Empire; Professor Jahn on Ludwig's *Germania Princeps;* Professor Griebner on natural law; Professor Krause on the history of legislature; Dr. Wernher on jurisprudence and feudal law; and Counselor Mencken on canon law. Attending lectures was only part of his studies, for he was conscientious in examinations and the "repetitions," the later a sort of review and discussion session. The instructors appreciated his accurate and precise answers. In addition he read lectures privately, as, for instance, Lauterbach's compendium of the pandects and Gundling's abridgment of the history of the Empire.

In the area of what was then termed philosophy he attended public lectures in logic and ethics and read privately in the field. He heard Dr. Vater's lectures upon the experimental aspect of natural philosophy. He studied some mathematics which he disliked.

He pursued his language studies under private tutors, thus continuing the excellent training he had previously received. Some of his diary and correspondence were in French, which was also the language used at the dining table. He improved his proficiency in Latin. He kept up his Greek by diligently reading the New Testament in the original and by occasionally writing a Greek letter to certain friends. He studied some Hebrew; but, as was the case earlier, he had little enthusiasm for it. What language he used in his correspondence seemed to vary with his mood. His letters to his mother were either in German or French, as were hers to him. His diary, besides the French, as stated above, has also many German and Latin entries. All his life Zinzendorf was to have the habit of indiscriminately throwing foreign words of a half-dozen languages into his German addresses and writings.

Conscientious as he was in pursuing the legal studies laid out for him, they were not his first love. This continued to be the study of theology. According to his own testimony:

My mind inclined continually toward the cross of Christ. My conversation always turned to that subject; and since the theology of the cross was my favorite theme, and I knew no greater happiness than to become a preacher of the gospel, therefore subjects not related to that I treated superficially; and what I know of civil law is not to be credited to any extraordinary application. I learned divinity at Wittenberg. But since I was not allowed to attend public theological lectures, I read them at home in my leisure.[2]

He spent many hours in the study of hymns. If for any reason one of the lectures in his assigned courses was not held, he took advantage of the opportunity to read the Bible, especially the Greek New Testament, and various theological books. Among these were works of Spener, Gediken, Kromajer, Sekkendorf, Schelweg, Lange, and, above all, Luther. He also spent much time in reading sermons on the church year. Especially helpful in advising him in his theological reading was Professor Wernsdorf, with whom he struck up a warm friendship. Wernsdorf's irenic spirit in the midst of the current theological controversy made a profound impression on Zinzendorf.

His diary shows that his studies, individual instruction under tutors, correspondence, and private devotions kept the young student pretty well occupied. Under date of February 28, 1718, we read:

This week I began the plan of spending a whole hour, from six to seven in the morning, as well as in the evening from eight to nine, and for fifteen minutes at a quarter of ten, in prayer. Also I resolved to pursue the study of civil law with all my energy, since I expect all sorts of interruptions this coming summer.

Examinations with Mencken. At ten o'clock I fenced. At eleven I studied the pandects. At twelve I dined. At one I played badminton [*schlug volants*]. At two I drew. At three I attended a lecture in the history of the Reich. At four I danced. At five Bardin [French tutor] was here. At six I studied civil law. At seven I dined. At eight I prayed. At nine I studied Hoppi's examination.[3]

Knowing that the spiritual climate of Wittenberg was a threat to his Halle brand of Pietism, Zinzendorf put up his guard in the form of a somewhat legalistic pattern of private devotions. Besides his daily program of prayer and Bible study he would occasionally spend a whole night in prayer. For a time he set Friday aside as a fast day, and later, finding Friday too inconvenient, he changed the day to Sunday. He says of himself that at Wittenberg he became a strict Pietist. As at Halle, his religious life brought him into conflict with many of the students.

[2] Spangenberg, *Leben Zinzendorfs*, p. 72.
[3] Gneomar Ernst von Natzmer, *Die Jugend Zinzendorfs*, p. 135.

Adding to the opposition was his championing of Halle's point of view. He warmly defended Francke and his colleagues against distorted criticism, losing no opportunity to acquaint others with what he thought to be a true picture of Halle. He distributed Halle literature, wrote tracts himself, and translated Francke's treatise on prayer into French.

He kept up a voluminous correspondence, especially with former Halle associates. To a large extent this correspondence was a continuance of the fellowship of the prayer circles which did not exist at Wittenberg. The actual beginning of the Order of the Grain of Mustard Seed came during the count's second year at Wittenberg in 1718, and because the group was no longer together, largely through correspondence. The permanent name came even later. Only long afterward were the actual rules and regulations of the order brought before the public eye. What finally brought this about was the death in 1737 of one of the members, Abraham von Rumswinkel, a Prussian official stationed in Amsterdam. Among his possessions was the ring worn by members of the order and a copy of its statutes. A certain Professor Voget of Utrecht, coming into possession of these statutes a year later, had them published, together with the erroneous explanation that they were the rules of an order of the Herrnhuters, or Moravians. It was a period in the history of the Moravian Church when many tracts were being issued against the followers of Zinzendorf. The statutes which the accompanying explanation construed as political were intended to be anti-Moravian propaganda.

The Order of the Grain of Mustard Seed was, of course, simply a Christian compact entered into by like-minded individuals who had certain ideals which they thought could best be accomplished without publicizing them. Members pledged themselves to remain true to the teachings of Jesus and to conduct themselves accordingly, to love their fellow men, to refrain from worldly things such as dancing and gambling, to seek at all times the welfare of others, to work especially for the conversion of the Jews and the heathen. Members wore a ring with the inscription in Greek, "No one liveth unto himself." A green silk ribbon, embroidered with a cross and a mustard tree, was also part of the insignia of the order. There were no officers, no dues, no meetings. The members pledged themselves to live for certain Christian ideals and regarded the affair simply as a personal matter. Spangenberg says that he knew personally that Zinzendorf was diligent through the years in his correspondence concerning the Order of the Grain of Mustard Seed. Some of those in the fellowship of the order were John Potter, archbishop of Canterbury; Thomas Wilson, bishop of Sodor and Man; Cardinal Noailles of Paris; and General Oglethorpe, governor of Georgia. Just how seriously these men took their membership is not known. Concerning the count himself, he said in later years that as "knights" of the Order of the Grain of Mustard Seed he and his friend von Watteville were under obligation to receive the Moravian refugees when Herrnhut began.

Meanwhile the count dutifully took private fencing and dancing lessons, resolving, however, to use these arts only to the extent to which they contributed to wholesome bodily exercise. He took the same practical attitude toward chess and balloon, the latter a form of football played with an inflated leather ball. Only reluctantly did he allow himself to be drawn into these pastimes. More to his liking than these lighter social activities was to have his rooms frequented by visitors, among them members of the faculty. Invariably the discussions were along religious lines. Nothing did the young count love better than to be in the midst of an argument, in the course of which he was by his own admission very tenacious of his opinions.

Zinzendorf's correspondence with his mother reveals much about the university student. For one who saw her son so infrequently, Lady von Natzmer had remarkable insight into his character. Their exchange of letters conveys the impression that she was a stabilizing influence upon him during the Wittenberg period. Never blind to his faults, she combined deep maternal affection and objective common sense in her advice to him. With restraint, and yet with firmness, she sought to check his immature ventures and eccentricities.

Illustrative is the youth's reaction to the death of his granduncle, Baron von Friesen, about a year after the count had been at Wittenberg. Zinzendorf had elaborate plans for observance of a period of mourning, which were to include black clothing, and furniture and windows draped with symbols of mourning. When he mentioned this to his mother, she replied in no uncertain terms how ridiculous the idea was. She pointed out that he had many relatives who would in the natural course of events precede him in death and that to go into special mourning for each of them would exhaust his resources. She asked him how he would mourn for a father and mother if he was so elaborate in noting the passing of only a granduncle. She furthermore reminded him that he was at the university not to put on a stately show but to prepare for something worthy.

Well did Lady von Natzmer know her son when upon occasion she took him to task for his conceit and tendency toward illusions of grandeur. Patiently she listened to his requests that he be without a tutor. But she did not yield and refused to suggest such a course to his guardian. When the young count would express his impatience with his uncle's rules and regulations, she reminded him that they were for his welfare.

Zinzendorf took his diary very seriously and sent a copy of it regularly to his grandmother. Upon his offering to do the same for his mother and stepfather, the former replied that it was unnecessary. She told him frankly that with his limited experience the contents would not be important enough to warrant the trouble of making an extra copy. Apparently she was seeking to avoid further feeding his vanity. She had little sympathy with his much correspondence and other writing, feeling that he was thereby dissipating his energy. Thus she advised him:

There are times for learning and times for the practical application of learning. It is your duty now to be faithful in the first. Later on you can pursue the practical application so much better. A well-built house must have deep foundations. Then one can build much upon it.[4]

When after only a year and a half of study the count suggested that he had been at the university long enough, Lady von Natzmer knew what to say. She told him that she would not like to include him among the people who, though they could say that they had been to the university, had never really learned anything solid. She knew from conversation with wise and sensible people that no one can possibly complete a course in law in even three full years.

Though Zinzendorf was older than his years in many ways, in others he was just an average youth who needed the usual advice on how to conduct himself sensibly. The parental letters contain the familiar warnings to be more careful with money, to study conscientiously, to be careful about associates, to write more legibly. Concerning money there was cause for special admonition, for the count never did learn how to handle it wisely. However, to his credit it must be observed that his weakness was not in expenditures on himself but in careless generosity toward others.

That an eighteen-year-old student, though a count, should have

[4] *Ibid.*, p. 145.

been seriously regarded as a mediator in the theological dispute between Halle and Wittenberg seems incredible. Yet such was the case during Zinzendorf's last year at the university, between November of 1718 and April of 1719. To be sure the effort miscarried, but it showed the daring of his imagination and the high regard those men who knew him well had for him. Entering Wittenberg with the viewpoint of Halle, Zinzendorf had come to appreciate the merits of both schools. The growth of mutual confidence between him and Francke at Halle was duplicated in his association with Professor Wernsdorf of Wittenberg.

The tragedy of a divided Lutheranism had been made more apparent by the Reformation bicentennial of 1717, and the desire for reconciliation was widespread. Clergymen, professors, and statesmen frequently expressed themselves on the subject. In fact not only did some project the possibility of a united Protestantism, but even a religious unity which would include the Roman Church as well.

Prior to the Reformation observance Professor Löscher, onetime Wittenberg faculty member, had approached professors Stryk and Lange of Halle in an unsuccessful attempt to effect an understanding. Following this stalemate Zinzendorf, perhaps somewhat presumptuously, looked upon his close connection with both institutions as a divine call to serve as peacemaker. That this was not entirely presumption on his part is shown by the response his proposal received from both Francke and Wernsdorf.

Already in August the count had written a tract entitled *Various Thoughts on Peace to the Quarreling Lutheran Churches,* which upon coming to the attention of Professor Wernsdorf a few weeks later had elicited the theologian's warm praise. A personal conference with Wernsdorf assured Zinzendorf that he could count on the professor's co-operation in an attempt at reconciliation. Immediately the count contacted friends in Halle, including Francke himself. Playing a leading role were his two former associates Söhlenthal and Wallbaum, who were still at Halle, the latter being especially close to Francke. Not making much headway writing, Zinzendorf sought to arrange a personal meeting between Francke and Wernsdorf, in preparation for which he was busy in preparing a tentative agenda for discussion. Just when the negotiations had gotten to the point where Wernsdorf and the count himself were to go to Halle together, his family intervened with advice to abandon his grand scheme. Lady von Natzmer wrote a strong letter on the subject under date of December 10. His grandmother also sought to dissuade him during the course of his visit at Hennersdorf during the Christmas season. The sentiment of his family was that church disputes were none of his business, and, even if they were, he was too immature to deal with them.

However, the youth was not so easily dissuaded, and a few months later he was still engaged in the project. But the principals involved seemed to lose faith in the matter. Zinzendorf was especially disappointed in Wernsdorf, and from this point on there was a strained relationship between the two. What little hope the count still had for success in the effort was for a second time dashed by family interference. This time General von Natzmer himself, under date of April 18, wrote a letter in which he expressly forbade the count to go to Halle. Thus ended in failure his first effort on behalf of the unity of a divided church.

Later that year Löscher and Francke met at Merseburg. They were brought together by the court preacher Philippi. Zinzendorf had no part in this meeting, but it is reasonable to assume that his earlier efforts may have indirectly helped to bring it about. Be that as it may, nothing came of the Löscher-Francke conference.

The close of the episode in which the count assumed the role of a peacemaker coincided with the end of his Wittenberg studies. Three years earlier, upon leaving Halle, he had delivered a valedictory on "The Quarrelsomeness of Learned Men." Both incidents were prophetic of what was to be almost an obsession with him, the unity of Christian believers. But as is invariably the case, peacemakers are like prophets in their own country. Neither Halle Pietists nor orthodox Lutherans had much appreciation for him. The peace-loving Moravians were not really accepted by the church world until after the count had passed on.

6

WANDERJAHR, 1719-20

To Zinzendorf's first three phases of training and formal education at Hennersdorf, Halle, and Wittenberg respectively, there was
added the fourth and final phase, that of his *Wanderjahr.* It was fully as
decisive as the other three had been. The opportunities of this period
of leisurely study and travel, which the average young man of his status
would have turned to advantage in the pursuit of a secular career, only
strengthened the count's conviction that he was destined for something
else. The desire to follow a religious calling had become more pronounced as his university days drew to a close. Yet obedience to family
tradition still prevailed, as it was to prevail for some years longer; and
he set out upon his travels, theoretically at least as a future statesman.

One improvement in his situation was that Crisenius was no longer
his tutor. Finally, after seven years of recurring strained relations between the two, the count's family had seen fit to dismiss the man. His
place was taken by Riederer, who had served as tutor of the count's
older half brother, Frederick Christian. Zinzendorf had come to have
high regard for this tutor, whom he had learned to know during his
visits at Gavernitz.

The journey began in the middle of May. At Leipzig, Zinzendorf and
Riederer were met by Frederick Christian, who was to accompany them
for several weeks. The first stop of importance was at Frankfort on the
Main, where the count took special pleasure in recalling it as the scene
where his beloved Spener had begun his great work. From there the
travelers proceeded to some of the cities of the Rhine. In his lack of
appreciation of nature Zinzendorf was a child of his era. He saw in the
Rhine Valley in the month of May only "cliffs, vineyards, and castles."
More impressive to him were places of historic interest.

Indicative of the frame of mind in which he set out to see the world
was his experience in the magnificent art gallery in Düsseldorf. Among

all the masterpieces the one which left its mark upon him was a thorn-crowned *ecce homo* (today hanging in a Munich gallery) by Domenico Feti. Beneath it was the Latin inscription: "This I have suffered for you, but what have you done for me?" He thought that he could answer very little and prayed to the Saviour to draw him into the "fellowship of his suffering" whenever he was disposed to wander from it. Such an experience was hardly to lead him toward the goal his travels were supposed to achieve; namely, to round him off as a man of the world.

Arriving at Utrecht on his nineteenth birthday, he noted the occasion by a prayer of thanksgiving to his Saviour for his gracious preservation and with the expressed wish not to live longer than he should serve him. Zinzendorf was to study in Utrecht for three months, but not before he had spent a few weeks in visiting other Dutch cities. Among them were Gouda, Rotterdam, Delft, Gravenhage (The Hague), Leiden, Haarlem, and Amsterdam. The busy commercial life of these cosmopolitan places impressed him. Of more interest to him, however, were the contacts with persons of differing religious denominations in the free atmosphere of a tolerant nation. He met and worshiped with his own Lutheran coreligionists, and with Reformed, Mennonites, Arminians, and Anglicans. In each of these communions he found something which struck his fancy.

Upon the return to Utrecht, Frederick Christian left for Saxony and Zinzendorf began his brief term at the university. Here he continued his legal studies by attendance upon the lectures of Vitrarius. He began to study the English language. As a matter of deep personal interest he had frequent conversations with a distinguished authority in the field of medicine, a subject which was to Zinzendorf a lifelong hobby. Needless to say, he continued his avid reading of theology. The pattern begun at Halle and followed at Wittenberg was maintained with consistency at Utrecht. Sundays were especially devoted to an intensive reading of the Bible. Concerning this he said: "I will abide by my old method of spending Sunday for the benefit of my heart; the people may think of it what they please."

Of more import for the future than any academic work during his residence in Utrecht was the free exchange of opinion with the many prominent persons to whom the count's rank gave free access. Among them were Count Fugger and Baron Wolfskehl of the Roman Church; Count Lippe and his tutor Geudern, of the Calvinists; and the Barons Schell, Putbus, and Negendank, of the Lutherans. These he remembered for the vehement religious dispute in which they engaged on a certain occasion. Others whom he learned to know were Count Teklenburg; Count St. Paul; Prince Tremouille; the latter's sister, the Countess of Oldenburg; and the two Counts Danneskiold. Among scholars, besides Dr. Vitrarius, he came to know Counselor Neuhaus whom he admired for his piety; Baron Hammerstein of Amsterdam, a lover of the sciences; and Jacob Basnage, divine and historian.

On one occasion in the company of Prince von Nassau-Siegen he met the Saxon lord von Grone, who in the course of the conversation spoke of the conversion of the Duke of Zeist and the part which Francke had played in it. Zinzendorf used the opening as an opportunity for further religious discussion, whereupon he was immediately recognized by Grone as the youth who three years before had delivered the speech at Halle on "The Quarrelsomeness of Learned Men." This led to a lasting acquaintance characterized by the exchange of religious views.

The effect of all these contacts is appraised by Zinzendorf himself:

I came to the university of Utrecht with the theory of the Wittenberg divines, and the practice of those at Halle, which made me appear to be a peculiar kind of young lord on his travels. Here I had contact with the Calvinists and also with several kinds of philosophers, to whom I reacted at first with great impetuosity, but became gradually so moderate as patiently to hear what they had to say. As we came out of very different schools, I was soon convinced that I must either keep some of my speculations to myself, or find better arguments to support them, because I had not courage enough in these disputes to produce many weighty maxims and fundamental points. And I often thought at first hearing, that my opponents supported their erroneous opinions with stronger reasons than I could produce in defense of the truth. This perplexity, though it did not cause me to fall, yet made me retreat a little, and when I could do it with an easy mind I allowed my opponents the last word by which means I obtained the character of a modest young man.[1]

Zinzendorf left Utrecht on September 2, and after a leisurely trip via Amsterdam, The Hague, Antwerp, and the Belgian cities along the Schelde, he arrived in Paris toward the end of the month. Here he took lodging at the Hôtel des Escarelles in the Rue St. Honoré. His life in the French capital for the next six months was to be pretty much a repetition of his stay in Holland. With the highest social circles open

[1] Spangenberg, *Leben Zinzendorfs*, p. 110.

to him, he continued to feel out of place. Only when he could convert a situation into an occasion for religious discussion was the young count in his element.

Soon after his arrival in Paris he struck up a friendship with Baron Nicholas von Watteville, brother of his schoolmate Frederick, who at the time was also living in the city. Watteville says:

We soon become very good friends and visited each other daily. But as to the disposition of our hearts, we differed greatly, notwithstanding our friendship. I loved the world, but he not. He introduced me to cardinals and bishops, but I never could persuade him to go with me to the opera.[2]

Nor was Zinzendorf particularly interested in the sights of Paris which were so attractive to tourists. A few hours sufficed for him to visit nearby Versailles with its great buildings and gardens. On the other hand, he was deeply impressed with the Hôtel Dieu where hundreds of sick people were being cared for.

As part of his more formal training under his tutor's supervision, he spent many of his morning hours at the riding school and his afternoon hours in studying jurisprudence and the French language. As in Holland, spells of sickness kept him indoors for some of the time, in which case he occupied himself in religious reading and writing.

The common rules of courtesy made it impossible for him to escape entirely the social functions of his class. We find him becoming acquainted with some of the foreign nobility in the capital, such as the Swedish ambassador. He was warmly received by the Duchess Charlotte Elizabeth of the Palatinate, mother of the regent of France. She recalled her acquaintance with the count's father and uncle forty years earlier and revealed a homesick attachment for her native Germany. Others in this circle of acquaintances were the princes of Gotha, Schwartzburg-Sonderhausen, and Baden, Baron Stosch, Lord Tschirnhausen, and Lord Stairs.

Despite the count's distaste for the life of high society, he displayed a curious inconsistency in the seriousness with which he looked upon rank. He confessed that the deference shown to him in Paris was a dangerous temptation. When on one occasion the usual courtesies due him because of noble status had not been observed at court, he lodged a complaint with the marshal of the court against the master of cere-

[2] *Ibid.,* tr. Nyberg, I, 115.

monies and demanded satisfaction. Soon after, however, he regretted his action and begged God's forgiveness for his pretensions. He "promised his Saviour to be his poor follower, and wholly to abandon the world." At this stage of life he still knew few people in the lower classes of society.

The most significant experience of Zinzendorf's stay in France was his contact with Cardinal Louis de Noailles of the Jansenist faction of the Roman Catholic Church. French church life at the time was in a state of tension because of the controversy between the Jesuits and the Jansenists. Through the efforts of the former the pope had been persuaded in 1713 to condemn Quesnel's *Moral Reflections on the New Testament* by the bill Unigenitus. Noailles, having previously approved of Quesnel's work, led in protesting the Unigenitus, though controversy was foreign to his gentle and peace-loving disposition. The matter was approaching a showdown when the count became acquainted with the cardinal in November of 1719.

The introduction was made by Father de la Tour, head of the Fathers of the Oratory in Paris, who had been struck with Zinzendorf's unusual interest in religious matters. The first interview with the cardinal in the company of La Tour lasted two and one half hours. So gracious were the two clerics that the count felt his own Protestant faith to be in danger. Shortly following the visit he wrote a frank letter to the cardinal, telling him to give up any hopes that he might have of winning him over to Catholicism. This frankness brought a prompt reply in Noailles' own handwriting, clearing up certain points which had been raised in their discussion, assuring the count of his friendship, and inviting him to visit him often.

The mutual attraction between the count and the cardinal lay in the fact that they were kindred spirits in their concept of Christianity. Both had a deeply Christocentric faith expressed in personal obedient devotion to the Saviour. This tie made it possible for them to discuss in friendly fashion the differences between their churches. The cardinal acknowledged corruptions within his church and yet regarded Rome as the head of the one true church. He classed Protestants as schismatics who ought to return to the church from which they had separated, if they wished to follow God's will. Observing the count's zeal to serve Christ, he pointed out how much good he could do if he were reconciled to Rome. Father de la Tour likewise kept up his efforts in the same direction. Zinzendorf wrote to his friend Count Reuss, "Father de la Tour does his utmost to convert me to his church."

Personal visits between Noailles and Zinzendorf were supplemented by exchange of thought in writing. The latter wrote a Latin treatise of twenty-one pages setting forth for the cardinal the chief points of his religion. The conclusion was this:

When God enters into judgment with a sinner, then nothing avails but the righteousness of Jesus, through faith in his blood; and our salvation does not depend upon the pope or any other man, but merely and alone on the merits of Christ.[3]

As their acquaintance ripened, their appreciation of each other deepened. Realizing that neither could change the other's opinion on the externals, they spent more time sharing the essentials of their Christian experience. The cardinal became interested in Zinzendorf's family and friends. He listened with pleasure to excerpts of letters the count had received from his grandmother, mother, and aunt. Zinzendorf also introduced the cardinal to the Barons Watteville, Grone, and Haase.

This friendship continued over a period of months, until it was broken off by further developments in the French church. The cardinal's peaceable disposition, his loyalty to the church, the infirmities of age, and other factors combined to move him to a compromise acceptance of the Unigenitus early in the year 1720. Zinzendorf, hearing of Noailles' proposed action, was anxiously concerned; and thinking that there might still be opportunity for the prelate to stand firm, he wrote him to that effect. The cardinal replied with the assurance, "I will not give up the truth." Soon after, however, when it was clear that he had yielded, Zinzendorf wrote a memorable farewell letter, intended to end their relationship.

Is it then done, my lord! Alas! the fortitude which defied all danger and amazed the enemies of truth, now yields to the weak hope of an unwarrantable peace. I, who have known you, and your good intentions, can scarcely believe it. What will those people say, who at a distance have admired your virtues, when they hear that you have condemned one of the best books in the world, which you yourself have so emphatically recommended unto the flock, which God hath committed to your care. . . .

I know I am not qualified to teach you; but since my eyes shall see you

[3] *Ibid.,* p. 155.

no more after this lamentable occurrence, I hereby bid you adieu forever. I return you humble thanks for the friendship with which you have been pleased to honor me; and since it is possible that my frankness may sometimes have been displeasing to you, I beg your pardon a thousand times on that account. . . .

When our dear God and heavenly Father, after this miserable life, according to the greatness of his mercy, shall bring us together in a future world, I am persuaded that you will be inclined to forgive the excess of my zeal, and that you will be as fully convinced of the truth of my faith, and of all I now have the honor to tell you for the last time, as I am at present. Believe me, my lord! that I love you inexpressively, and that I honor you sincerely, and that it is with the most poignant grief I now take my leave of you.[4]

The above letter did not prove to mark the end of their friendship, though they never met in person again. Zinzendorf soon resumed his correspondence with the cardinal and in 1725 dedicated to him a French translation of Arndt's *True Christianity*. Noailles died in the year 1729.

Zinzendorf's friendship with the Catholic clergy was not confined to Noailles and La Tour. Moved by the sincere evangelical preaching of a Dominican friar, Anton Dionysius Simon d'Albizi, in the church of the Premonstrants, he became acquainted with the father after the service. Later Albizi introduced him to some more principals in the Jansenist affair, namely, to two of the appealing bishops who had opposed the Unigenitus. These were the Bishop of Boutagne and the Bishop of Montpellier. He also met the Abbé Pompone, who had sided with the appealing bishops. Another prelate whom he had met at court was Cardinal de Bussy.

These Paris contacts left Zinzendorf with a lasting respect for Roman Catholics. Never again, if such had ever been the case, was he able to think of true Christians in terms of denominations or factions, but only in terms of their common loyalty to the Saviour.

[4] *Ibid.*, p. 161.

7

A BROKEN ENGAGEMENT

The end of his residence in Paris in May of 1720 was also the end of Zinzendorf's attendance at a university. But there was still to be another year of leisurely travel before his coming of age and entrance into state service. An otherwise happy period, the year was to be clouded by the tension between the count and his relatives with respect to his future. During this time of waiting, in the face of increasing family opposition, there was a deepening of his conviction of a vocation to the religious life. Yet at no time did this difference of opinion strain filial ties. The young man's faith in the overruling providence of God and his regard for the Fifth Commandment saved him from rebellion and embitterment.

THE COUNT AS A YOUTH OF TWENTY

The high light of the year was a romantic episode involving his cousin, eighteen-year-old Theodora von Castell. The count went from Paris to Strassburg and thence to Switzerland. At Strassburg he wrote a cordial letter to Father d'Albizi, an indication that he was to maintain his contacts with his recently acquired Roman Catholic friends in France. At Basel he stayed for a week with the two Wattevilles, Frederick and Nicholas, the latter having also just returned from France.

En route from Schaffhausen to Zurich he became acquainted with the two venerable clergymen Mayer and Werefels.

From Switzerland he went by way of Nuremberg to Oberbürg, where he stayed through the summer with his paternal aunt the Countess Dowager von Polheim. There he occupied himself with his endless correspondence and other writing. In reflecting upon his recent experiences, he shows even less relish for secular life than he had the year before. In response to his brother Charles von Natzmer's congratulations upon his return from Paris, he wrote: "My dear Charles, you cannot imagine how insipid the world has been to me in my travels. Oh, what a poor, miserable thing is the grandeur of the great ones!"

It was in these weeks that the time of his being under a tutor also ended. Contrary to his relations with his previous two tutors, those with Riederer had been highly satisfying on both sides. Apparently the man had the insight and tact necessary to supervise the high-strung count. He continued in the service of Frederick Christian Zinzendorf.

From Oberbürg the count went to Castell to visit the second of his two paternal aunts, the widowed mother of Theodora. Intending to spend only a week there, he was forced by illness, described as a fever, to remain over two months and into late January. It was during this time that he fell in love with his cousin. In accord with proper procedure he consulted her mother, who expressed her approval of a match between the two. Her guardian also gave his consent, and Zinzendorf made a formal proposal to Theodora. Her reply, which he interpreted as favorable, was actually very noncommittal, couched in these terms: "If God should incline me to it more than at present, I will not resist." Even if she had responded more favorably, the count was not ready to enter upon a formal engagement without first consulting his relatives. He knew that his mother approved, for he had corresponded with her about it. Seeking his grandmother's consent also, he made a quick trip to Hennersdorf in late January. She expressed uneasiness because of their blood relationship but had no further objections.

On the journey back from Hennersdorf the matter took a strange turn. Zinzendorf was delayed at Plauen because of a mishap due to high water in the Elster River. He wrote of his narrow escape to his friend Count Henry von Reuss at nearby Ebersdorf. Reuss immediately sent him an invitation to Ebersdorf, which the count accepted. In the course of the visit his friend confided that he too was looking for a girl to marry. In the presence of Reuss's mother the two reviewed a list of eligible countesses, including Theodora, whose affair with Zinzendorf apparently was not yet known to his friend. At this point the mother advanced the observation that of all those who had been proposed Theodora had been most highly recommended, but that she was not eligible for "reasons best known to Zinzendorf."

This remark struck home in a strange way. Not so much in a spirit of gallantry as with the feeling that God may have so ordained it, Zinzendorf resolved to relinquish his prior claim to the hand of Theodora. Though reluctant to take advantage of his friend's generous spirit, Reuss was convinced by his insistence in the matter. Zinzendorf, to show that he really meant what he said, offered to take his friend with him to Castell. Upon their arrival the matter was soon concluded with Theodora and Henry being formally engaged on March 9. At the ceremony of betrothal, conducted by Counselor Bonin, the count offered a moving prayer and read a discourse of Francke's upon the text, "Whatsoever a man soweth, that shall he also reap."

The incident naturally attracted widespread attention because of its unusual nature. The behavior of the count in renouncing Theodora to his friend seems less strange when we weigh the facts carefully. The girl had never committed herself to him in the first place. Nearly fifty years later the then-widowed Theodora wrote a statement to Spangenberg for inclusion in his biography of Zinzendorf. She plainly says that she had no inclination to accept the count's proposal, but that she yielded to pressure from her mother, not to the extent of saying yes, but to the extent of encouraging her suitor by leaving it an open question. She goes on to say that after he had left her home she had even less heart for the marriage than at first. She begged her mother to so inform the count. She concludes in this vein: "The misundertanding lies in the fact that Count Zinzendorf said the matter was agreed upon, and I on the contrary said that the matter had not yet been decided."

Also to be taken into account is that the two were first cousins. Perhaps the doubts expressed by the grandmother had a deeper effect upon the count than appears on the surface. Furthermore, he was well aware that his life's ambitions were out of line with what a girl like Theodora might expect in her husband. All of which together meant that when he was returning to Castell and was delayed at Ebersdorf, he was perhaps doubtful of the wisdom of his proposed marriage. He was, therefore, in reality not gallantly breaking an engagement in deference to a preferred suitor but gracefully withdrawing from a situation in which he felt he did not belong. With an inborn flair for the dramatic, he was able to conclude the whole matter by entering whole-heartedly into the betrothal ceremonies. To the girl's mother he wrote:

> I see in your letter that you esteem it a praiseworthy deed in me to give up the Countess Theodora to my dear Count Reuss. I have no doubt that it is the will of God, which I respect with submission, and cheerfully put up with my own loss, if his wise and gracious purposes be but answered.[1]

The following year he married von Reuss's sister.

Zinzendorf a month away from his majority was further than ever from being reconciled to the prospect of state service. In this frame of mind he described himself to his aunt Henrietta in a letter from Pölzig under date of April 23, 1721. In part he says:

> I am resolved to disengage myself from everything that is great in life, and to lay aside all state and grandeur, to give up all ambitious views, and to act according to the inclinement of my heart . . . which leads me to the choice of a retired life wherein, though I may draw upon myself the con-tempt of the world, yet being contented with what is allotted me, I shall be happy in the enjoyment of peace and quietness.[2]

The count goes on to explain that all of his projects undertaken at the university and during his travels were for no other motive than the glory of God. He himself did not conceive of them as extraordinary, though the world may have thought them so. He appeals to Henrietta to try to understand him, reminding her that many of the things she her-self does quite naturally are looked upon as unusual by many. This letter was but one of many attempts to break down objections to his de-parture from family tradition.

Shortly thereafter the count, en route to see his mother in Berlin, visited his old friend Francke in Halle with the intention of investigat-ing the prospects of throwing in his lot with Halle's far-flung benevolent activities. Halle's distinguished patron, Canstein, had died two years before, and no one had yet presented himself in his place. Before Zin-zendorf could approach Francke on the subject, Francke approached him. The count accepted the offer enthusiastically, but subject to his family's consent. Failure to get this consent was the basis for a temporary estrangement between him and Francke.

---

[1] Spangenberg, *Leben Zinzendorfs*, tr. Nyberg, I, 190.
[2] *Ibid.*, p. 196.

Zinzendorf was with his mother on the occasion of his twenty-first birthday. Legally this birthday changed his status. It brought him into control of a considerable estate, but it changed relatively little his obedience to parental wishes. In Berlin both mother and stepfather remained firm in their opposition to the idea of a count becoming a minister. During the summer months with his grandmother at Hennersdorf he experienced even firmer resistance. In late October he went to Dresden to become aulic and judicial councilor in the electoral government of Saxony.

From Hennersdorf came strong pressure for the count to take his place among the titled rulers of the land. However, it was undoubtedly the associations surrounding Hennersdorf which at the same time stirred his imagination to conceive life plans which were to be the way out of his unhappy predicament. Beside his wish to become a pastor there developed in the maturing Zinzendorf a second choice. In this he pictured himself as the owner and proprietor of a country estate which would also be a religious community encompassing employees, neighbors, and guests. His grandmother had been the central personality in such an establishment ever since he could remember. To the young man, just back from two years of travel which had filled him with growing distaste for the secular world, the summer of 1721 at Hennersdorf must have enhanced such a dream. He lost no time in giving it substance. Before he left for Dresden he had begun building his manor house on land which his grandmother agreed to sell him. What this step eventually led to was beyond even Zinzendorf's imagination to foresee.

8

FINDING A LIFEWORK

The Dresden period in Zinzendorf's career turned out to be five years of transition at the end of which he and his life's work had finally found each other. Steps in the transition were the purchase of the Bertheldorf estate close by his grandmother's Hennersdorf, his marriage, the coming of the Moravian refugees, and his quitting government service.

He got off to a slow start in the capital because of his extreme caution in taking the oath of office. Included in the oath was a reference to the articles of faith of the Lutheran Church. These he felt it necessary to study carefully over a period of some weeks, following which he drew up a declaration in writing stating in what sense he could take the oath of religion. It was during this interval that he was at the point of not remaining in Dresden at all but of seeking a position at the Danish court in Copenhagen, where he had a warm friend in Crown Prince Christian, a distant relative. Again his grandmother thwarted his scheme. Finally before the end of the year he assumed the office for which he had come to Dresden.

Apparently the misunderstanding with Francke had been cleared up; for soon after Zinzendorf had entered upon his work, Francke sent him a congratulatory letter and an assurance of his continuing prayers on the count's behalf.

At the outset of his work Zinzendorf expressed the desire to his superior, Chancellor von Bunow, that he be assigned mainly to business pertaining to communications with foreign governments. Though the chancellor assured him that he would keep his request in mind, it does not seem to have been carried out; for the count's own recollection of his five years of court service between 1722 and 1727 was that he did little more than effect a few settlements between contending parties.

With the major portion of his energy going into matters closer to his heart's desire, nothing much more could have been expected.

Hardly settled in Dresden, where he was accompanied by his recently acquired steward, John George Heitz, the count began holding religious services in his apartment on Sunday afternoons. Heitz, a native of Switzerland, had been in the employ of Zinzendorf's aunt at Oberbürg and though of the Reformed Church was by virtue of his piety a kindred spirit. These services, usually lasting from three to seven o'clock, soon attracted a growing circle of adherents, many of whom were of separatist tendencies. The meetings were supplemented by personal evangelism in which Zinzendorf laid emphasis upon devotion to Christ. Always he discouraged separation from the state church, little as that church had to offer spiritually. It was in this period of his life that Zinzendorf first came into close contact with persons outside his own social circle.

Superintendent Löscher, administrative head of the Lutherans in Dresden, had known Zinzendorf at Wittenberg and recognized his loyalty to the church. Otherwise the meetings probably would not have been tolerated. Late in the year 1726 they were finally forbidden. The count himself sensed the incongruity of his situation. Thus he expresses it:

In Dresden I had liberty every Sunday to keep public meetings at my house. The oddity of it was that, though I was a preacher, and my heart lived entirely in the gospel, yet in obedience to my parents I must wear a sword and attend the administration.[1]

Again he wrote in a letter: "I bear my present circumstances with patience, because I know that I am but a guest in this place and a pilgrim in the world." It was late in the year 1721 when he was in this mood that he wrote what is perhaps his best known hymn, "Jesus Still Lead On," sung today in over ninety languages. Representative of the hymn are these lines:

> Jesus still lead on,
> Till our rest be won,
> And, although the way be cheerless,
> We will follow, calm and fearless;
> Guide us by Thy hand
> To our fatherland.[2]

[1] Spangenberg, *Leben Zinzendorfs*, tr. Nyberg, II, 25.
[2] Jane L. Borthwick, tr.

Devout and resolute as these sentiments may be, they hardly reflect the disposition usually found in young men just beginning their life-work.

The work in Dresden was to occupy Zinzendorf during only part of each year. In April of 1722 the purchase of the estate from his grandmother was completed and he began to turn his attention to its development. Included in the property was the old village of Berthelsdorf, which had existed as a church parish since the year 1346. The combined legacy which had come to him from his father and uncle covered the major portion of the purchase price. Had Zinzendorf insisted on claiming his full share of the inheritance, he would have had more than enough to pay for the property. The share from his father was 20,000 thaler and from his uncle 10,000 thaler. However, the latter was part of the property in possession of the count's half-brother Frederick Christian, who demurred at paying the sum. Zinzendorf agreed to settle for only 21,500, much to his more practical mother's displeasure. This amount was 6,000 short of the purchase price, for which he went into debt.

The incumbent pastor of Berthelsdorf was having difficulties in the parish but died very suddenly soon after this, before there was any occasion for dealings between him and the new owner. The count lost little time in securing a successor in the person of John Andrew Rothe, a fellow Pietist twelve years out of the University of Leipzig, whom he had first met at Hennersdorf and again at Dresden. Rothe, a highly gifted man, had never held a parish of his own because of his scruples against the practice of asking for one. In the meantime he had been serving as tutor to the children of Baron von Schweinitz at Leube. He had already demonstrated his abilities as a preacher in the Trinity Church at Görlitz.

On May 19, 1722, in a formal ceremony, including a three-hour sermon by the neighboring Pastor Schwedler of Niederwiese, the count took possession of his new property. The residents with handshake pledged their loyalty to him as their lord of the manor. On the same day he extended the call to Rothe to become their pastor. With his steward Heitz in charge of the property, he was able to divide his time between Berthelsdorf and Dresden.

The next step was marriage. The affair with Theodora had evoked serious thought on the part of Zinzendorf as to whether he, with his distaste for the ordinary life of the world, should marry at all. It is interesting, but perhaps only coincidental, that the time of such thinking should have come so shortly after his close association with Cardinal

THE ZINZENDORF HOME IN BERTHELSDORF

Noailles and other Roman clergy in France. Even though the subject may not have been part of his conversation with these men, the example of the celibacy of consecrated men in the Roman Church must have appealed to the idealistic young count. At any rate he studied both the Old and New Testaments on the subject to marriage, prayed earnestly over the problem, and consulted trusted friends about it. His decision was to marry but to choose only a partner who shared his ideals. He found that person in the young Countess Erdmuth Dorothea von Reuss, sister of his friend Henry.

The countess, born on November 7, 1700, daughter of the pious Henry X von Reuss and his wife, Erdmuth Benigna, was the fifth in a family of eight children, of whom three had died in infancy. Henry was the only brother. It was in the castle at Ebersdorf, where the widowed mother lived with her children, that Zinzendorf first met

Erdmuth. It was the occasion, referred to previously, when he was en route back to Castell to confirm his tentative engagement to Theodora.

How well the two became acquainted in the course of this first meeting is not known. Decisive for the future, however, was the religious life of the Ebersdorf household, which surpassed even that of Hennersdorf in its espousal of Pietism. This had been intensified by the attendance of the young Count Henry at Halle. At the time of Zinzendorf's visit he had recently completed his studies. Both the twenty-year-old Erdmuth and her older sister, Benigna Marie, were known for their devout participation in this *ecclesiola* in their home. Zinzendorf in later life credits Ebersdorf with suggesting the basic plan which went into the establishment of Herrnhut.

Romantic love had but a minor place in the courtship between the count and the countess in the year prior to their formal engagement on August 16, 1722, and their marriage a few weeks later on September 7. In expressing himself to his grandmother, Zinzendorf said: "I shall never marry in the spirit of this world, nor choose anyone who in the least conforms to its ways." To his future mother-in-law he wrote in the June preceding the marriage:

I foresee many difficulties in this case; as I am but a poor acquisition for any person, and the dear Countess Erdmuth must not only enter upon a life of self-denial with me, but also co-operate with me in my principal design, namely, to assist men in gaining souls for Christ, under shame and reproach, if she will be of any service to me.[3]

On the day of his engagement he wrote a poem which later became one of the hymns of the Moravian Brethren. This speaks of the love between him and his future bride as but an image of Christ's love for his church.

The Zinzendorf marriage took place at Ebersdorf with the court chaplain Schubert officiating in the presence of relatives from the families of Reuss, Solms, and Castell. It was destined to set a pattern for the kind of marriage soon to become common in the Renewed Moravian Church; namely, marriage entered upon because of a common devotion to the service of Christ. It was to set a pattern also in relegating normal home life to second place in favor of the call of duty. Separations due to travel on the part of both parties were to be long and frequent.

Life for the countess was not easy during that first year, nor for that

---

[3] Spangenberg, *op. cit.*, II, 44.

THE COUNTESS

matter during any year of their partnership. The young couple did not leave Ebersdorf until late November, after which they moved into their Dresden quarters furnished for them by his grandmother Gersdorf. This first home was a third-floor, four-room apartment rented from Burgomaster Schwarzbach for one hundred dollars a year. The count's lack of enthusiasm for his employment was reflected in his income, for he reported later that they lived off his wife's pin money. This was probably one of the chief reasons they soon left Dresden before the end of the year for their winter stay in the country at Hennersdorf. The house which Zinzendorf was having built at nearby Berthelsdorf was not yet ready for occupancy, which necessitated living with the grandmother. The Berthelsdorf estate, not having had a resident owner for two hundred years, was in rundown condition and at this stage was still a liability rather than a source of revenue. Living with her husband's relatives, judging from her correspondence with her mother, was no easier for Erdmuth than living with in-laws has been for countless other brides. The baroness herself was easier to get along with than Aunt Henrietta, by this time a strong-minded spinster in her late thirties.

The summer of 1723 found the Zinzendorfs back in Dresden. Finally in August they were able to move into the first home of their own, the new manor house at Berthelsdorf. Over the doorway to this house, which he called Bethel, the count had inscribed these words in golden letters, the first set on the left and the second on the right:

> Hier übernachten wir, als Gäste:
> Drum ist dies Haus nicht schön, noch feste.
>
> So recht: wir haben noch ein Haus
> Im Himmel: das sieht anders aus.

> "Here we spend the night as guests:
> Therefore this house is neither beautiful nor permanent."
>
> "Quite right: we have also another house
> In heaven where things are different."

Cited, but not written out, were the scripture passages Zech. 9:12 and II Cor. 5:1-2.[4]

Wise was it for Zinzendorf to have turned over the management of their financial affairs to the countess at the very outset of their marriage.

---

[4] Uttendörfer and Schmitt, *Die Brüder*, p. 103.

Ten years later, in 1732, she was given actual legal title to his property. Her wise management eased the financial stringency of those first years. Not only was she far more capable in practical matters than he, but she also undoubtedly saved their estate from confiscation by having the property in her name at the time of his banishment from Saxony.

DOORWAY OF THE HOME
IN BERTHELSDORF

Contemporaneous with the foregoing events was the first coming of the religious exiles from Moravia to Upper Lusatia, an event which intruded itself into Zinzendorf's life in such a way that it is difficult to see it other than the hand of Providence. The Pietist awakening had spread beyond the confines of Germany to the Roman Catholic lands under Austrian rule, converting a considerable number of people to an evangelical point of view. Being restricted in free worship, they began to look across the borders of their country to friendlier Protestant territory. Some living in Bohemia near Silesia would actually cross over for worship in the few so-called "churches of grace" in which Protestants could worship in peace according to the Treaty of Westphalia. With the victories of Charles XII in 1706 there was an extension of Protestantism in Silesia. However, the real solution was emigration for the evangelicals in Bohemia and Moravia, among whom were descendants of the almost extinct *Unitas Fratrum*.

A key individual in this revival was Christian David, born in Moravia in 1690. Reared a Roman Catholic, he had a religious experience in early manhood which ultimately led him into the Lutheran Church. With his naturally restless dispositon accentuated by his search for spiritual peace, he worked as an itenerant carpenter and served for a time in the Prussian army. In 1717, attracted by the Pietist pastor Schaeffer, he chose Görlitz in Silesia as his home. In his wanderings the problem of freedom of worship for his countrymen remained one of his major concerns. It was this which finally brought him into contact with Zinzendorf in Dresden in May of 1722, through Rothe, the count's future pastor at Berthelsdorf.

Immediately sympathetic with the plight of Christian David's fellow seekers, the count promised to find a place for several families whom David specifically recommended. He was not yet at this point quite prepared to offer his own recently acquired estate as a permanent asylum but did give assurance of a welcome there until another place could be found. Especially did he hope for some place near Ebersdorf in the domain of Count Reuss, who was already harboring some dissenters. Christian David, however, moved so rapidly that the die was cast within the next month without Zinzendorf's knowledge.

The impulsive David proceeded at once to Sehlen in Moravia to inform his friends of his conversation with Zinzendorf. Two brothers, Augustine and Jacob Neisser, of a family keeping alive the traditions of the Bohemian Brethren decided to emigrate immediately. Two days later, on May 25, with their wives and children and two close relatives, they were on their way afoot to Saxony. The party of ten, six adults and four very young children, was led personally by Christian David. Friends entertained them en route, and at Görlitz the families were temporarily lodged with Pastor Schaeffer; while the two brothers and David went on to Hennersdorf to interview Lady Gersdorf.

She gave them a cold reception when they appeared on June 8 but was persuaded by the family tutor Marche to refer them to Zinzendorf's steward Heitz at Berthelsdorf. Heitz first thought of settling the newcomers on one of the farms of the estate. Further consultation with Lady Gersdorf, during the interval when the Neissers returned to Görlitz for their families, resulted in the decision to locate the refugees on a still unoccupied portion of the count's property. In the meantime an empty dwelling was found for their immediate use. The baroness gave them a cow to supply milk for the children.

The first task for the party was to build a house of their own. For this the shrewd Heitz, foreseeing a growing settlement and seconded by Marche, selected a strategic location where the highway from Lübau to Zittau skirted the base of a hill known as the Hutberg. Christian David, again losing no time, was there on June 17 to fell the first tree that went into the building of the new settlement. That same day Heitz sent a letter to Zinzendorf in Dresden informing him of this quick sequence of events. The count approved, though little realizing what a decisive moment it was to be for him. The next month in another letter to him Heitz revealed that he had already named the spot "Herrnhut," with the hope that a community might arise there which should not only be "unter des Herrn Hut" (under the Lord's watch) but also "auf des Herrn Hut" (on the watch for the Lord).

For the next year or so the coming of the exiles meant relatively little to Zinzendorf. Other details concerning his estate, his marriage, his religious activities in Dresden, kept him fully occupied. His first contact with the Moravians was in late December when he and his bride, accompanied by Frederick von Watteville, were approaching Berthlesdorf on their way to Hennersdorf for their winter stay in the Gersdorf home. Seeing the new house in the woods beside the road and learning that it was the home of the Neissers, the count stopped to offer them his good wishes and before leaving knelt in prayer with them in their humble home. Knowing little or nothing of the history of the Bohemian Brethren, Zinzendorf in 1722 looked upon these settlers simply as religiously earnest people whom he was happy to welcome to the free atmosphere of the Berthelsdorf parish. Five years later he had learned that much more was involved, and that he had not just an *ecclesiola* on his hands but also a denomination.

During the years 1722 to 1727, at the end of which he finally got a leave of absence from the court, Zinzendorf spent less than half of his time in the capital. Directing the destinies of Berthelsdorf and Herrnhut was becoming his vocation. When in Dresden, he continued making his home the meeting place of informal conventicles.

An interesting venture begun late in the year 1725 was the publication of a weekly periodical called the *Dresdener Socrates,* so called because the count sought, like Socrates, "to bring his fellow citizens to reflect upon themselves, and by his example to show them the way to the attainment of real and lasting contentment." The outspokenness of the paper in its criticism of the life of the state churches moved the authorities to confiscate the third issue. Technical grounds for this action was that the publisher was anonymous. Thereupon Zinzendorf announced himself as publisher, and the *Dresdener Socrates* lived on to reach a thirty-second number in December of the next year. The printing was done on the press he and his associates had set up first at Berthelsdorf and then at Ebersdorf. The material of the *Dresdener Socrates* was published in book form in 1732 under the title of the *German Socrates.*

Issuing from this same press in 1726 was the Ebersdorf Bible. It was the regular Luther translation with Luther's foreword and his preface to the Epistle to the Romans. But in addition it contained comments by Arndt, and what proved to be objectionable to many, some interpretations by both the count and his pastor, Rothe. The result was that the Ebersdorf Bible drew upon itself a storm of criticism.

From Ebersdorf came also a French translation of Arndt's *True Christianity,* done by Samuel de Beauval, and which, as before stated, was dedicated to Cardinal Noailles. Frederick von Watteville presented it to the cardinal in person. Noailles was highly pleased with the work and the count's tribute in dedicating it to him but foresaw that it would be forbidden in France. A ban against its sale followed promptly. Besides the Bible and Arndt's work there were printed in this period a catechism, a hymnbook, religious poems, and other items. The distribution of inexpensive Christian literature as an effective means of spreading the gospel was always highly regarded by the count.

The one person, above all, holding him to his halfhearted discharge of state duties in Dresden was the Baroness von Gersdorf. Release from her dominance came with her passing on March 6, 1726, at the age of seventy. To refer to her in this way is not to imply that the count resented her hold upon him. Curiously, much as he disliked what she forced him to do, he never once betrayed that he doubted her judgment. He looked upon what his family made him do as God's discipline, in which all things work together for good. Between the baroness and him there was warm affection. For her last birthday he composed this ode:

> Pattern of grace! whose faith and practice shew'd
> To me and others what we owe to God;
> How can I possibly, Christ's name pass by,
> Since thy whole life of him did testify?

Toward the close of her life there was evidence that she was beginning to recognize that her grandson was on the threshold of great achievement, not as statesman, but in his chosen field. A semi-invalid for her last twelve years, she had herself carried out into the country to the growing village of Herrnhut a few days before her death. There she gave her blessing to what she saw. The count himself preached a sermon at her funeral.

His grandmother's passing made it easier for Zinzendorf in the months following to gain his mother's approval for his taking leave of Dresden. Technically it was only a leave of absence; and in the interval between the spring of 1727, when it began, and late 1731, when he finally severed his connection with the Saxon court, he was occasionally occupied with matters of state. These were so minor, however, that the end of the Dresden period is correctly dated 1727.

In April of that year the Zinzendorfs went to Berthelsdorf, where they stayed only two months; for in June they moved into the new *Herrschaftshaus* at Herrnhut. Baron von Watteville had in the meantime leased the manor house they were vacating. With them was their infant daughter, Benigna, born on December 28, 1725. Three months after they settled permanently at Herrnhut, Christian Renatus was born on September 19. Their first child, Christian Ernest, born on August 7, 1724, had lived only three months. He was the first of the eight Zinzendorf children, of the twelve born to the couple, to die in infancy.

9

A BROTHERHOOD EMERGES

By the time Zinzendorf left Dresden to give full attention to what was happening on his country estate, Herrnhut had already grown to three hundred persons. As early as August of 1723 he and three intimates entered into an association which came to be known as the "Covenant of the Four Brethren." The three joining him in this were his long-time friend Frederick von Watteville; his own pastor, John George Rothe; and the neighboring pastor Melchior Schaeffer of Görlitz. In effect the Covenant of the Four Brethren was a practical application of the principles of the Order of the Grain of Mustard Seed. Watteville, following his schooling at Halle, had passed through deep spiritual unrest and was still seeking peace of soul when he accompanied the Zinzendorfs to Hennersdorf the previous Christmas. That winter he had experienced a heart-warming conversion. Now the high talents and considerable wealth of this Swiss nobleman were at the disposal of Christian benevolence. Rothe's fervid piety and eloquent preaching were beginning to revitalize the old Berthelsdorf parish and having stimulating effects on other parishes nearby. Schaeffer for some time previously had been having a similarly fruitful pastorate in his parish.

The four pledged themselves to the cultivation of holiness in themselves and throughout the land, to

FREDERICK VON WATTEVILLE

carry on personal correspondence toward this aim, to enlist pulpits in promoting religious revival, to publish devotional literature, to work for the reformation of pastoral methods and the inner life of the church, to promote the work of itinerant personal evangelists, to provide for the establishment of Christian schools. It can readily be seen that in these aims they were not originating anything but were merely enlisting themselves in projects, most of which Spener had advocated fifty years before. Their fields of labor were not far to seek. They chose to intensify and expand what they were already doing in Dresden, Berthelsdorf, and Görlitz. Of course, Berthelsdorf meant Herrnhut too, for the parish church was where the settlers worshiped.

The Four Brethren were not long in engaging a printer, Gottlieb Ludwig by name, from Pirna, for their proposed publication house. That was to have been set up at Berthelsdorf; but before it could get into operation, the Saxon cabinet in May of 1724 withheld its permission. Count Henry von Reuss of Ebersdorf came to the rescue by allowing the press to be set up in his more autonomous territory of Köstritz. There it remained for two years. Zinzendorf and his colleagues did not limit their publishing efforts to their own press but also engaged other printers as occasions required.

Little time elapsed before they made a beginning with their schools. In fact these antedated their covenant of 1723, for Lady Gersdorf had several years before established an orphanage at Hennersdorf. About the time that the Four Brethren were making their covenant, she gave some money for a charity school at Berthelsdorf. Another of the first efforts was a girls' school in the Berthelsdorf home of Lady Johanna Sophia von Zezschwitz, who in 1724 was married to Watteville.

That the cluster of institutions which the count envisioned had been inspired by what he had observed in Halle is readily detected in the projected plans for a large building with rooms enough to house several enterprises. There were to be an academy for the sons of noblemen, such as Zinzendorf and Watteville had themselves attended; a bookshop; and an apothecary shop. It was this last which was one of Halle's best sources of income to help carry the projects in which there was no profit. Subscribing two hundred dollars each, getting another hundred from a Captain von Schweinitz, and borrowing seven hundred more, they scraped together the money necessary for a start. They decided to locate the institution at the base of the Hutberg where the Moravian refugees were building their homes.

The project became important, not by developing as expected, but by accidentally becoming a turning point in the rise of Herrnhut. The cornerstone laying for the building took place on May 12, 1724, which happened to be the same day on which there arrived in Herrnhut five young men from Zauchenthal, Moravia. Their departure from their homes was the fruit of the religious revival in general and of Christian David's work in particular. This awakening, as it spread, had drawn increasing suppression from local authorities in various communities. Emigration became more of an issue than ever. Besides, a new factor arose in the case of some of those involved. The Neissers and the other few who had already left their homes had been content simply to move to a country where they could earn their living and worship God according to their Protestant convictions. Now some were entertaining the thought of reviving the church of the Bohemian Brethren. Among these were the five young men of Zauchenthal—three of them named David Nitschmann; another, Melchior Zeisberger; and the last, John Töltschig. All of them were the sons of well-to-do parents and had much to lose in leaving.

Having defied the regulations against taking part in private religious services, they were equally ready when the occasion arose to defy the edict against emigration. During the night of May 2, 1724, they fled their native village, intending to go to Lissa, Poland, where some semblance of organization of the Bohemian Brethren had been maintained within the Reformed Church. It was their hope to help this remnant effect the re-establishment of their pre-Reformation denomination.

En route to Poland and safely out of the reach of Austrian authority, they decided upon a detour to Herrnhut, about which Christian David had spoken in such glowing terms. The little collection of small houses and the meager field of grain struggling for growth in the still untamed surroundings did not impress them upon their arrival on that May 12. Rothe's initial cold reception changed to warmth when he learned more about them, and the Neissers were overjoyed to see them; but the newcomers were still disappointed. They soon met the count, but he seemed little interested in them, preoccupied as he was with preparations for the cornerstone laying. During their first hours in Herrnhut the five young men were quite sure that not much of significance for them was in progress.

Then at three o'clock they heard Zinzendorf speak. They saw Watteville kneel on the cornerstone and heard him pray. The moving address, setting forth the purpose of the building, and the heart-warming prayer changed those five men of Moravia into Herrnhuters. David Nitschmann, the carpenter, eleven years later became the first bishop of the Renewed Moravian Church. David Nitschmann, the weaver, became known as "the syndic" because of his service to the Moravian Church as a negotiator with various governments. The third David Nitschmann died in an Austrian prison as a martyr in 1729, following his arrest on a journey home to help his fellow religionists. John Tölt-schig became a leader in the establishment of the Moravians in England. Melchior Zeisberger was one of the early Diaspora workers and during his long life occupied a place of influence among the Brethren in Germany.

The building erected upon that cornerstone was a college for young

COMMUNITY HOUSE IN HERRNHUT

noblemen only a year and a half, after which it became an orphanage. Its largest room was the first place of worship for the people at Herrnhut, apart from their parish church in Berthelsdorf. Eventually it became the *Gemein Haus* (community house) of the village. The five upon whom its beginning made such a transforming impression were the first of a growing number of Moravian immigrants who saw in Herrnhut the future realization of their dream of the renewal of the church of their fathers.

It was under the inspiration of Halle that Zinzendorf had entered upon his program of making his estate the center of a network of religious and educational effort. Therefore, it was in a confident mood that he visited Halle, shortly after the cornerstone laying, to report his undertakings to Francke. Expecting encouragement and helpful advice, the count met with just the opposite. Francke's colleague, Anton, was enthusiastic; but Francke himself apparently had expected to be taken into confidence sooner and looked upon his friend's scheme as a rival to his own institutions. Nevertheless, Zinzendorf and Francke personally retained their high regard for each other. Their last visit together in Halle in October of 1726 was a happy occasion. With the death of Francke the following year the rift between Halle and Herrnhut widened.

The rapid growth of Herrnhut during its first five years created both internal and external problems. The Moravian immigrants, practically all from the German areas of their homeland, were joined by many native German Pietists and other religious enthusiasts who were not Pietists. It became necessary to screen carefully applicants for settlement. Those who came for other than sound religious reasons were sent on their way. Those who did find a haven in Herrnhut found that learning to live together was not easy, for along with zeal they had brought diversity of opinion. More than once the infant village was near shipwreck on the rocks of discord.

Christian David's success in recruiting immigrants from Moravia met growing resistance from Austrian authorities. David Nitschmann the martyr was only one of scores who experienced the strong arm of the law. The count was beginning to be embarrassed, for it appeared as if he personally were fomenting rebellion in a foreign country. Actually David's frequent trips to Moravia were against his express wishes. In an attempt to ease the tension Zinzendorf, in 1726, made a personal visit to Austria to consult with Cardinal von Schrattenbach, bishop of Olmütz, and with his brother, Count Otto von Schrattenbach, an officer in the imperial service. He accomplished nothing in appealing for the right of Protestants to emigrate, though the appeal was based upon a provision of the Treaty of Westphalia. Nor was his request for the liberation of Nitschmann listened to. Zinzendorf learned afterward that he himself had been in danger of arrest and that only the brevity of his stay had saved him. It was the first of many journeys he made throughout the rest of his life on behalf of his Herrnhuters.

Other troubles came from neighboring landowners who complained that Herrnhut was luring their tenants away from their homes and undermining the loyalty due their superiors. Unfriendly parish clergy joined in these complaints as Rothe's eloquence filled the Berthelsdorf church to the point where this edifice had to be enlarged. The withholding of governmental sanction for a printing press no doubt stemmed from this opposition. Efforts were made at the capital to have the extrachurch activities at Herrnhut suppressed. But if the count had enemies in Dresden, he also had friends; and the new community remained free to go its way.

The internal troubles of Herrnhut were more serious. Some of the newcomers were Lutherans, others were Calvinists, and still others complete dissenters from established churches. The immigrants from Bohemia and Moravia had been outwardly Roman Catholics. Their private religious lives had found expression in conventicles in which had been practiced some of the simple biblical piety of the Bohemian Brethren, and which had more recently been quickened by the Pietism that had arisen within Lutheranism. Though grateful to their Lutheran benefactor, they were reluctant to lose their identity by joining the Berthelsdorf church outright. Adding to the village's problem in late 1726 was the arrival of a company of Schwenkfelders who were no longer tolerated in neighboring Silesia. These were the followers of Casper Schwenkfeld, a Silesian nobleman who was a contemporary of Luther. Disagreeing with the reformer on a number of items, particularly the Lord's Supper, he had founded a sect of his own.

From the start of Rothe's pastorate it was obvious that he and Heitz would clash. Pietists though they both were, the Lutheranism of the one could not come to terms with the Calvinism of the other. Subjects of disagreement included election, auricular confession, and the form of the bread to be used at Communion. Watteville's tact was helpful in softening the differences between the two during the year when both were on the scene. The problem was solved with Heitz's departure in August of 1723.

Later, as the Moravian refugees grew in number, the friction between them and the regular parish members deepened. A point of difference was the nature of confession before the Communion. The Moravians preferred a general confession to the individual one which Rothe had introduced into the parish. Zinzendorf persuaded Rothe to yield, but other questions arose from time to time. Generally the Moravians, in line with their tradition, leaned toward a less liturgical form of church life than they experienced in the Lutheran Church.

The count, as much as his court duties permitted, sought personally to smooth out these differences. Toward the close of the year 1725, for instance, he spent the greater part of three days and three nights in heart-searching conferences with the Herrnhuters, in which he learned to know their convictions and in which he freely shared his own. Particularly helpful was a series of biblical studies which he conducted following these conferences. That this effort had its good effect is revealed in an exchange of letters between Zinzendorf and Francke. The latter, having learned of what was going on, cautioned his friend in a very kindly spirit against tolerating sectarianism, reminding him of his obligation as one in high position to uphold the Augsburg Confession. Under date of March 2, 1725, the count was able to reply: "The Lord has bestowed grace so that after sufficient instruction all have been united for some months and remain in brotherly affection." Christian David in telling later of the beginning of Herrnhut adds his testimony as to the count's effectiveness in pouring oil on troubled waters.

About the same time—namely, in early February of 1725—an attempt at better human relationships was the introduction by Rothe, with Zinzendorf's backing, of certain "apostolic offices" into the congregation. Rothe after a church service asked a number of persons of both sexes to remain, for they were the ones chosen for special duties. After each had expressed himself willing to serve, he was assigned to his particular office by lot—one of the earliest, if not the first, instance of the use of the lot in Herrnhut. Thus some were exhorters, some teachers, some visitors of the sick, some almoners, some overseers. Both the regular members of the Berthelsdorf parish and the immigrants were represented. Among the former were Baron von Watteville and his new bride, the tailor Mordelt, the gardener Hahn, and the peasant girl Anna-Lena. Among the immigrants were Christian David, Jacob Neisser and his wife, and George Jäschke. The results were not an unmixed blessing. Though the next year and a half were not particularly difficult, Herrnhut was far from being an ideal religious community. Many of the villagers were not yet ready to take advice and discipline from those of their peers whom the new arrangement had invested with authority.

The restless spirit of Christian David was a matter of growing concern to Zinzendorf and his colleagues. Appointed a visitor of the sick, he paid little attention to this responsibility but left on one of his evangelistic journeys whenever he felt so led. Nor could the community rely upon his badly needed skill as a carpenter. For the next two years the man who had done so much to bring Herrnhut into being played pretty much of a lone hand, though his itinerations were still bringing newcomers.

Events began moving toward a crisis with the arrival in Herrnhut of the fanatic John Sigmund Krüger in August of 1726, the time when Zinzendorf was on his mission to Austria. Krüger during the previous year had been in the service of Count Reuss as a counselor at Ebersdorf, a position for which Zinzendorf had recommended him. There he had become involved in the theological disputes with the court preacher Schubert, with the result that he was barred from Communion. Later he wrote and had printed, without authorization, on the Zinzendorf press at Ebersdorf a very unorthodox pamphlet on the person of Christ. The writing was immediately confiscated and Krüger dismissed from Ebersdorf. Though not agreeing with the man's posi-

CHRISTIAN DAVID

tion, Zinzendorf was not in accord with the arbitrary suppression of the publication. This and the fact that the count had been earlier impressed with the man's spirituality account for his coming to Herrnhut. The affair proved to be one of the many instances of Zinzendorf's generous spirit bringing him grief.

Krüger came not as a humbled man without a job but as a messiah. He intended, as he said, "to go among the Jews and proclaim Jesus, the one and threefold God." Like many another self-styled prophet, Krüger was not long in attracting a following. Among his first and most ardent disciples was Christian David himself. Krüger appeal, besides that of his appearance of extraordinary piety and his stirring messages, rested upon the underlying frustrations of the community. Many shared David's view that the routine religious life of a Lutheran parish was hardly worth the sacrifices which they had made in leaving their homes. When Krüger preached separation from the church, particularly abstinence from the sacrament of Communion, he struck a responsive note.

A visit to Herrnhut of Pastor Steinmetz in December of 1726, at Zinzendorf's invitation, had the opposite effect of that hoped for. Steinmetz, in charge of a church in the border city of Teschen, had long been a spiritual adviser of the evangelicals in Moravia; and the count felt that perhaps a word from him would help. The people apparently misinterpreted the pastor's talk on brotherly love and gained the impression that he was on their side in their opposition to the churchliness of Zinzendorf and Rothe. Shortly thereafter the majority of the Herrnhuters were completely on the side of Krüger, who was calling Zinzendorf "the beast" and Rothe "the false prophet." Christian David's defection went to the extent of his building a cottage for himself and digging his own well outside the boundaries of the village.

At the end of 1726 when the trouble was at its height, Krüger suffered a mental breakdown of such a severe nature that he had to be physically restrained. On January 15, after a temporary recovery, he left Herrnhut for good, except for a brief visit fifteen years later. The man never fully recovered and lived a pathetic existence, wandering from place to place as a beggar.

The sad exit of Krüger was the turning point in the crisis, but it was to be some months before peace was achieved. In all of this the patience of Zinzendorf was remarkable. With only a few definitely on his side—notably, Watteville, David Nitschmann the future bishop, Martin Dober and the physician Gutbier—he still refrained from exercising his powers as a landlord and took no action against the dissidents. Rothe was less patient and refuted the separatists and theologically unorthodox from the pulpit. The count in objecting to this felt that it only added fuel to the fire. By nature he was opposed to enforcing religious conformity by external regulations. His one major concern was that nothing be done at Herrnhut at variance with the Augsburg Confession. If Zinzendorf could be blamed for the trouble of the infant community, it was not because of his dominance but because of his almost naïve lack of interference. When the village eventually did arrive at an amicable settlement of its discord, it was only after he had asserted himself more firmly as lord of the manor.

As a result of their differing points of view on how to proceed, the count and his pastor came to an agreement on a division of labor between Berthelsdorf and Herrnhut. Rothe was to have a free hand in the former, with Zinzendorf assisting him only as patron. In Herrnhut, on the contrary, Zinzendorf was to act as assistant pastor and catechist and as such to deal with the Moravians in his own way. This arrangement was made immediately following the count's release from state service and was announced on the Sunday after Easter, 1727.

With Zinzendorf now living in the community, in Berthelsdorf from April to June, and after that permanently in the newly erected *Herrschaftshaus* in Herrnhut, he was able to appraise the situation more clearly. In order to devote himself completely to the matter in hand, he entrusted his business affairs to his wife and Watteville. Similarly Marche, the former family tutor, had gradually been assuming the role of legal advisor. The count, with his hands free, first concentrated on mingling with the Herrnhuters in the manner of a new pastor getting acquainted with his parishioners, though he was not yet an ordained man. It did not take him long to see what was needed. He discovered that the problem of Herrnhut was to allow the Moravians to retain their identity, as the continuation of the old *Unitas Fratrum,* within the framework of the state church. This meant the setting up of a system of church discipline which had been one of the distinctive features of the old Unity. To do this without violating the church law of Saxony was a delicate matter. Rothe as pastor and Marche as legal expert were helpful. Within a month Zinzendorf took the step that he had previously been reluctant to take, to draft a set of rules for Herrnhut, providing both for its life as a civic community and as a suborganization within an established-church parish.

May 12, 1727, became a milestone in the history of the Renewed Moravian Church, for that was the day on which Herrnhut's new constitution was formally adopted. For the occasion the count summoned the three hundred residents to a mass meeting at which he spoke for three hours on the evils of schism and the aim of the proposed agreement which he was presenting. The one part dealing with their civic responsibilities was entitled *Manorial Injunctions and Prohibitions,* and the other, drafted in the form of forty-two statutes, relating to their association as a fellowship of Christians was entitled *Brotherly Agreement of the Brethren from Bohemia and Moravia and Others, Binding Them to Walk According to the Apostolic Rule.* The injunctions and prohibitions were of the form usually followed for newly created districts and had, therefore, a legal character. The forty-two statutes, on the other hand, were a set of rules for a voluntary religious organization and were of significance in serving as a pattern for future Moravian communities.

The unanimous and warm acceptance of the regulations is a tribute to the tact that had gone into their formulation. Catholic in spirit, they allowed for differing opinions. The emphasis was upon practical Christian behavior, for which they were sufficiently explicit to escape being vague generalities. The forty-two statutes began in this vein:

It shall be forever remembered by the inhabitants of Herrnhut, that it was built on the grace of the living God, that it is a work of his own hand, yet not properly intended to be a new town, but only an establishment erected for the Brethren and for the Brethren's sake.

Herrnhut, and its original old inhabitants, must remain in a constant bond of love with all children of God belonging to the different religious persuasions—they must judge none, enter into no disputes with any, nor behave themselves unseemly toward any, but rather seek to maintain among themselves the pure evangelical doctrine, simplicity, and grace.[1]

The conclusion of the day's events of May 12 was a pledge to abide by the new order, a pledge made individually to the count with symbolic handclasp by all present. Particularly impressive was it that Christian David, won back in the previous weeks, was among them. One of the valuable extant accounts of Herrnhut's troubled time and its solution is a letter which David wrote to Heitz a year later. His appraisal, surprisingly objective for one so deeply involved in the chain of events, gives full credit to Zinzendorf's love and impartiality in transforming discord into harmony. Rothe comes off with less credit in David's opinion, which is to the effect that if the count had intervened sooner when Rothe's ineptness was evident, much of the dissension might have been avoided.

There was also on that memorable day the beginning of village organization, the first step being the election of twelve elders. Emphasizing that the elder's function is purely spiritual was the provision that none of noble rank or of high education be eligible. Accordingly, the first elders were men who worked with their hands and who represented such skills as carpenter, weaver, cutler, potter, cobbler. Christian David was among those chosen, a fact which moved him deeply. Of these

---

[1] *Memorial Days of the Renewed Church of the Unitas Fratrum,* p. 111.

twelve, four were chosen by lot on May 20 as "chief elders." These four were Christian David; Melchior Nitschmann, the weaver; Christopher Hoffmann, one of the Schwenkfelders; and George Nitschmann, like David, a carpenter. These were the prototypes of generations of Moravian missionaries and itinerant Diaspora evangelists serving humbly wherever their church sent them.

Soon there were night watchmen, inspectors of public works—such as fields, gardens, streets, well—watchers by the sick, almoners of the poor, and other special appointees. The night watchers announced the hours with hymns from six stations in the community. Reminiscent of the count's Halle school days was his organization of bands or classes, known as *Bunden,* of seven or eight members who had a special spiritual affinity for one another.

The events of May 12 initiated a month's long period of religious revival in which previous discords were dissolved, so that Herrnhut during the summer of 1727 became a brotherhood. The count himself, as warden of the congregation, was the central figure in this ascending tempo of spiritual life. At the heart of the system of congregational oversight were the frequent conferences he held with the elders. Next in order were his conferences with the various other officers. His right-hand man was Watteville. Pastor Rothe, too, was caught up in the heightened spirituality, and his sermons became an increasingly effective influence as the summer progressed. Visitors from surrounding communities were attracted in growing numbers to the services of song, prayer, testimony, and preaching in both Berthelsdorf and Herrnhut. This gave rise to the so-called strangers' meeting, which in the beginning was a Sunday-afternoon meeting for the visitors who could not be accommodated at the morning service and which became an institution of long standing at Herrnhut.

Zinzendorf had been well aware of the fact that in the Moravian refugees he had on his hands more than just a group of religious enthusiasts. Yet there was little specific material concerning the church of their fathers available to him. The refugees themselves had but vague knowledge of their own history. This accounted in part for his reluctance to allow them to depart from the established Lutheran worship. During the weeks of July 22 to August 4, while conferring with a relative, Baron Gersdorf, at Hartmannsdorf in neighboring Silesia, the count began to change his mind on the subject. In the course of this visit he chanced upon a copy of the *Ratio Disciplinae,* the Latin version of the constitution of the Bohemian Brethren, in the city library at Zittau. To this, Bishop John Amos Comenius had added a historical preface in 1660. Zinzendorf, always an opponent of sectarianism, upon reading this constitution and history realized for the first time that here had been not a sect but a fully established church antedating Lutheranism itself.

Immediately he prepared a German excerpt of this small volume for the Herrnhuters, and he communicated it to the congregation upon his return. The people were at once struck with the similarity between the organization of the church of their fathers and the statutes to which they had so recently subscribed. They saw in this the hand of God, which further strengthened the morale of the community.

The high point of the revival was a Communion service on Wednesday, August 13, generally regarded as the spiritual birthday of the Renewed Moravian Church. The Communion was a special one called by Rothe, and in which he and the count played leading roles, following a remarkable upsurge of community religious feeling that began with the morning service on the preceding Sunday. Rothe began the memorable day with a preparatory address at Herrnhut, after which the congregation walked the mile to the Berthelsdorf church. There, following the reception of two girls into the congregation by confirmation, the count led the kneeling worshipers in fervent prayer and in the confession. Three other prayers followed. Pastor John Süss of Hennersdorf pronounced the absolution and administered the elements, Rothe preferring to partake as one of the congregation. The service was accompanied by a remarkable sense of the presence of the Holy Spirit, the reality of which experience was borne out by the fruits which followed.

Christian David and Melchior Nitschmann happened to be absent on a mission to Sorau in Hungary and had been specifically remembered in the above-mentioned prayers. While at Sorau, the two had gone to nearby Sablat to visit David Schneider, whom Christian David felt he had previously misled by his separatist views. There the latter also examined the belfry of the orphanage as a pattern for a similar one at Herrnhut. At ten o'clock, while he and Nitschmann were with Schneider in the orphanage, there came upon the two Herrnhuters a powerful impulse to pray, upon which they at once acted. When they returned to Herrnhut, they asked immediately what had happened on the morning of August 13. They learned then of the Communion serv-

THE BERTHELSDORF PARISH CHURCH

ice and that they had been prayed for at the very time when they had felt the urge to pray in Sablat.

Testimony is eloquent concerning the crucial importance of August 13 to the Moravian movement. Christian David wrote: "It is truly a miracle of God that out of so many kinds and sects as Catholic Lutheran, Reformed, Separatist, Gichtelian, and the like, we could have been melted into one." Spangenberg, though not a participant, spoke for the Brethren when he said, "There were we baptized by the Holy Spirit himself to one love." David Nitschmann wrote, "From that time on, Herrnhut became a living congregation of Jesus Christ." Zinzendorf himself referred to the day in relation to the congregation as "its Pentecost."

It is incorrect to assume, however, that the Pentecostal experience of August 13, 1727, had put an end to all disunity in Herrnhut. Deep religious experience does much to ease some of the ordinary frictions of living together, but it also creates areas of irritation which may not exist in the case of the unwakened. So it was with Herrnhut. While the over-all picture is that of a flourishing, harmonious community in dead earnest, there still were shadows. The difference is that after 1727 the Moravian Brotherhood had sufficient momentum to handle its problems in stride. The progress to be described in the following chapter was not without accompanying tensions, but there was an *esprit de corps* which made incidents of what might earlier have been grave crises.

The most delicate problem was the status of the Herrnhut congregation with reference to the Lutheran parish of Berthelsdorf. The more Herrnhut grew, the more difficult it was to look upon it as a mere society. It was obvious to many that Zinzendorf had gone far beyond the idea of the Pietist society. Unfriendly critics accused him of fostering a sect. The presence of outright dissenters like the Schwenkfelders, though these had been brought to temporary conformity, did not ease matters. Neighboring pastors, perhaps out of jealousy, pressed the issue. Rothe himself began to be sensitive to these criticisms and to cool toward Herrnhut, though it was not until 1737 that he eventually left for a new parish.

During the absence of the count at Jena in the summer of 1728 Rothe was persuaded by some of his clergy critics to make an attempt to abolish both the name and regulations of the Brethren's Church. The idea was to amalgamate completely with the Lutheran parish. By using the plea that such a step would not only forestall persecution in Herrnhut but also make it easier for the persecuted evangelicals still left in Bohemia and Moravia, Rothe convinced Christian David and other elders of the wisdom of such a move. It so happened that some of the Brethren who would most likely have objected to the proposed move were, like Zinzendorf, away on a mission for their church. David and Andrew Beyer, as leaders of the faction that wished to discard the Moravian discipline, went to Jena to confer with the count. If they were expecting his approval of the plan, they were disappointed. Zinzendorf and the brethren who had gone to Jena with him were vigorously opposed, expressing themselves in a letter dated August 13 and signed by David Nitschmann, George Böhnisch, and Matthias Miksch. A few days later the count put teeth into his objections by sending a letter in which he reminded the Herrnhuters of his rights as feudal lord.

Several considerations entered into his thinking. He was convinced that such action did not represent the wishes of the majority of the Moravians, who, deprived of their ancient name and discipline, would again become restless and leave Herrnhut and the state church completely. The concessions which it was now proposed be abandoned were among the inducements that had attracted many of the refugees in the first place. Furthermore, he rejected as unworthy the argument that it would avoid persecution. Also, probably by this time Zinzendorf had come to see the practical value of the church discipline under which Herrnhut had been living for a year. His views were seconded by the Jena students in fellowship with the Moravian movement. This group, in a *Letter of Union* drawn up by Spangenberg and signed by 102 students and professors, urged the Herrnhuters not to be ashamed of their forefathers but to maintain their brotherly union and discipline.

That such a major difference of opinion did not seriously disrupt the community, as it might have at an earlier date, is a tribute to the deepening maturity of the Brotherhood, to the gentle tact of the count, and to his attention to legal details. He was absent until October 12, and upon his return the strained situation was evident. The first night he talked with his secretary Tobias Frederick until three in the morning. He delayed speaking publicly to the congregation for a number of days. If he felt any resentment toward Rothe because of his part in the affair, he kept it to himself. When the count did address the congregation, on October 17, he did so on the text Gal. 5:9-10: "A little leaven leaveneth the whole lump. I have confidence in you through the Lord, that ye will be none otherwise minded: but he that troubleth you shall bear his judgment, whosoever he be." Appropriate as these words may have been, they were not chosen beforehand by Zinzendorf but turned to at random as he entered the place of worship. The Herrnhuters were persuaded to retain the name of Brethren.

The disputed point was next discussed at an elders' meeting, at which Christian David's part in it was acknowledged to be not so much a willful departure from policy as a mistake in judgment. Yet it was deemed best for him to resign as elder, which he did in fine spirit. At the same time there was a change in the personnel of the four chief elders. In order to clarify the situation the statutes comprising the *Brotherly Agreement* and the *Manorial Injunctions and Prohibitions,* first read to the congregation on May 12 of the preceding year, were reworked and presented simply under the title *Manorial Injunctions and Prohibitions.* The reason for this step was that the *Brotherly Agreement* had been interpreted by many as a confession of faith, which, had it been such, would have made it illegal. The *Manorial Injunctions and Prohibitions,* on the other hand, were entirely in accord with Saxon law. The signatures of the residents were not asked for under the new interpretation, for it was to be assumed that all inhabitants were subject to the laws of the community. These revised rules of November 6, 1728, called for loyalty to Lutheran forms of creed and worship but made specific provision for the retention of certain customs of the Bohemian Brethren in addition.

The matter thus ended happily, but Zinzendorf was not yet quite satisfied. Therefore, the following summer he had prepared a notarized document, commonly known as the *Notariats-Instrument,* which put a final legal conclusion to the whole affair. His procedure was to call together the German pastor and the Bohemian pastor of nearby Gross-Hennersdorf, his own parish minister, the justice of Berthelsdorf, and the men of Herrnhut. He had these last named affirm a set of declarations, which he then had drawn up as a notary's instrument, or deed; and on August 12, 1729, it was signed by eighty-three men of forty-seven different families. The document was ratified by the count as lord of the manor and by Pastor Rothe as parish minister on September 27 following. In this deed there is a narrative of the beginning of Herrnhut, emphasizing that the Brethren are neither separatists nor a new sect but are the descendants of a historic church recognized by Luther and Calvin. The paper expresses allegiance to the Augsburg Confession and the hope for the good will of the civil authorities.

Spangenberg in giving the account of this episode notes several items in the deed which are expressive of the count's thinking, as when the Brethren say: (1) that they will acknowledge none of their descendants as a brother or a sister who has not been converted; (2) that they will recognize as a true church of Christ only such a one in which the Word of God is preached in purity and simplicity, and in which the members live accordingly; (3) that they will not be separated from anyone who believes in Jesus his Lord, not by his own reason or strength, but by the power of the Holy Spirit, even though such a person may through ignorance of misguidance misinterpret some parts of Scripture; (4) that the lack of discipline among awakened people is a great defect, that the congregation is not to be blamed when anyone does not allow himself to be disciplined, that the blame lies upon the individual himself; (5) that they will not discard the names of brethren and sisters, for these names are scriptural, but that the addition of the names Bohemian and Moravian is to be regarded as sectarian; (6) that they are not content to rest upon the goodness of their fathers, but that they themselves seek to be spiritually alive; (7) that they will not love their lives above eternal things, for it is better to sacrifice one's life than to deny spiritual truths.

Zinzendorf's own words best explain why he acted as he did:

That gratitude toward the church to which I belonged and its reformers, whom God had sanctioned, required it. I should certainly have been no friend to Luther if I had let this opportunity slip of uniting the brethren with us. Besides, I clearly saw that if I suffered them to depart, some of them would go over to another great church, with the loss of their ecclesiastical constitution, by that the awakened would divide amongst all the smaller sects, and produce infinitely more confusion in general, than profit individually.[2]

[2] Spangenberg, *Leben Zinzendorfs,* tr. Jackson, p. 82.

10

THE DEVELOPING
HERRNHUT COMMUNITY

It had taken five years, from 1722 to 1727, for the Brotherhood, later to be known as the Renewed Moravian Church, to come into being. The next five years saw the emergence of most of the features which determined the peculiar role of the Brethren in the church world of Europe and America for the next two centuries. At the very center of this development was Zinzendorf himself. The year 1727 marks the time when Zinzendorfian Pietism began to diverge from its parent stock. In the years immediately following, Herrnhut became the kind of village which was to serve as a model for the twenty or more Moravian "settlement" congregations founded during the next fifty years. These communities were a blend of Pietism, the discipline of the Bohemian and Moravian Brethren, and the genius of an individual.

As soon as the count had convinced himself that Herrnhut could maintain its identity within the framework of the state church, he lost no time in giving shape to the raw materials in his hands. Overnight the village became a closely knit religio-socio-economic unit. Though Zinzendorf dominated the picture by virtue of his rank and personality, organization was remarkably democratic. A town meeting and a church council regulated secular and religious affairs. A communal court of justice supervised farming, handicrafts, and business, and acted as a board of arbitration in disputes. The elders, whose offices were among the earliest, continued their duties of spiritual oversight, though their numbers fluctuated from the original twelve. There was a constant turnover in personnel, not only among the elders, but in the case of most of the offices. Zinzendorf believed that no offices should be created until there were people qualified to fill them. He observed that an individual might lose his gifts or prove to be better fitted for some vacancy which presented itself. Hence, the number and the kind of offices were constantly in a state of flux. As in the New Testament church the emphasis was upon charismatic leadership which disregards social background and special training. Eventually one chief elder replaced the original arrangement of four.

The division of the congregation into small bands, begun in July of 1727, underwent extensive development, giving rise in about a decade to the more formal "choir" system based upon age, sex, and marital status. The bands met daily for worship and discussion in the room of the chosen leader, at work, under a tree, as the spirit moved them, in quite informal fashion. The unrestrained atmosphere of these congeniality groups served both as confessional and means of maintaining community discipline and morale. The count moved freely among the groups, from the smallest children on up, speaking to them or praying and singing with them, sometimes according to plan, sometimes in impromptu fashion.

A step of far-reaching consequence was the move of the unmarried men to a dormitory of their own in February of 1728, thereby bringing into existence the familiar institution known as the Single Brethren's house. It was more than a residence, for it was the focal point of handicraft industries and the training of apprentices. An important activity of this first group of Single Brethren was the spinning of wool. Here, too, many busied themselves with study in preparation for mission service. Two years later, in May of 1730, a group of eighteen single women, under the leadership of fifteen-year-old Anna Nitschmann, followed the same course, and the Single Sisters' house came into being. In neither case was celibacy held up as the ideal state, but both Single Brethren and Single Sisters pledged themselves to make matrimony secondary to service for Christ and church. Most Moravians eventually married, but many on special assignments postponed marriage until such time as it fitted into their life's work. At an early age children, too, were moved into dormitories for their upbringing, out of which arrangements grew the numerous boarding schools of the Brethren.

These social patterns grew partly out of practical necessity and were partly deliberate. It was the most efficient way for a poverty-stricken company of exiles to maintain themselves. Beyond that, Zinzendorf saw in these groupings the ideal method of Christian nurture. Though more than a decade was to pass before the system was in full vogue, already in these early years he had the thought that the merits of

Christ's life have a special import for each of the age and sex groupings. Some observers have felt that the theory came afterward, but the utterances of the count as early as 1729 reveal otherwise, as for instance his hymn *"Auf Maria Verkündigung,"* which makes reference to children, maidens, youths, married couples. After the community had begun its world-wide mission activity, the advantages of such a system became more obvious. It gave to Moravian missionaries, even to those with families, freedom of movement second only to the celibate missionaries of Roman Catholicism. They could rest content that their children were in devoted hands.

The division into small bands multiplied the number and variety of religious services. Their informal atmosphere encouraged innovations, such as the love feast, the cup of covenant, foot washing, festival days for each of the groups, song services. It was the Single Brethren who in 1729 held the first cup-of-covenant service in which they passed the cup from hand to hand, in imitation of Christ and the apostles, as they made a covenant to be true to Christ. It was also the Single Brethren who inaugurated the Easter sunrise service on the two-year-old cemetery on the Hutberg in 1732. In the early days of the love feast it was common for the service to be in the count's house on days of special significance, on Sunday evenings, or in connection with weddings. Of a private character, they were attended by a small company. They soon assumed a more inclusive aspect and were celebrated frequently by the whole congregation as well. There was much of the social, festive nature about these early love feasts as contrasted to the later, more liturgical form.

The deep religious life of the Hernnhuters could not help finding expression in song, as had been the case with their hymn-singing forefathers. For this the count was in his element, and he was the founder of the famed *Singstunde*. Aiding him in this was his musically gifted secretary, Tobias Frederick. The song service commonly opened with the singing of entire hymns and continued with the singing of single stanzas, skillfully but spontaneously chosen to form a unified theme in song. Hymnbooks were seldom used, except by visitors, since the count was of the conviction that a hymn must be memorized in order to express adequately the individual's Christian experience.

The use of a scriptural text as a daily watchword, now widely observed by the reading of the *Daily Texts,* came out of the evening song services of the year 1728. In the early part of the year at these services

Zinzendorf delivered addresses on a scripture text or a hymn stanza. On May 3 he suggested that the stanza he had used be considered the watchword for the following day. This became a daily practice. Later Zinzendorf, with the assistance of the elders, made a collection of texts out of which an elder drew one each evening for distribution throughout the settlement the next morning. This was the procedure until 1731, when for the first time the texts were printed in advance, which has been the case ever since.

A feature of Herrnhut's prayer life was the hourly intercession, begun on August 27, 1727, by twenty-four brethren and twenty-four sisters. Carried on without interruption for a hundred years, it was a program according to which someone was engaged in intercessory prayer every hour of the day. The intercessors met weekly for conferences, an important part of which was the reading of letters and messages from their brethren in distant places. Thus they were provided with specific projects and persons for whom to pray.

FIRST PLACE OF WORSHIP INSIDE THE COMMUNITY HOUSE

The community began its day with a worship service at dawn. Later morning services were held for the aged and infirm and then for the children. The day closed with the song service. On Sundays there was a full round of worship: the early morning prayer; the series of meetings for the various bands or later choirs; the eleven o'clock church service at Berthelsdorf, moved later to Hernnhut; the afternoon service for those unable to attend in the morning and for visitors, at which the count or some other layman reviewed the sermon the pastor had delivered that day; and services before retiring. Herrnhut knew no such thing as the separation of the religious and the secular life in the highly disciplined, hard-working, praying congregation. Only the hours of eleven to four were left for sleep, and during these hours the nightly watch was counting off the hours with song, and those of the hourly intercession were on their knees. In Herrnhut, too, spiritual leadership was charismatic, not based upon formal training. Illustrative is the case of Martin Dober the potter:

At five he led the congregation in morning worship in the chapel of the orphanage. In attendance were some distinguished and learned people. At nine o'clock he might be visited by a count, a nobleman, or a professor, who found him barefoot in his shop. For him that was quite proper. They seated themselves before his potter's wheel and paid heed to his words. That was an expression of the Holy in old Herrnhut.[1]

The use of the lot for important decisions was common among Pietists in general. Zinzendorf and his Brethren in freely following this practice made its use one of the marked features of the inner life of Herrnhut and the whole Moravian Church for a century and a half. One of the earliest instances that we know of was Rothe's assignment of certain duties to designated persons in 1725. The first four elders in 1727 were chosen by lot. In 1728 the practice was introduced as a customary way of arriving at decisions in church councils and conferences. It was first used for marriage in 1732; and, soon after, its voluntary use in this connection was frequent. Zinzendorf appealed to the lot in many instances where he himself was involved.

All this free religion, thanks to the count, was scrupulously kept within the bounds of the established church. The Brethren were required to be as faithful to Sunday-morning church worship as to their own meetings. They partook regularly of Holy Communion, in the beginning quarterly, later monthly. They followed the liturgical order of worship throughout the year, according to Lutheran form. They looked upon Rothe as their pastor.

A combination of factors made it inevitable that what happened at Herrnhut should spread. The settlement had a contagious brand of Christianity. Beyond that, its leader was a count with entry to the ruling circles of many lands and whose restless nature moved him to

---

[1] Heinz Renkewitz, *Zinzendorf*, p. 37.

make use of this advantage. Pietism had set a precedent of earnest Christians' meeting in small groups, the *ecclesiola,* which maintained fellowship through travel and correspondence. The Moravian exiles were uprooted pilgrims who took readily to a vocation of itinerant evangelism. It is not surprising, therefore, that almost immediately following the awakening of 1727 Herrnhuters were on the march. They went out singly, in twos, or occasionally in larger groups to make contact with like-minded Christians. The aim was simply to cultivate fellowship among the children of God. Out of this grew a network of societies within the established churches, to which eventually the term "Diaspora" was applied. The spiritual warmth which these societies brought into the large state-church congregations was among the major contributions of the Moravian Brethren to continental Protestantism. This Diaspora was really Zinzendorf's first love, and more than any other element checked the development of Moravianism as a denomination.

From the beginning, as we have noted, Herrnhut evoked the interest of evangelical Christians. Visitors were numerous enough to require a special service for them within a few years. Guests were invariably present in the Zinzendorf home. A *Gasthof* was one of the early institutions of the village. Requests came to Herrnhut for men to conduct services in other parishes. Responding first to such calls from the immediate vicinity, the Brethren soon found themselves venturing farther afield. With amazing rapidity the itinerant messengers—we can scarcely call them evangelists, for they did not preach—established a network of societies throughout Germany and beyond. On September 27 Gottlieb Wried and Andrew Beyer set out upon a tour which took in Lichtenstein, Kalditz, Köstritz, Jena, Saalfeld, and Bayreuth. On this journey they made contact with Professor Buddeus of Jena and Prince Christian Ernest of Saalfeld. At Jena they made a deep impression upon the young student August Gottlieb Spangenberg, an impression which was to have far-reaching consequences.

Christian David and David Nitschmann the future bishop itinerated in Austrian territory. Andrew Beyer, after returning from his first extensive visits, set out again, this time to Teschen in Silesia. Augustine Neisser went to Sorau, Hungary. Melchior Nitschmann and George Schmidt visited Moravia in 1728. There they were imprisoned, and Nitschmann, still in prison, died the following year. Schmidt, after six years of confinement, was released and became one of the pioneer missionaries in Africa. Wencelaus Neisser, John Töltschig, and David Nitschmann the syndic were sent to England in order to establish a connection with the Society for the Propagation of Christian Knowledge. Not accomplishing this objective, they did, nevertheless, make a contact with a friend of Zinzendorf, Countess Lippe-Schaumberg, which indirectly led to the work of the Moravian Church in the British Isles a decade later. Melchior Zeizberger visited Stockholm. Christian David, already mentioned as itinerating in Austria, and Timothy Fiedler in 1729 made the first visit to the Baltic provinces, the prelude to the largest Diaspora field numerically. En route to Riga and Reval, David and Fiedler stopped in Berlin to visit Daniel Ernest Jablonsky, Reformed court preacher and grandson of John Amos Comenius. Jablonsky, though a Reformed clergyman, had been consecrated a Moravian bishop in 1699, and at this time was one of the two surviving bishops of the ancient Brethren's Church. Additional regions visited by these and other brethren were Württemberg, Switzerland, Pomerania, the Palatinate. Certainly the coverage was extensive.

Nor was the count himself content to remain at home. In November of 1727 he responded to an invitation to visit the above-mentioned Prince Christian Ernest of Saalfeld. The intinerary made it possible for him to stop in Jena, Rudelstadt, Bayreuth, and Coburg, where he spoke to numerous individuals of all ranks and where he lost no opportunity to attend religious services, at many of which he spoke. In Jena he strengthened the ties which Wried and Beyer had established a few weeks earlier. The hearty response among Jena students encouraged him to make several more visits the following year. Out of this group there were many besides Spangenberg who eventually entered the service of the Moravian Church. Zinzendorf had a similar happy reception in Halle, where he also visited in 1728. A guest in the home of Professor Lange, he was sought out by students and faculty alike, though opposition to him had already begun to crystallize. The next few years saw various other similar travels.

Personal contacts were followed up with a vigorous program of correspondence. The Herrnhut diary of February, 1728, for instance, reveals that there were at times a hundred or more letters on hand. On November 13, 1728, some fifty letters arrived from friends in Halle and Jena. These made a deep impression upon the people to whom they were read in the course of one of their meetings. Out of this custom of reading letters to the congregation developed another type of service, the so-called Prayer Day, or Congregation Day. This was a monthly festival, usually on a Saturday, for the reading of reports and letters from those out in the field and the growing circle of scattered friends of Herrnhut. After the beginning of foreign missions the sharing of mission news and prayer for mission enterprises became the prominent feature of the Congregation Day.

A closer look at Zinzendorf himself during these formative years of the Moravian movement finds him growing along with his projects. A remarkable aspect of his life is the continuity of his interests, for the things which fired the imagination of the boy were the same things which fired the imagination of the man. We saw already in the school-boy and the university student one who was tireless in correspondence, keeping a diary, scripture study, literary activity, organizational schemes pertaining to religion, personal counseling, travel. Maturity in no way took the edge from this drive to be everlastingly doing or organizing something. Herrnhut served as a channel for his diverse energy on a greatly expanded scale. It was to be expected that he still continued doing things which brought down upon him censure or ridicule. Fortunately, with his growing involvements, his capacities to cope with them were keeping pace. The measure of the man is to be seen in a sample of his diary for 1729:

February 1. A very blessed night in which in deep humility before his presence I prayed for everyone in Herrnhut by name.

16. I wasted much time in reading. I am not yet free of the lust for reading.

March 9. On the journey to Zittau I spoke earnestly with our servant Christoph and was deeply humbled by his testimony concerning himself. He is far in advance of me.

April 14. There came news in the mail that dear Melchior Nitschmann passed away in prison. This gave me an opportunity to examine my own hope, for with him went half of my heart.

May 5. I went up the Hutberg and laid before the Lord the 130 localities where his name is especially known. At the same time I went through the various sects and inner leadings with the Lord.

10. On Tuesday I was in Hennersdorf and talked of committing oneself to the Lord in childlike faith without longing for

> temporal things. I was so carried away in relating certain experiences that I said things I should have kept secret.
>
> July 12. David Nitschmann and Christian David were at my table. We took stock of ourselves and told each other what yet remained to mar the image of Christ. I let them tell me first what I lacked and then I told them what they lacked.[2]

An unusually gifted speaker, particularly as an extemporaneous one, Zinzendorf had some definite convictions on the subject of preaching. He believed that a supreme qualification for a preacher was to be first exclusively occupied with the things of God, and that the heart should always be full enough for the mouth to speak out of its abundance. It was this kind of preaching and personal religious conversation on the part of the count, on every conceivable occasion, which infused vitality into the Brotherhood. If present at baptismal services conducted by Rothe in Berthelsdorf, he directed scriptural exhortations and admonitions at the parents. At weddings he took pains to discourage worldly display and to maintain Christian simplicity. For the Single Brethren and the Single Sisters, too, he had homiletical advice. In the presence of death he constantly maintained that children of God ought to look forward to it joyfully. Speaking to children was especially dear to him. The divisions of the community into bands or classes multiplied the count's opportunities of speaking to people according to their differing needs. Yet he acknowledged his own limitations by keeping away from difficult or controversial passages of Scripture. He felt that as an unordained catechist he should confine himself to the well-known and commonly accepted Christian truths. He remained faithful to this principle even after his ordination.

As a youth Zinzendorf knew few people outside his own class. It was different beginning with the religious services he conducted in his Dresden apartment; the folks who came there to share Christian experience were from all strata of society. Conscious though he may have been of rank in secular affairs, the count saw no such distinctions in the spiritual realm. Since religion was his all absorbing interest, it was a simple matter for him to be at ease with anyone. Herrnhut meant a more radical departure, but with his impulsive enthusiasm he could easily make the transition from nobility to peasantry.

The countess found the adjustment harder to make. In her case

---

[2] Spangenberg, *Leben Zinzendorfs*, p. 541.

family tradition had accomplished what it had failed to do in the case of her husband, leaving her with a reserve which she could not readily cast aside. What he could do on impulse was for her a matter of gradual development. She did, of course, stand beside her husband in his enterprises, eventually occupying a position of leadership in her own right. But it did take her several years to be one with the people of Herrnhut, a fact which appears to have evoked some impatience on the part of the count. She was, however, one of the women who were first assigned special responsibility for spiritual oversight among their own sex. She belonged to one of the small bands as early as 1729. Her main responsibility was running the extensive Zinzendorf household on a limited budget. For years there was no line of demarcation between the family's personal expenses and the enterprises of the Brotherhood. In the beginning the count took the refugees generously into his employ as servants or personally paid the expenses of their evangelistic and missionary journeys. Spangenberg describes the household as it was in 1728:

His consort, who was also his faithful helpmate in the work which the Lord had assigned him, undertook this year, the office of matron, to the benefit of many of the brethren and sisters who served the community. From this time her house became the abode of many of the Saviour's servants, and a resting place for pilgrims. . . .

According to outward appearance, her house was like any other little court, surrounded with attendants of both sexes, for every species of employment; but he who considered it attentively, soon found that the whole had reference to the Saviour's cause. For she took many of the brethren and sisters into her service because they were employed in the church; although there were others, also, who had a family, and carried on their business, yet, at the same time ministered to the church, and ate their own bread.

The count, moreover, paid attention to the observance of good order amongst his domestics. He appointed Tobias Frederick his major-domo; and drew up a series of domestic regulations, which were read to them all. . . .

The count also this year laid out his garden in Herrnhut, with the intention of affording work to the poor when unable to earn anything.[3]

This same biographer makes little more than incidental mention of the birth of the Zinzendorf children. The countess had borne six of her twelve children by 1732 and had already seen four of them die. Servants there may have been plenty of, but Erdmuth Dorothea still merits deep admiration and sympathy.

[3] *Ibid.,* tr. Jackson, p. 97.

11

INTO ALL THE WORLD

Rapid as was the development of Herrnhut, the lively imagination of the count usually ran a step or two ahead of it. As the Brethren grew in their capacity for service, he saw to it that they were confronted with something into which to channel it. In the foreign-mission enterprise he found for his Moravians a project which would keep on challenging them indefinitely. Missions proved to be his greatest monument. Their beginnings demonstrated the usual Zinzendorf gift for the dramatic. Attending the coronation of Christian VI in Copenhagen in 1731, Zinzendorf met a Negro slave from the Danish West Indies. He had him come to Herrnhut as soon as possible to tell his story of the need for the gospel among his fellow slaves. A year later two of the Moravians launched the first mission.

Seemingly impulsive, the count's actions were consistent with his life plans; for the mission story had its beginning long before. The Danish-Halle missions in India had inspired the fifteen-year-old boy and his comrade Watteville to vow to work for the conversion of the heathen. They remembered that vow as the Order of the Grain of Mustard Seed took shape. It was still in their minds as they became party to the Covenant of the Four Brethren in 1723. Looking for a possible missionary outlet, John and David Nitschmann, as emissaries of Herrnhut in Copenhagen in 1727, had made it their business to inquire about Hans Egede's work in Greenland. They returned with a manuscript account of his undertaking. At the very first of the prayer days which began on February 10, 1728, and which developed into the Congregation Day, the subject under discussion concerned Turkey, Ethiopia, Greenland, Lapland, and other lands. The following day twenty-six of the Single Brethren banded themselves into a mission prayer group and the day after that moved into their own dormitory. There Zinzendorf himself directed their studies in writing, languages, geography, medicine, and Bible study. Meanwhile the success of the itinerant messengers on the home front encouraged the community to venture farther afield. The count's visit to Copenhagen unexpectedly opened the doors.

The coronation was the immediate reason for going to Denmark. Zinzendorf saw in it an opportunity to explore something more important. What he had in mind was some official appointment at the Danish court. It will be recalled that ten years before he had hoped for such a position in place of the one at Dresden. The Pietistic inclinations of the Danish royal family was in contrast to what he had encountered in the Saxon capital. The more congenial atmosphere of the Danish court, he felt, would leave him freedom to preach the gospel and to continue his personal direction of Hernnhut.

Zinzendorf felt himself too deeply involved in Herrnhut's affairs to go without consulting the community itself. Conversations with individuals uncovered overwhelming sentiment favoring the journey, since the count's colleagues by this time had been infected with his spirit. He still hesitated and had the question put to a vote at a congregational meeting. One hundred thirty-eight brethren voted for the trip, four against it, and the remaining fifteen declined to express an opinion. Not yet convinced, Zinzendorf consulted the lot, which confirmed the congregation's vote.

On April 25, accompanied by several others, among whom was David Nitschmann the future bishop, he set out for Copenhagen. The itinerary included a stop at Halle, where he had a visit lasting far into the night with inspectors Freyer and Baumgartner and numerous other admirers at the university. In Rendsburg he struck up what was to be a lasting friendship with George John Conradi, superintendent of the Lutherans in Schleswig-Holstein. Following an address by Zinzendorf at a gathering which included several pastors, Conradi performed on the harpsichord. This divine said: "When it gets to the point that counts preach and hold song services, general superintendents can at least accompany them."

Zinzendorf's experiences in the Danish capital, where he had quarters not far from the royal palace, were a repetition of what he had often encountered previously in court circles. He was graciously received and entertained at a round of functions preceding the coronation, including an invitation to the royal table itself, an invitation extended to only a few select guests. The high favor shown him by the king and queen put him in a position which attracted the attention of less-favored persons. These fell over one another in being attentive to him. Meeting Zinzendorf personally was for some of the people attending the coronation a bit of a surprise. Expecting to meet an odd personage, they found, instead, an individual of talent and charm in full command of the social graces. Yet he reacted no differently than he had twelve years before in Paris. He was bored. To the countess in Herrnhut he wrote in one of his letters: "I am hardly in a mood to write, because I have to report mostly worldly honors which inconvenience me."

He had not been in Copenhagen long before he had a direct inquiry from King Christian through his chamberlain, whether he would become one of his ministers, were the post offered him. This was a full-time position and not what Zinzendorf had in mind. Therefore, he answered immediately in the negative, citing his commitment to Herrnhut as a reason. At the same time he and some of his pietistically inclined friends presented his own original plan to be employed in some lesser capacity, leaving room for free-lance religious activity. This unusual proposal got little response, and the matter which had been uppermost in his mind when he left Herrnhut came to nought.

One honor he did accept, though reluctantly. He permitted the king at a private audience in the castle at Fredericksburg to bestow upon him the Order of the Danebrog, a recognition for distinguished service, either military or civilian. Coming to the castle by invitation, he was informed by Chamberlain von Pless of the king's intentions. The announcement troubled him deeply, his first reaction being concern over its effects upon his religious activities. The night before the scheduled event was one of sleeplessness and tears. He had practically resolved to decline the honor but was persuaded otherwise by his friend the Margravine of Culmbach. Moments before he was to appear before the king, she called him to her quarters and begged him to avoid the sensation which his refusal would arouse. In due course he was invested with the insigne of the Danebrog, a white-enameled gold cross suspended by a white ribbon with a red border.

The affinity between the religious outlook of the count and the Danish sovereign is shown in the latter's request that Zinzendorf recommend someone for the position of court chaplain and professor of divinity at Copenhagen. Not only did the king agree to the appointment of Chancellor Reuss of Tübingen, as proposed, but he also had Zinzendorf carry on the necessary correspondenece. Another service the count performed for Christian was the drafting of plans for an academy along the Halle pattern. Perhaps he had in mind that Zinzendorf might be induced to direct the institution himself; for after the latter had left Denmark, the scheme was abandoned.

The two months' stay in Copenhagen was not a matter limited to the affairs of the upper circle of society. For almost a decade the count had been on everyday terms with artisans and peasants, and experience had confirmed for him something that he had always instinctively felt, that spiritual gifts are independent of social rank. He put his time to good use in becoming acquainted with all classes. Meanwhile the several Herrnhuters who had accompanied him were likewise busy in cementing the ties of the scattered Pietist fellowship. Denmark from that time to the present has always been friendly soil for the Moravian Brethren, thought it has only one Moravian congregation, and that not organized until 1773.

From Denmark, under Frederick IV, had come the initiative for the Danish-Halle mission which had sent Ziegenbalg and Plütschau to India in 1706. Now this same country was about to become the point of departure for the first two mission fields of the Moravians, one in the Tropics and the other in the Arctic. Through his companions from Herrnhut, especially David Nitschmann, Zinzendorf became acquainted with Anthony Ulrich, the West Indian Negro body servant of Count Laurwig of Copenhagen. The man's tale of the spiritual destitution of his fellow Negroes on the plantations of his native St. Thomas struck a responsive chord in the count. Anthony himself, since coming to Denmark, had received Christian instruction and had been baptized. He spoke longingly of a sister and a brother on the island and of his confidence that they too would become Christians if given the opportunity. Zinzendorf was moved to the point of dispatching Nitschmann immediately for the West Indies, but he soon realized that the project was not as simple as that. Equally appealing to him was the challenge of Greenland, rekindled by his meeting with two Eskimos from that Danish outpost. Also, news from official quarters that Egede's mission efforts had failed and were about to be abandoned deepened the count's desire to act upon what he had in mind already in 1727.

Zinzendorf left Copenhagen on July 1 and three weeks later was back in Herrnhut, after various visits with distinguished friends en route. Among his stops were two further audiences with the Danish royal couple in Schleswig, where they had gone following the coronation. Back home among the Brethren, he reported the high lights of his journey. To him these were not the honors conferred upon him. More significant to him than the Order of the Danebrog was his meeting with two Eskimos and a Negro slave. In a stirring address to the Herrnhut congregation on July 23, he repeated Anthony's story. Two of his hearers, independently of each other, felt it directly aimed at them. The one, Leonard Dober, spent the night tossing on his couch in thinking about it. Opening his book of scripture texts at random in the morning, he read: "It is not a vain thing for you; because it is your life; and through this thing ye shall prolong your days." Hesitant to accept the words as God's definite answer, he consulted that evening the one person to whom he felt closest spiritually, Tobias Leopold. The conference between these two young men in the woods on the edge of Herrnhut was a deep emotional experience for both, for Leopold divulged that he too felt the Lord's call concerning the matter. Rising from their knees, the two then joined the rest of the Single Brethren in their vesper hymns in the streets of the village. As the singing brethren stopped before the Zinzendorf home where Pastor Schaeffer of Görlitz was a guest, the count and the visiting pastor stepped to the door. The former spoke to his friend to this effect: "My dear Sir, there are among these brethren messengers that will go forth to the heathen in St. Thomas, Greenland, Lapland." Dober and Leopold had additional confirmation for their resolve.

The following day, July 25, they drafted a letter to the count, offering themselves for mission service. Leopold did the writing, and his letter, now preserved in the Herrnhut archives, is the first recorded offer of service in Moravian missions. It concluded in this vein: "Dear Brother, please keep the matter private, think it over, and let us know your opinion. May the Lord lead us in the right path, rough though that path may be." It was not, however, the kind of sentiment to keep private, and Zinzendorf, after having conferred with the two, read their letter at the evening service with telling effect but without revealing the names of the authors.

More was yet to follow. Four days later Anthony Ulrich came to Herrnhut in the company of David Nitschmann, by previous arrangements of Zinzendorf. He repeated his story to the congregation. Not only did he dwell upon the spiritual need of his people, but also called attention to the fact that anyone preaching to the slaves would have to live among them, which would mean virtually becoming a slave himself. The long hours and the strict curfew laws made access to the plantation laborers difficult for one who did not share their lot. Some of the brethren upon hearing this lost their enthusiasm for the proposed mission. Leopold and Dober were not among them. If anything, they were strengthened in their resolve. Yet a year was allowed to pass before the congregation acted.

Zinzendorf himself was probably as responsible as anyone for the delay, not because he was among the fainthearted, but because he wished to give his volunteers full opportunity to count the cost. Neither at this time, nor later, did he urge his Moravians to enter mission service. Any candidate that revealed any degree of hesitancy was not enrolled in foreign service. He spent much time in the following months becoming thoroughly acquainted with the candidates for mission service, especially Dober. He chose him as a companion on a tour of Thuringia, during the course of which he helped prepare the man for his undertaking.

Dober's and Leopold's continuing resolution during a whole year convinced Zinzendorf and others that the time had come for action. The church council appealed to the lot, which confirmed Dober's appointment but directed Leopold to stay home a while longer. The council acceded to Dober's request for David Nitschmann as his companion, since he was the one who had first met Anthony in Copenhagen. The lot confirmed that Nitschmann should go.

A month later, on August 18, 1732, the congregation made of the evening song service a farewell occasion for these pioneers. Perhaps as many as a hundred hymns were sung in that epoch-making service. Then on August 21, at three in the morning, the count took the two departing missionaries in his carriage as far as Bautzen, a distance of fifteen miles. There, with imposition of hands, he laid upon them the Lord's blessing and sent them on their way. In the pockets of each were about three thaler, plus a small token which the count had thrust into their hands as they parted. Other assets were their dedication and the skills of their respective crafts. Dober was a potter, Nitschmann a carpenter. The former was a single man; the latter left a wife and child behind. A month's journey on foot took them to Copenhagen. After another month of breaking down opposition to their venture and waiting for passage, they set sail for St. Thomas, where they arrived on December 13. The mission they began continues to the present day.

Greenland was not forgotten and was occupied only a few months later than St. Thomas. The immediate effect of the announcement of the sentiments of Dober and Leopold to the Herrnhut congregation on that July day of 1731 had been to raise up two volunteers for Greenland. They were Matthew Stach and Frederick Böhnisch, both immigrants from Moravia. Like the former two volunteers, they discovered that each had independently of the other come to the same conclusion. Their period of waiting was a year and a half; and when their time had come, the lot, as in the other instance, fell upon only one. Stach was chosen to go, Böhnisch to stay at home. Not two, but three brethren were sent to begin this mission. Besides Matthew Stach there were his cousin, Christian Stach, and that indefatigable wanderer Christian David. These set out on foot for the Danish capital on January 19, 1733. Their ship sailed on April 10 and cast anchor at Godhaab on May 20. From this beginning the mission in Greenland continued until the Moravians turned it over to the Danish state church in the year 1900.

The Brethren at this point had much to learn about converting the heathen, for in 1732 missions were still only a small experiment among Protestants. Something had been learned from the Danish Halle mission, from Egede in Greenland, from the missionaries of the Society for Propagating the Gospel of the Anglican Church, and from a few others. For years the count had been a keen follower of what had been done by these pioneers, learning as much from their failures as from their successes. The result was that from the outset he had some very definite convictions on how his missionaries should approach the heathen. During the first generation of Moravian mission effort the men on the field acted almost exclusively in accord with personal directives from their leader. By the time of his death these instructions had set a pattern of mission theory and procedure which had proved itself so effective as to be continued.

Zinzendorf observed that the heathen did not need to be convinced of the existence of God, something which they already believed. The one thing they did not know was that the Saviour had died for them. He felt that Egede's failure in Greenland had been in presenting a theology before he presented a gospel. Therefore, he instructed his missionaries to begin with a Christocentric approach. Already in a letter of April 12, 1732, to an English missionary friend of the Society for Propagating the Gospel, some months before Dober and Nitschmann left Herrnhut for the West Indies, he expressed his theory of missions along three lines: First, the missionary is never to lord it over the heathen but to live humbly among them. Second, the missionary is to come directly to the point and preach the crucified Christ. Subjects as the Creation and the Fall can be discussed later. Third, the aim is not to convert whole nations but to look out for individual seekers after truth. He drew an analogy from the episode told in the book of Acts about the Ethiopian eunuch of the court of Queen Candace to whom Philip expounded the gospel only after being requested to do so.

The last point, which he called his "firstfruits" idea, bulked large in his thinking. He believed that the time for wholesale conversions to Christianity would have to await the conversion of the Jews. Until such time there would be only a few Candace souls, chosen by God, to be the firstfruits of their respective nations. In 1747 he had the gifted Moravian artist Valentine Haidt portray his idea on canvas for the chapel at Herrnhaag. The picture shows twenty-two converts from as many different racial and national groups, in native costume, arrayed before Christ on his throne in heaven. Each of the individuals appearing in the picture represents the first one of his or her tribe to have died as a Christian, hence the "firstfruits unto God and to the Lamb" (Rev. 14:4). This picture, now in Herrnhut, remains a dramatic portrayal of Zinzendorf's mission policy.

The result of this policy on mission growth was much the same as in the case of the church on the home front. As long as the count lived, the number of converts was small. With thousands of people under the care of Moravian missions at the time of his death, there were only about a thousand baptized members. For instance, Frederick Martin in 1736 gained seven hundred converts in the West Indies but baptized only thirty. Of course, this was at a time when Zinzendorf was still expecting the Moravian Church to disappear as a denomination and when he was still planning eventually to turn his converts over to established churches.

Even had the Brethren been able to support their early missionaries by sending them money from the home churches, Zinzendorf would not have permitted it. He believed it highly important that the missionary earn his own living in order to teach the natives the dignity of labor. He demanded that his personnel be strict in their obedience to both the civil and ecclesiastical laws of the country in which they were working. He forbade any activity in political affairs or meddling in controversial issues, such as employer-employee relationships. Finally,

Zinzendorf imbued his missionary staff with a spirit of self-effacement. No missionary biographies were ever published as long as he remained on the scene. Missionary letters and diaries were commonly multiplied in handwritten copy and passed around to be read at missionary meetings but not printed for general consumption. It was only after his death that Moravian mission literature served as an inspiration to readers outside of Moravian circles.

The count laid down exacting standards for mission service. Fortunately he had the genius to infect his followers with his driving energy and enthusiasm. His warrior band of apostles to the heathen never lacked for volunteers.

12

GROWING OPPOSITION

The inevitable was bound to happen sooner or later. Zinzendorf was not to stay long in good standing in the Lutheran Church, to which he asserted his loyalty all his days. The church of his time was not in position to know just how to incorporate within itself an organization like his Moravian Brethren. Organized religion alone was not responsible for its inability to absorb the vitality of this new thing. Not only religiously, but politically and socially as well, eighteenth-century Germany was not yet prepared for it. The accumulating opposition to the count first crystallized into a definite faction beginning about the middle of the year 1728, following his visits to the universities of Jena and Halle. From then on, in academic circles and among parish clergy, there never ceased to be a strong anti-Zinzendorf party as long as he lived. For years after his death the Moravians were the heirs of this opposition to him personally. His detractors were recruited alike from Pietists and Orthodox; though the former, being more nearly his rivals, were probably more vocal.

It could not have been otherwise but that there be opposition. In the first place it was odd for a count to make religion his vocation. To sponsor religious activity was one thing. To step into the pastor's realm was quite another thing. Who had ever heard of a person of his position acting as a catechist for refugee peasants? Worse still, he allowed these uneducated and unordained men to speak freely on religious subjects, even sending them on missions to other parishes. To be sure, they never actually preached or administered the Sacraments. Yet they were introducing novelties into church life. The strictly regulated regime at Herrnhut gave the appearance of a denial of the belief in salvation by faith. If Zinzendorf were as loyal to his church as he claimed to be, what about his fellowship with separatists, such as the followers of Dippel, Rock, and Schwenkfeld? There was to be noted, too, his association and correspondence with Roman Catholics.

Added to these and other religious questions were the political implications of his activities. His disregard of class distinctions smacked of subversion. Local authorities became uneasy about the restlessness he might stir up among the peasantry. Their fears were augmented by the objections from Austria to the emigration of evangelicals.

Those opposing him in the universities, according to Spangenberg, who as a Jena student was a firsthand observer, were suspicious of his theology. But they disliked more his innovations in the church. They had good reason to conclude from his extensive travel and correspondence, as well as from the tone of his addresses, that he was not satisfied to have just one Herrnhut but would soon be seeking to set up other places on the same pattern. It was clear to the Pietists that he did not want the religious life of converted people to be limited to conventicles for prayer, testimony, and Bible study. He was serious in his interpretations of scripture passages like Rom. 12:6-8 and I Cor. 12:4-11, which speak of diversities of gifts. He believed that laymen should be given an opportunity to exercise these gifts by having an active part in church affairs. He did not hesitate to point out to others the happy results of the Herrnhut experiment. Many objected to Zinzendorf for no other reason than his extraordinary zeal. He countered with the observation that what is credited with being moderation and good sense is often only fear of what others think.

Though his opposition did not deter him in the least from carrying out his projects, it did trouble him deeply, for he had an inherent aversion to religious controversy. Early in his adult life he resolved to leave attacks upon him unanswered. He said: "I hate controversy with God-fearing people and zealous professors as always. I will not seek to justify myself against them, neither by letter, nor by mouth, nor in print." He stuck by this principle with reference to himself but did not refrain from replying to attacks upon his friends.

Paradoxically much of Zinzendorf's unpopularity stemmed from his unceasing activity on behalf of the unity of evangelically minded Christians of all communions. A unique venture for a Protestant was his sponsorship, in late 1727, of a combination hymnal and prayer book for Roman Catholics. The immediate factor behind this undertaking was his warm friendship with a parish priest in Schweidnitz, Silesia. Struck with the profound effect of certain hymns upon the man, Zinzendorf proceeded to make a collection of songs which he felt belonged to the church universal. Prominent in this compilation were hymns of the seventeenth-century Silesian mystic John Scheffler, who had gone over from the Lutheran to the Roman Catholic Church. The count had scrupulously avoided all controversial doctrines and had stuck to his "heart religion" in the publication. It was welcomed and used by quite a number of Catholics.

Soon Zinzendorf conceived the idea of going a step farther by writing to the pope himself on behalf of such a hymnal on a more ambitious scale. The count's personal contacts and extensive correspondence with both Roman clergy and laymen had given him insight into and appreciation for their church. Such a letter to Benedict XIII, whom he regarded highly, did not seem to him at all presumptuous or out of line with his own Protestant convictions. The letter was drafted but never sent, because Zinzendorf foresaw some problems it would involve, the first one being the proper way for a Protestant to address the pontiff. Carelessly used as a bookmark, the unsent letter fell into the hands of the count's former steward Heitz, who happened to be visiting at Hennersdorf. Heitz, then at odds with his onetime employer, left with the letter in his pocket. Upon the prompt request of the count's wife he returned it, but not before copying it. Word of it got around, and years later it was even printed and presented as evidence that Zinzendorf had actually sent such a letter. His enemies made capital of it as proof that he was a menace to the Protestant church.

If Zinzendorf was unconventional because of his fraternization with Roman Catholics, he was equally so because of his fraternization with those at the opposite pole, as demonstrated in his visits to Berleberg, Schwarzenau, and Isenberg in 1730. In Berleberg there were many people who were disturbed by the teachings of the eccentric Pietist John Conrad Dippel. Zinzendorf was invited there by the reigning count in the hope that Herrnhut's solution for religious discord might be one for Berleberg. Through a series of meetings and tireless work with individuals, Zinzendorf did effect a remarkable degree of unity in the realm during his two weeks' stay. Dippel himself attended the meetings, and the two found themselves in deep agreement on the doctrine of Christ's complete atonement for the sins of the world. Subsequent teachings of Dippel, however, forced Zinzendorf to repudiate him.

In similar fashion at Schwarzenau the count succeeded in persuading some separatists to return to the sacraments which they had given up sixteen years before. From there he went to Wetteravia, where, upon invitation from the elders, he visited churches of the Inspired, also known as French Prophets, followers of John Frederick Rock. Two of the Herrnhuters had previously visited the region and had been cordially received. As in his contact with Dippel, Zinzendorf found that he had much in common with Rock; and the visit was followed with several years of friendly relationships, eventually to be broken off because of the separatist tendencies of the Inspired.

A year later when the teachings of the mystic Madame Guion had taken hold of some of the Herrnhuters, Zinzendorf attacked the problem by reading the works of this woman and holding meetings, at which he spoke on the subject. His attitude toward mystics of this type was that they were less to be avoided for their errors than for their bizarre expression of common truths. As a result of the count's fair way of confronting it, Madame Guion's influence in Herrnhut was of brief duration. His actions were consistent with his views on the character of an apostolic church, expressed during these years:

A chief characteristic of such a church is the intertwining of faith and godliness. Its true members know how to bear with and be kind to others and to strangers. With themselves they are uncommonly strict and severe. . . . They acknowledge themselves unworthy of divine grace, freedom and blessing, and carry their treasure about with them as if it were only loaned to them and might easily be lost. They shun persecution at a distance and gladly prevent it, but at close quarters they meet it boldly and stand immovable.[1]

The man of thirty had the same convictions as the precocious youth who had set himself to the task of reconciling quarreling theologians. As earlier, these convictions frequently got him into trouble.

His championship of people whom he felt had been treated too harshly or unjustly added to his difficulties. Typical is the case of a certain Victor Christoph Tuchfeld, a preacher who had got himself imprisoned in Berlin. Converted by Halle divines, Tuchfeld felt impelled to go further than they in religious reform. Specifically he did not think that freedom of speech in the church should be confined to the clergy. He advocated preaching in the streets according to the example of the primitive church. He spread his views in Halle, Berlin, Potsdam, and other places. When he became abusive toward the church to the point of preaching separation, he was arrested. He had been imprisoned for three years when Zinzendorf, in late 1729, interceded

[1] Spangenberg, *Leben Zinzendorfs*, p. 647.

for him by a letter to King Frederick. In his plea the count made no attempt to justify the man's conduct, which he acknowledged was in error, but expressed the opinion that the man could be set straight in a more scriptural way than imprisonment. He offered to receive the man at Herrnhut and there, with the help of experienced persons, seek to moderate his misguided energy. Frederick responded graciously to Zinzendorf by soon afterward setting Tuchfeld at liberty. The man did not come to Herrnhut, except for a brief visit, but later became a court chaplain in Berleberg. Such meddling did not add to the count's popularity with churchmen jealous of their authority.

A similar case was that involving his old friend Pastor Steinmetz of Teschen, Silesia, who had been so instrumental in encouraging the evangelical revival before there was a Herrnhut. In 1728 Steinmetz and some of his colleagues in their Lutheran parishes were put under severe restrictions by the authorities, for Silesia was then under Roman Catholic Austria. Zinzendorf, upon hearing about it, interceded by a letter to Father Tönnemann, the emperor's confessor. When the reply asked for particulars, Zinzendorf followed his first letter with another to Tönnemann and one to the emperor himself. Though his pleas were politely acknowledged by Tönnemann, who expressed a desire to keep peace between Roman Catholics and adherents of the Augsburg Confession, the situation did not improve for the Protestant pastors. When two years later Steinmetz was forced to quit his charge, Zinzendorf, through the Margrave of Bayreuth, secured a position for him as church superintendent of Neustadt on the Aisch.

Some of Zinzendorf's uncomfortable moments came more directly from within Herrnhut itself. Despite the attempt to screen applicants for residence in the village, persons temperamentally unfitted for such a community did manage to gain admittance now and then. One such was a certain baron who in 1729 made his home in Herrnhut. Within a few weeks he was a source of trouble, both because of his unworthy conduct and because of the dissatisfaction he created in others. The elders had little difficulty in persuading the man to leave, but the problems he left behind were not so easily disposed of. When mild measures failed, the count was moved to preach a strong sermon against members of the disaffected faction and to excommunicate some of them. Since, on this occasion, most of the Herrnhuters were on the side of Zinzendorf, the incident was not serious within the congregation. It was much more regrettable with reference to the outside world, for those who felt that they had been mistreated spread the report that the count dealt in curses and excommunications. The gossip even went to the extent of pointing the finger of suspicion at his morals. The elders, instead of shying away from such an accusation against their patron, conducted a thorough investigation, which completely absolved him.

Besides letters and pamphlets directed against the count and Herrnhut, some of the itinerant messengers were mistreated. A few neighboring towns levied fines upon them or imprisoned them for conducting religious meetings.

On the brighter side of the picture the opposition moved many admirers to rise up in the count's defense. These wrote letters of encouragement to him. Conspicuous among these friends was the aforementioned Daniel Ernest Jablonsky of Berlin, whom the Brethren had visited on their way to the Baltic States. He wrote:

> I have observed with great sorrow, from printed circulars, that your harmless institutions, which the Christian world ought to regard as a shining light, are vilified and despised by an evil and perverse generation. Yet it cannot be otherwise. If you were of the world, the world would love you. Since you are not of the world, the world hates you. . . . You must not lose courage. . . . It cannot be easier for Christ's servants than it was for Christ himself.[2]

Words of this kind, coming from the court preacher in Berlin, must have been of great help to the morale of the count. Nevertheless, he remained uneasy about the ultimate fate of Herrnhut. In consequence, what he so strongly resisted in the fall of 1728, he himself proposed in early 1731; namely, to dispense with the community's religious statutes and to merge completely with the Lutheran parish. The objections to this step were more vigorous than anticipated; and when neither the count nor the opposition would yield, it was agreed to submit the question to the lot. Two texts were used, I Cor. 9:21 and II Thess. 2:15, which read respectively: "To them that are without law, as without law, (being not without law to God, but under the law to Christ,) that I might gain them that are without the law"; and "Therefore, brethren, stand fast, and hold the traditions which ye have been taught." The not quite four-year-old Christian Renatus Zinzen-

[2] *Ibid.,* p. 581.

dorf drew the latter, and Herrnhut retained its *status quo*. Far from being disappointed at the rejection of his proposal, the count was strengthened in his faith that God had a special mission for Herrnhut.

How shall we interpret this reversal of himself on the part of Zinzendorf with respect to the rules which the Brethren had set up for themselves? It was, no doubt, simply an honest question as to strategy in the face of what was turning out to be a more difficult venture than he had anticipated. Zinzendorf had been convinced that the adoption of a special ecclesiastical discipline in 1727 was a necessity in order to keep the immigrants together. He still felt that way the following year. But now, more than two years later, the situation looked somewhat different. In the face of the growing criticism of Herrnhut's peculiar regulations the count had grounds for questioning the advisability of retaining them. Also he may have reasoned that the Moravians no longer needed them but had developed as a community to the point where only the ordinary Lutheran church laws would suffice. Had the suggested change been adopted, the future course of the Moravian movement might have been different. Be that as it may, the outcome of this incident was another step forward to the ultimate separation of the Moravians from the state church.

The enemies of the count did not let up in their attacks. Uneasiness over the continued immigrations from Bohemia and Moravia, the jealousy of neighboring clergymen, and the deepening bitterness of Pietists in Halle were the focal points of trouble. Herrnhut was not the only place which had taken in immigrants. Zinzendorf's aunt Henrietta, who had succeeded her mother as proprietor of Hennersdorf, had received a few. Refugees were to be found in many different communities in eastern and northern Germany. Yet most of the blame for their fleeing their homes was fastened on the count. What finally brought the matter to a head was the coming to Herrnhut of some seventy immigrants about the time he returned from Copenhagen in July of 1731. The result was the lodging of a formal complaint against Zinzendorf and Herrnhut by the imperial ambassador at the Saxon court. The privy council at Dresden thereupon appointed a commission to investigate Herrnhut.

Zinzendorf, learning in advance that the inquiry would be in charge of George Ernest von Gersdorf, prefect of Upper Lusatia, extended to him a cordial invitation to examine everything at Herrnhut thoroughly. Von Gersdorf and his secretary were at Herrnhut from the nineteenth to the twenty-second of January, 1732. In the course of these four days they mingled freely with the inhabitants, attended a variety of church services, and had extended interviews with individuals. Zinzendorf gave the examiners a documentary statement concerning the affairs of the community. Though the government made no formal statement on the commission's findings for over a year, it left the impression that Herrnhut would be granted a clean bill of health on the two points on which the investigation centered, its Lutheran orthodoxy and the legality of receiving the refugees. In the meantime, however, the land-owners of Upper Lusatia were forbidden to receive any more immi-grants from Austrian territory.

The manner in which the state left the affair hanging in air put Zinzendorf in an uneasy position, particularly so when disturbance broke out among the Bohemians on his aunt's estate that summer. Dissatisfied with her refusal to grant them freedom to worship at Herrn-hut, some of them fled to Herrnhut. Sympathetic as he was, Zinzendorf could not accept them, both because of lack of facilities and because of Henrietta's refusal to release them from her jurisdiction. As a result they wandered aimlessly about the country. Again the count was sus-pected of responsibility for the incident. Rumors spread of his im-pending arrest. How imminent that was is not known, but under date of October 28, 1732, the elector of Saxony issued a rescript order-ing Zinzendorf to divest himself of his estates and quit the realm with-in three months. It is more than likely, though there is no documentary evidence for it, that his own relatives were behind this severe measure. Long enough had they been subject to embarrassment because of his unconventional behavior. There may be some significance in the fact that von Gersdorf, who had investigated Herrnhut, was a relative of Zinzendorf's.

The order to sell his property meant little to the count, for ever since his marriage, ten years before, he had planned to put everything in his wife's name. Even before the edict he had taken steps to carry out this resolution, so that already on November 13 the countess became the legal owner of both Herrnhut and Berthelsdorf. A month later, on December 19, the residents formally transferred their alle-giance to her. Earlier in the year he had resigned what minor position he had retained at the Saxon court after the leave of absence granted him in 1727. Zinzendorf subsequently referred to the months immediately following the order to sell his estates as his first exile; but, as it turned out, that designation was four years premature.

The sudden death, on February 1, 1733, of Frederick Augustus II brought a friendlier ruler to the throne. The long-awaited report on Herrnhut appeared in the form of an edict of toleration on April 4, granting the refugees freedom to stay in Upper Lusatia. This was followed with written approval of the transfer of Zinzendorf's property to his wife, together with permission for him to remain in Saxony. This turn of events occurred after he had already left Herrnhut, and what he thought was his first exile proved to be just another of his many journeys, in this instance to Ebersdorf and Tübingen.

The trend of affairs had been to focus attention upon the dual nature of the Berthelsdorf-Herrnhut parish and to make it increasingly clear that Herrnhut needed a pastor of its own. Rothe's growing coolness toward the Moravians added to the problem. But the growth of the parish called for another pastor, even if Rothe had been more sympathetic to the tradition of their fathers. The man chosen was Professor Steinhofer of Tübingen, who was agreeable to the proposal if the theological faculty would approve it. He himself was in hearty accord with the peculiar church discipline at Herrnhut but wanted some statement from a body of competent theologians as to the propriety of such an arrangement within a parish subscribing to the Augsburg Confession. Since the Tübingen faculty had the matter under advisement about the time the count was preparing to leave Herrnhut, he took advantage of his supposed exile to confer personally with them.

Tübingen's opinion, issued on April 19, 1733, was most favorable; the theologians saw nothing in Herrnhut's situation contrary to Lutheran regulations. Yet Steinhofer's appointment did not materialize because of the Saxon government. It forbade the presence of an assistant pastor. Steinhofer could have become Rothe's successor but not his assistant. In the face of this embarrassing development Steinhofer accepted a post at Ebersdorf.

This disappointment took the edge off the satisfaction derived from the edict of toleration of April 4. Herrnhut was much in the same position as before. Zinzendorf had reason to be dissatisfied, for, after all, the tone of the edict was that the Herrnhuters would be "tolerated" as long as they "behaved quietly." The Schwenkfelders, whom he had been harboring at Upper Berthelsdorf since 1726, had not fared so well. To them had come the order, at the time the Herrnhuters had been granted toleration, to leave Saxony in small groups. Zinzendorf could not help wondering how long it would be before the Moravians were in the same predicament.

Accordingly his strategy was to prepare for the worst. Later that year he divided the Herrnhuters into two groups, the native Germans and the immigrant refugees. Then he began to cast his eyes about for possible places where the latter might colonize in the event of their being exiled. The prior departure of his first missionaries to the West Indies and to Greenland naturally turned his attention to the New World.

In the meantime there was added to the Moravian Brotherhood the one man who ranks second only to the count himself as the leader of the early Renewed Moravian Church, Augustus Gottlieb Spangenberg. It was in 1727 that two itinerating brethren had first met the twenty-three-year-old instructor at the university of Jena, where he had obtained his master's degree the year before. He was a leader among the large group of Pietists at the university and from the moment of this first contact with the Moravian Brethren was enthusiastic about their type of Christianity. A key person in Spangenberg's life was Professor Buddeus, who at the outset of his young friend's student days had persuaded him to change from a study of law to theology. Spangenberg's attraction to the Moravians was strengthened by Zinzendorf's visits to Jena later in 1727 and again in 1728 and 1729. Concerning his first impression of Zinzendorf he said, following a meeting at which the count spoke: "I was present and kept silent, but my heart rejoiced." A practical result of the awakening among the Jena students was the establishment of free schools in the suburbs of Jena for poor children, to whom Spangenberg gave much of his time. Zinzendorf greatly encouraged the group in this effort. In the spring of 1730 Spangenberg and a close friend, Godfrey Clemens, visited Herrnhut. As a result his connections with the Moravians and with Zinzendorf personally became increasingly intimate. The count began to value his counsel and sent him his diary and other papers relating to Herrnhut. Declining an appointment as professor of theology at Halle the following year, Spangenburg did accept the superintendency of the orphan house there in 1732. Before assuming his duties in September, he paid another visit to Herrnhut.

Spangenberg's Halle position was an ill-fated venture almost from

the start, for after a cordial reception from young Francke the differences between these two Pietists became all too apparent. One of the
points of friction was Spangenberg's continued attachment to Zinzen-
dorf, though, ironically, it was the latter who had helped arrange the appointment. Like the count, Spangenberg did not confine his religious associations to conventional Lutherans. Men like Gichtel and Tuchfeld found in him a warm friend. There were differences of opinion, too, centering around the confession and the administration of the Communion. At various times Spangenberg was cited before the directors of the orphan house to explain his actions. The breaking point came with his visit to Ebersdorf, where he partook of the Lord's Supper with Zinzendorf, then en route to Tübingen. On February 27, 1733, he was relieved of his duties as superintendent and on April 2 dismissed by royal mandate from the university. A few weeks later he arrived in Herrnhut to throw in his lot with the Moravians.

AUGUSTUS GOTTLIEB SPANGENBERG
*Drawn from the original in the
Moravian Archives, Bethlehem, Pa.*

The coming of Spangenberg gave impetus to the count's plans, directly and indirectly. The Halle fiasco, blamed on Zinzendorf, closed many doors still half-open to the Brethren. To the ranks of the ortho-
dox Lutherans, who were against the count from the start, were now added large numbers of Pietists. Zinzendorf was now more than ever compelled to go his own way, for which Spangenberg's high qualities of leadership were immediately put to use. With the congregation's approval he became Zinzendorf's assistant, compensating for the disappointment, a few months later, over the miscarriage of the plans for Steinhofer's coming. From this time on, Spangenberg's career was

occupied with one special assignment after another in the service of the Brotherhood. One of the first of these was to accompany a band of eighteen missionaries as far as Copenhagen, the port of embarkation for St. Croix.

Spangenberg's expulsion from Halle focuses attention upon a basic theological difference between Halle and Herrnhut. In calling Zinzendorf a Pietist, we must note that he began to differ early with Halle. The emphasis of the latter was upon the struggle of repentance which preceded the believer's deliverance from a guilty conscience and his entrance upon the peace of mind which followed. Both this painful struggle (*Busskampf*) and the next stage, the break through (*Durchbruch*), the Hallensians insisted upon as a universal necessity in the process of being saved. The count, having practiced the presence of Christ from his tenderest years, could not fit this pattern to his own experience. Even if he could have done so, he objected to ascribing uniformity to God's ways of dealing with individuals. His conception of the believer's relationship to the Saviour had a much more joyful and personal note in it than was the case with his early teachers.

13

A COUNT BECOMES A MINISTER

The deep felt call to enter the ministry had never left Zinzendorf, and the events of the years just described made it more compelling than ever. Of course, he had been exercising all the functions of the ministry, short of administering the Sacraments, ever since he began holding services in his Dresden apartment in 1721. But even with all of his defiance of convention, it took him until 1734 to take the final step of ordination. Prior to about 1733, as long as he was able to find Lutheran clergy who were sympathetic to his projects, he felt that it was sufficient for him to retain the status of a lay patron. A decade of experience under such an arrangement proved how awkward was his position. Though there were still friendly pastors willing to co-operate with him, the state through its church officials was putting barriers in their way, as in the case of Steinhofer. Thus far the missionaries in Greenland and the West Indies were only laymen, and the question of how to serve their converts would soon be arising. Should the Moravians be forced to leave Herrnhut, there would be the problem of providing them with a pastor. It seemed unlikely that a Lutheran pastor would be permitted to serve them in such a situation. All of these considerations led to the point where the count felt that he could no longer delay his own ordination.

He had not trained for the ministry at the university, but the theology he had studied on his own was much more a part of him than were the legal studies to which he had so unwillingly been subject. At school and ever since, theologians had been his intimates. He had learned much from his own pastor and colleague, Rothe. Preparation for taking clerical orders was no problem for Zinzendorf. Yet he did avail himself of further training and counsel at the hands of three eminently qualified men in Herrnhut during the year preceding his ordination. One was Spangenberg. A second was Steinhofer, who visited in Herrnhut during the summer of 1733, when it was still expected that he would become pastor of the Moravians. The third was another Tübingen professor, Oettinger, who spent some months in the community. These men sat with the count in a series of intensive Bible conferences. The group even attempted a new translation of the Bible. A beginning was made with Paul's first letter to Timothy, after which the project was dropped. Spangenberg informs us that they were agreed at the outset that the translation was only an experiment and that when they compared their results with Luther's they unanimously admitted that the great reformer had done a better job.

This preparation was begun before Zinzendorf had actually announced his decision to seek ordination. He discussed his plan thoroughly with the leaders of the congregation, some of whom tried to dissuade him because they feared the consequences. His wife was among those who warned him—prophetically as it turned out—against what would happen. The matter was finally debated at a meeting of the elders and settled affirmatively by the lot. Once more the count had received sanction for what he believed to be God's will.

A few weeks later he had what amounted to a decisive religious experience. He was standing up well against his critics and those who differed sharply with him, but not without constantly examining his own inner life and convictions. It was about this time that Dippel's attack upon the doctrine of the atonement moved him to analyze his own conversion. He said:

Some time before I entered the ministry something special occurred in my inner life. They [the Pietists] had said that I had never been really converted. At the same time Dippel came forth with his attack on the atonement. . . . As I came to look closely at my own conversion, I noted that in the necessity of the death of Jesus and in the word "ransom money" (*lytron*) there was a special secret and a great depth, where, though the philosopher trips, revelation stands immovable. That gave me an insight into the whole teaching of salvation. . . . Since that year 1734 the propitiatory sacrifice of Jesus became our special and only testimony, our universal remedy against all evil in teaching and practice, and remains so to eternity.[1]

This conviction of Zinzendorf's was reinforced by an incident trivial in itself. Among some papers he was burning in the fireplace were

[1] Jacob Wilhelm Verbeek, *Des Grafen von Zinzendorf, Leben und Character*, p. 142.

the watchword and hymn verse for February 14, 1734. As the material turned to ashes, one little segment remained unconsumed. On it were the words: "He shall choose our inheritance for us, the excellency of Jacob whom he loveth" (Ps. 47:4) ; and

> O let us in thy nail prints see
> Our pardon and election free.

Shortly thereafter he composed the hymn beginning:

> Jesus, our glorious Head and Chief,
> Sweet object of our heart's belief!
> O let us in thy nail prints see
> Our pardon and election free.

Zinzendorf and the Brethren from this moment began to preach their "blood and wounds" theology, exalting the suffering Saviour. Highly effective in winning converts, this approach ushered in the most creative period of the Moravian movement. It can be credited with some of the greatest Moravian successes both in the mission field and on the home front. But it was also a type of theology susceptible to morbid distortion and was the cause, a decade later, of a regrettable episode in the church's history.

A theological examination at the hands of some university faculty was the usual prerequisite to ordination, but Zinzendorf's admission to such an examination was very uncertain. Few faculties would have risked their status by being a party to it, because he was a count and because of the notoriety he had gained for himself in the theological world. When Zinzendorf was wondering what to do, a wealthy merchant of Stralsund, Abraham Ehrenfried Richter, wrote to Herrnhut, and requested a tutor for his children, who had recently lost their mother. The reputation of the Brethren was already such that they were being asked to fill assignments of this kind. The count immediately seized upon the situation as an answer to his problem.

Stralsund was under Sweden, and two of its theologians, Langemack and Sibeth, had royal appointments as examiners for the university of Greifswald of candidates for the ministry. Langemack was also superintendent of the Lutherans of the area. The count reasoned that theologians under Swedish jurisdiction might be less prejudicial to him than those in Germany. Thus it came about that at the end of

March a Herr von Freydek presented himself to Langemack in Stralsund as Richter's tutor and a candidate for clerical orders. This name was not exactly a fiction, for "Lord of the Barony of Freydek" was one of Zinzendorf's titles which had belonged to his family for generations. As Freydek he won the complete confidence of the superintendent, and within a few days he had an invitation to preach in one of the city's pulpits.

In the course of a subsequent theological conversation Zinzendorf and the Herrnhuters came under review and the Stralsund pastor made known his intention of refuting them in print. When asked by Zinzendorf whether he had actually read any of the writings of the people whom he planned to refute, the cleric quite frankly admitted that he had not, but that he had read what a Doctor Weidner had said about them. The count persuaded Langemack to read some of his utterances within the next few days. Seeing the man's opinion about him changed thereby, he promptly revealed his identity, but with the request that it be kept from the public. The two came to know each other intimately in the course of the weeks which Zinzendorf spent in Stralsund. Sibeth too was favorably impressed and later in April joined Langemack in subjecting the count to a three-day, detailed theological examination conducted in Latin and German. Zinzendorf preached five times, as Herr von Freydek by permission of his examiners, during his stay in the city. Reviewing the experience some years later, he said: "I told them by word of mouth, in writing, and in five sermons, whatsoever I have, in all my life, believed and taught, both in theory and practice; nay all the mistakes I ever had made. . . . But they retained their favorable opinion of me."

On April 26, a few days before he left Stralsund, Sibeth and Langemack gave him a complete certificate of orthodoxy from the Lutheran point of view. In the document they specifically acknowledged certain features of the Herrnhut church discipline as allowable nonessentials, not in contradiction to the Augsburg Confession.

Zinzendorf's presence in Stralsund had a remarkable effect on Langemack, an invalid who for over five years had felt himself too weak to preach. The count's final sermon closed with a reference to the woman who, according to the gospel record, had anointed the head of Jesus and of whom Jesus said: "She hath done what she could." Having to stop abruptly because his time had run out, Zinzendorf ended with the challenge: "You also do what you can." Langemack, deeply moved, was conscience-stricken by his own lack of faith concerning his illness. It was the beginning of a change in his life, and following a later visit from one of the Herrnhuters he again entered upon the full duties of his office.

Another striking aftermath of the Stralsund episode was the case of Richter himself, the unwitting instrument of it all. Zinzendorf actually served him as a tutor in between his other activities, and Richter was one of the last to know Freydek's real identity. The merchant may have regretted losing a tutor, but he was sufficiently drawn to the count to follow him to Herrnhut a year or two later with his family and to establish residence there. He served the church on evangelistic missions in western Germany and among Germans in London. In 1739 he went to Algiers to work among Christian slaves. There he died of the plague the following year.

The Stralsund examination was a personal victory. Zinzendorf's orthodoxy had been vindicated by two theologians whose position was unimpeachable. With this hurdle behind him, he now sought a way leading to formal entrance into the ministry. He wrote of his intentions to the queen of Denmark, perhaps hoping for a lead from that quarter. He wrote another letter to his long-standing cleric friend Superintendent Löscher of Dresden, giving a detailed account of his theological thought as expressed to the Stralsund divines. Löscher had little to offer other than a few corrections on some minor points of theology. Before being received into the ministry, a candidate had to have a call to some parish or an appointment to some other specific task. This was as much of a problem for the count as had been admission to examination.

In the meantime the need for a training center for Moravian personnel was becoming more apparent. Already there had been more requests for catechists and tutors than the Brethren were able to supply. Herrnhut was still asking for a second pastor. Zinzendorf saw what looked like an opportunity for both his followers and himself when he heard of the abandoned cloister of St. George in the Black Forest of Württemberg. He would restore this cloister at his own expense, make of it a theological seminary, and as head of it be consecrated a prelate of Württemberg. This would be a type of ministry, in the eyes of those in ruling circles, less at variance with his rank than would be an ordinary pastorate. The king of Denmark, he felt, would not be embarrassed for having given him the Order of the Danebrog.

In July he sent Spangenberg to present the proposal to Duke Charles Augustus of Württemberg. Three months later Spangenberg received the polite reply that though the duke had high esteem for Zinzendorf, he could not grant the request because of the disturbances it might create in his kingdom. It was probably expecting too much of the Roman Catholic ruler to make such a concession to a Protestant, though a majority of his subjects were Protestants.

While in Württemberg waiting for the reply from Charles Augustus, Spangenberg on his own initiative conferred with Chancellor Pfaff of the Tübingen faculty, discussing with him in detail the case of Zinzendorf. Spangenberg asked specifically for an opinion on the count's plans to assume the duties of a clergyman. Pfaff, on September 19, issued a favorable written declaration concerning the matter, acknowledging Zinzendorf's obvious qualifications and citing precedent for his contemplated step. Zinzendorf, himself, before he knew of this, though it was already early November, wrote to the church directory of Württemberg at Stuttgart. Apparently he had already given up hope concerning the cloister project, for in his letter he said that he had resolved to take clerical orders according to the apostolic example of Stephanas, as recorded in I Cor. 16, that is, by ordaining himself. (The reference is: "Ye know the house of Stephanas, that it is the firstfruits of Achaia, and that they have addicted themselves to the ministry of the saints.")

This announcement evoked a favorable response, which the count must have received about the time he learned of Pfaff's equally encouraging reply to Spangenberg. Heartened, therefore, Zinzendorf hastened to Tübingen a month later to take the final step. His statement laid before the theological faculty on December 18 forms one of the finest confessions of his career. In part he said:

I was but ten years old when I began to direct my companions to Jesus, as their Redeemer. My deficiency in knowledge was compensated by sincerity. Now I am thirty-four; and though I have made various experiences; yet in the main my mind has undergone no change. My zeal has not cooled. I reserve to myself liberty of conscience; it agrees with my internal call to the ministry. Yet, I am not a free thinker. I love and honor the [established] church, and shall frequently seek her counsels. I will continue as heretofore, to win souls for my precious Saviour, to gather his sheep, bid guests, and hire servants for him. More especially I shall continue, if the Lord please, to devote myself to the service of that congregation whose servant I became in

1727. Agreeably to her orders, under her protection, enjoying her care, and influenced by her spirit, I shall go to distant nations, who are ignorant of Jesus and of redemption in his blood. I shall endeavor to imitate the labors of my brethren, who have the honor of being the first messengers to the heathen. I will prove all things by the only criterion of evangelical doctrine, the Holy Scriptures. Among the brethren at Herrnhut and elsewhere I shall endeavor to maintain their ancient church discipline. The love of Christ shall constrain me, and his cross refresh me. I will cheerfully be subject to the higher powers, and a sincere friend to my enemies. . . . I am poor and needy, yet the Lord thinketh upon me. He shall deliver the poor and needy.[2]

The Tübingen faculty, the very next day, graciously replied to this stirring plea and formally recognized him as a minister of the gospel. Its sentiment was that, though in ordinary cases a regular appointment is required, there was no reason why duly qualified men should not publicly proclaim the gospel, especially when done with the consent and at the desire of the church. Zinzendorf's first public act as a minister, on the same day on which he was approved as such, was to preach in the Cathedral Church of Tübingen and then in the St. Thomas Church.

Confronting the count was still the problem of ordination for others of the Brethren. Back in Herrnhut, where he returned on New Year's day, 1735, he faced this with more concern than ever; for in the year just past more new ventures had been projected. The Schwenkfelders had left for Pennsylvania and two of the Herrnhuters had gone along to help them get settled and to explore the possibilities there for the Moravians themselves. Spangenberg had gone to London with the first Moravian contingent bound for Georgia. En route, while in Holland, he had also negotiated with the Surinam Company about a colony and mission work in that South American land. The Brethren going to these various places, theologically untrained men who worked with their hands, were not the kind that Lutheran consistories would be likely to ordain before their departure. The missionaries of the Danish-Halle stations, in contrast, had been trained for the ministry and hence did not face this obstacle.

Dramatizing the issue was the return about this time of Leonard Dober from St. Thomas with a converted Negro boy, Carmel Oly. Dober, called home to assume the chief eldership of Herrnhut, had

---

[2] Spangenberg, translation by La Trobe in *Ancient and Modern History of the Brethren,* p. 237.

brought with him this firstfruit of the West Indian Mission, an African-born slave. The following August, Carmel Oly was taken to Ebersdorf and baptized by Pastor Steinhofer. Just why he was not baptized at Herrnhut, where he was "blessed" in preparation for baptism, is not clear. Perhaps it was a feeling of uncertainty about the attitude of the Saxon authorities. At any rate his presence focused attention upon the prospects of many other converts like him on the distant mission fields in the near future.

In this expanding dilemma Zinzendorf finally yielded to what had long been the desire of the Moravian-born Herrnhuters; namely, to revive the clerical orders of the church of their fathers. Just two bishops of the old Brotherhood remained, Jablonsky and Christian Sitkovius of Thorn, Poland, both of advanced age. With the former the Herrnhuters had been on cordial terms for over five years. His letters had given the count much encouragement. Jablonsky himself, even before Zinzendorf's ordination, had offered to consecrate one of the Brethren a bishop. Now the time had come to ask him to carry out this offer— that is, after the lot had so affirmed. David Nitschmann the carpenter, one of the five young men to reach Herrnhut on that decisive May 12, 1724, one of the first two missionaries, an itinerant evangelist of experience, was the man selected—again approved by lot. He was consecrated by Jablonsky in Berlin on March 13, 1735, in a private ceremony witnessed by several fellow Moravians. In the consecration certificate Jablonsky speaks in part as follows:

I, the undersigned, in accordance with this properly presented request, as Elder, Senior, and Episcopus of the Bohemian-Moravian Brethren in Great Poland, with the knowledge and consent of my colleague in Great Poland, Sir Senior Christian Sitkovius, did ordain the afore-mentioned Mr. David Nitschmann, on March 13, 1735, in the name of God, according to our Christian custom, with the imposition of hands and prayer, a Senior of the afore-mentioned congregations, and endowed him with full authority to perform the visitations called for by his office, to ordain the pastors and church servants of those congregations, and to take upon himself all those functions which belong to a Senior and Antistes of the Church.[3]

The step was even more fateful than Zinzendorf had anticipated. At the time he was still hoping to confine Moravian orders to missionaries. He emphasized to the community that, though one of them had become

[3] J. Taylor Hamilton, *History of the Moravian Church*, p. 71.

a Moravian bishop, it would mean no change for Herrnhut, which was still to avail itself of the services of the Berthelsdorf pastor. With a regular pastor at hand it was easy enough to abide by this principle, at least for a while. When the need arose for a pastor away from Herrnhut, the problem was quite different. The breach came when a few months later the first ordination performed by the newly consecrated bishop was that of John George Waiblinger, pastor elect of the proposed settlement of Pilgerruh in Schleswig. Moravian orders were not to be confined to the mission field after all. Nor did Nitschmann so confine himself in the discharge of his episcopal functions other than those of ordination.

If Zinzendorf had thought that his meticulous concern for certification of his Lutheran orthodoxy would make his entrance into the ministry more palatable to his critics, he was soon disillusioned. The feeling aroused by his ordination was hardly improved by the consecration of Nitschmann coming such a short time afterward. The year 1735, consequently, saw a mounting tide of opposition. Conspicuous among those who were vigorously antagonistic were his aunt Henrietta of Hennersdorf, Count von Brühl of Dresden, Baron von Huldenberg of Neukirch, and Count Christian Ernest of Stolberg-Wernigerode, all of the nobility. Among the clergy there were Anton and the younger Francke at Halle, the court preachers Marperger and Ziegenhagen at Dresden and London respectively, Chaplain Winkler at Ebersdorf, and Professor Urlsberg of Augsburg. Also frowning upon him for being a minister were his own mother and stepfather in Berlin, his wife's family, and his half brother Frederick Christian, head of the house of Zinzendorf. But most painful of all to Zinzendorf was the alienation of his onetime supporter King Christian of Denmark. Apart from what this meant to him personally, he knew that the ill will of Christian might endanger the mission in the West Indies.

He felt deeply enough about the situation to set out for Copenhagen, along with Bishop Nitschmann, to seek to clarify matters. Leaving Herrnhut on April 25, he arrived in the Danish capital on May 8. There he immediately communicated his arrival to a circle of his acquaintances in high places, including the king and queen. The king responded through Chamberlain von Pless, who gave the count a friendly invitation for an interview. However, this friendly reception did not turn out as Zinzendorf hoped. The king's word through von Pless was that there was nothing specific against him, but that some of the clergy were fearful that his activities were laying the groundwork for disturbances in the church. Therefore, the king suggested that a colloquy with the clergy would be the best means for coming to an understanding with them. Looking forward to such a meeting, Zenzendorf was disappointed when a few days later he was informed that the colloquy could not take place because there was no real complaint against him. Nor did he get to see the king to discuss the matter further.

The count cut short his stay in Copenhagen, leaving on May 16 for Herrnhut via Swedish ports on the first leg of the journey. At Malmö he visited the Bishop of Lund and another pastor who asked for him. During the six days his ship was marooned at Ystad by contrary winds, he spent his time in writing, especially letters to friends in Copenhagen, and in studying some of the books of the New Testament. He left Ystad on the twenty-third of the month and five days later was back in Herrnhut.

A strange sequel to his brief and very private stay in Sweden was a rescript from Stockholm, two weeks after his departure, forbidding him to settle in the country. Obviously wrung from the Swedish authorities by his enemies, the rescript was a distortion of fact in its statements that the count had been banished from Denmark after having been duly heard and refuted, that he was unable to remain in Saxony, and that because of this he was seeking residence in Sweden. On the surface his enemies had somewhat of a case, for the clergy in Denmark may have felt that he actually had been refuted, though not in formal colloquy; his banishment from Saxony had almost been effected two years before; and Diaspora workers from Herrnhut had been regularly visiting Pietist societies in Sweden since 1731.

As stated, Zinzendorf's policy was to leave personal attacks unanswered; but this one, he felt, involved more than just himself. Accepted by a gullible public, it could endanger his whole movement. Accordingly he wrote a detailed defense of himself and Herrnhut in a public letter addressed to the king of Sweden. This letter, thirty-four folio pages in length, was largely a point by point interpretation of the Augsburg Confession. It was printed at Regensburg at the end of the year and widely distributed among clergymen and heads of state representing the three great religious divisions of the Holy Roman Empire —Catholic, Lutheran, and Reformed. It was another of the count's supreme efforts to convince the powers that be that there was room within Lutheranism for what he was trying to do.

In the meantime Zinzendorf had also been busy with the affairs of the congregation. Noteworthy was his work on a new edition of the hymnal used at Herrnhut. In 1731 had appeared the *Collection of Ancient and Modern Hymns,* edited by Marche of Görlitz and prefaced by Zinzendorf. Much criticism had been directed at the Brethren because of this collection, for it was regarded by some of the clergy not only as the Brethren's hymnal but also as their confession of faith. Zinzendorf felt that by reprinting this book with the objectionable hymns removed he might silence some of the criticism. The new hymnal had 972 hymns of which over 200 were of the count's own composition. At the same time he issued an appendix to the collection, featuring the hymns written by the Brethren themselves. This was the first of twelve such appendixes that appeared within the next fifteen years. The count took special pains to encourage hymn writing on the part of those in whom he sensed the gift for it. One of his methods was to give to several persons themes on which to compose a hymn. Then he would have the group meet with him later to compare the results. Out of this sharing would often come new insights productive of fine hymns.

During the year 1735 also the work of the missions increased its tempo. In July ten brethren left to strengthen those who had previously gone to St. Croix. In August three others left Herrnhut to begin the mission in Surinam. The Georgia colonists who had left London in February were followed by a second company, under Bishop Nitschmann, embarking in late fall. In the ship with this second colony were the Wesley brothers, John and Charles. On the Continent three of the brethren were in Sweden investigating the possibility of work among the Lapps in the northern part of the country. One of the David Nitschmanns was in Russia to see what could be done in that empire.

Zinzendorf spent the closing months of the year on what he called his "witness journey." A leisurely walking trip through South Germany and Switzerland, the itinerary included such centers as Bayreuth, Regensburg, Constance, Zurich, Nuremberg, and Ebersdorf. Perhaps the count wished to test his effectiveness as a free-lance minister, which he now considered himself to be. John Nitschmann walked with him as far as Freiberg, after which he continued on alone. Dressed in ordinary clothes, without his usual servants, trudging through towns and villages, or availing himself of chance rides, Zinzendorf opened his heart to whomever he met. In turn many opened their hearts to him. To Spangenberg in America he wrote that his reason for traveling alone was to be able "to converse the more unreservedly with his Saviour."

A few days after Zinzendorf had left Herrnhut, the countess gave birth to a daughter, Marie Agnes, her ninth child. With this new arrival there were five surviving children in the household. The others were ten-year-old Benigna, eight-year-old Christian Renatus, three-year-old Christian Ludwig Theodor, and one-year-old Anna Theresa. Upon hearing the news of the birth, the count wrote to his wife:

You can easily imagine, my inwardly beloved wife, that it is a great joy to me that your Saviour has so graciously helped you, as I had faith would be the case. The Saviour has been very merciful to us and we should daily grow more in conformity to him. It is going well with me on my witness journey.[4]

The experiences on his witness journey must have given him inward assurance in his vocation. New Year's Day found Zinzendorf writing to King Christian, asking either for approval of his having entered the ministry or for permission to return the Order of the Danebrog. The brusque reply soon came that he should send the Danebrog to the king's master of ceremonies. Christian's brief explanation was that the retention of the decoration would convey the impression that the Danish court had a part in Zinzendorf's religious novelties. Of these he, Christian, did not approve. Six months later the then-exiled count, in a show of spirit, returned the Danebrog, not to the master of ceremonies, but directly to the king; because when he had received it five years before, it had been from Christian personally. Accompanying was a lengthy letter summarizing his life's purpose.

Sensing the crisis ahead, Zinzendorf occupied himself during the early weeks of 1736 with pastoral work at home. One of his first actions was to conduct a New Year's Eve watchnight service lasting until four in the morning. He spent long days in conferences with the elders and other church officers. With these colleagues he reviewed the spiritual life of many individuals. Those who showed signs of weakness were paired off with others who appeared stronger. Careful consideration was given to doctrine. Luther's method of teaching was cited, and it was agreed that his writings should be read more often in church. A few changes were made in the church rules. The state of the schools, choirs, discipline, buildings were carefully examined. The leaders expressed

[4] Spangenberg, *Leben Zinzendorfs*, p. 928.

themselves as determined as ever to continue along the lines of the developments of the past decade, and, as so often emphasized before, to avoid any separation from the state church.

Assured of the high morale at Herrnhut, Zinzendorf was ready to set off on another mission, this time to Holland, where he had been cordially invited by the dowager princess of Orange. It was quite a different journey from the recent one to Switzerland. The countess, young Benigna, and twelve others set out on the afternoon of February 15. The count himself, occupied in personal interviews with some sixty individuals, did not get away until after midnight. He caught up with the party at Bautzen. Not quite three weeks later all reached Amsterdam. En route the company had halted three days in Jena, where Zinzendorf publicly addressed students and townsfolk. Another pause had been at Hof, the home of his brother Frederick Christian. At Amsterdam a rented apartment served as headquarters during six weeks of activity.

A considerable congregation gathered around the nucleus of Herrnhuters during this stay, for the Surinam venture had resulted in the Brethren becoming widely advertised in Holland. Spangenberg, upon request, had given the Surinam Society a short account of the Brethren in writing. Deeply impressed by Spangenberg, a certain Isaac Lelong had this statement translated into Dutch and published. He soon followed this with a book entitled *God's Wonders with His Church,* which had a rapid sale. Consequently, when Zinzendorf began a round of services in his quarters, the crowd was larger than could be accommodated—a fact which added to the uneasiness he had over the advance publicity surrounding him. He discontinued these meetings when he saw that the numbers were getting out of hand. He did, however, accept a few invitations to speak elsewhere and kept up an endless round of appointments.

This Holland visit of 1736 was fruitful for the spreading Moravian cause. Zinzendorf's conferences with directors of the East India Company, one of whom was Amsterdam's Burgomaster van derBampen, paved the way for the beginning of a mission among the Hottentots a year later. With the directors of the Surinam Company he discussed further plans for the mission in the territory under their jurisdiction. At Leuwaarden, where lived the dowager princess of Orange, he made the necessary arrangements for a settlement of the Brethren in the barony of Ysselstein, said settlement to be called Heerendyk. Some of the company who had come with him from Herrnhut stayed behind to begin this venture immediately. The new settlement was planted as a strategic place for missionaries en route to and from their stations. Destined to be short-lived, Heerendyk did open the way, in 1746, for the settlement of Zeist, which continues to be the headquarters of the Moravians in Holland to this day.

From Holland the Zinzendorf entourage went to Cassel on the way back to Upper Lusatia. At Cassel they found David Nitschmann (not the bishop) with an ominous document in his hands, an order banishing the count from Saxony. The immediate instigator of it had been Baron Huldenberg of Neukirch, who for the past year had been complaining to the local authorities of Upper Lusatia and to the privy council in Dresden about the irregularities at Herrnhut. The specific charge which had been procured against Zinzendorf was that of persuading tenants to leave Huldenberg's estate and become the count's own vassals. The decree, dated March 20, reached Zinzendorf at Cassel on April 21. Just as disturbing to him as the action against himself was the news Nitschmann brought of a second investigation of Herrnhut to take place in the near future. At the moment it looked as if all of the Brethren faced the prospect of exile.

The count took the blow in stride. Having read the rescript of the king, he said to Nitschmann: "It matters little. I could not have returned to Herrnhut anyway for ten years, for the time has come to gather the pilgrim congregation and preach the Saviour to the whole world. Our home will be that particular place where at the moment our Saviour has the most for us to do." Travel plans were changed immediately, the party staying at Cassel for only an hour before it went on to Lichtenau. "My husband," said the countess, "walked most of the way and talked the matter over with his Saviour." In those moments he decided upon his immediate strategy. At Ebersdorf they separated, the countess going on to Herrnhut to await the investigation. Zinzendorf himself stayed in Ebersdorf, where among friends he could lay long-range plans. He needed friends, but his enemies can be credited with having done much for him. As the banished count he was at his best.

14

THE PILGRIM COUNT

Herrnhut was in less jeopardy than had been feared. The countess reached home a few days before the government investigators came to carry out their assignment. The four members of the commission—Captain von Loben and Chamberlain von Holzendorf of the nobility, and Superintendent Löscher and Dr. Heidenreich of the clergy—were in Herrnhut from May 9 to May 18. Their procedure and findings were essentially a repetition of those of the commission which had investigated the community four years earlier in 1732. Herrnhut was found to be worshiping in conformity with the Augsburg Confession and was assured that as long as she did so she would remain unmolested. As before, the special ritual and discipline carried over from the Bohemian Brethren were allowed to stand. Löscher himself, with a deep show of feeling, addressed the congregation and gave every indication that he was in accord with what he saw. Back in Dresden, where some were expecting him to recommend restrictive measures against Herrnhut, he publicly commended the Brethren from his pulpit. The action against Zinzendorf, however, remained in effect.

The good news of the favorable report on Herrnhut was relayed promptly to the count in Ebersdorf, and it was in high spirits that he went to Frankfort on the Main in late May. There he was cordially received and taken care of by enthusiastic coreligionists in this original home of Pietism. While in Frankfort he went to nearby Lindheim to spend a few days with Baron Karl von Schrautenbach, whose son Ludwig was later to be one of his associates and biographer. About this time, too, Zinzendorf's wife and family and a number of the Brethren joined him in the Frankfort area.

Some thirty miles east of the city lay the principality of Wetteravia, a territory under the counts of Ysenburg. These counts—Ysenburg-Büdingen, Ysenburg-Wächtersbach, and Ysenburg-Meerholz—were deeply in debt and looking for likely settlers to rehabilitate their run-down domain. From what they knew of Herrnhut, they looked upon the Moravians as good prospects. Among the enthusiastic admirers of Zinzendorf was the steward of Ysenburg-Meerholz, who with Rock had once visited Herrnhut. It was he who induced Zinzendorf in Frankfort to visit him in Wetteravia at the castle of Marienborn, a former cloister, and to consider it as a possible home for himself. While there Zinzen-dorf was struck with a neighboring castle, the Ronneburg, owned by Count Ysenburg-Wächtersbach; and it was this which he chose as the first home of the Moravians in Wetteravia.

Besides the fact that the Ronneburg was larger than Marienborn and could better accommodate the Pilgrim Congregation which Zinzen-dorf was projecting, the very wretchedness of the surroundings was a factor in the decision to locate there. The condition of the place was such that it discouraged even Christian David, just returned from Greenland. Doors and windows no longer hung in their places. Stairs were hazards. The roof leaked. Rats and mice had hastened the destruc-tion wrought by the elements. After inspecting it, David reported that Zinzendorf could not possibly live there. But the latter overruled him. The count saw immediately a mission project in the threescore families of poverty-stricken gypsies and Jews living in and around the outbuild-ings of this half-ruined medieval castle. This he began on June 17, the day after he took possession, by preaching on the parable of the lost sheep, the gospel for the day. The next step was to invite the neigh-borhood children into the castle, the boys to dine with his son Christian Renatus, and the girls to dine with his daughter Benigna. This was the prelude to schools for these children. To discourage them from begging, to which they had become accustomed, the count distributed food among them on specified days.

Later that year Marienborn was also leased, and this rather than the Ronneburg became Zinzendorf's headquarters. Two years later, on a tract of land below the hill on which stood the Ronneburg, the Brethren began the building of a village on the Herrnhut pattern and which they called Herrnhaag after the Haag Church nearby. Herrnhaag soon surpassed the mother community in size and with Marienborn occupied a dominant place in Moravian affairs for the next decade.

At the Ronneburg the Pilgrim Congregation had its beginning. Comprised of those who stood closest to the count, the Pilgrim Congrega-tion might be defined as the itinerant executive conference of the

Moravian Brotherhood. It was this group which helped Zinzendorf direct his rapidly growing enterprises. Yet it was more than the body which stood at the head of the church. It was in part a training school for those whom the count had recruited and commissioned for some

THE RONNEBURG

special mission. He regarded the Pilgrim Congregation as a spiritual union of those who, like himself, had a vocation to proclaim Christ to all the world. Among the members might be some missionary or Diaspora worker reporting back from the field. Learning from the experienced brother would be a neophyte about to venture forth. Consequently, its personnel and size were constantly changing. In effecting such changes the lot was invariably resorted to.

When the count traveled, the Pilgrims, or at least some of them, usually went with him, residing either in the same house at stopping points, or in separate quarters close at hand. The years of exile found this group in Wetteravia, England, Holland, Berlin and Switzerland, according to the strategy of the moment. Even when on the move, the Pilgrim Congregation adhered strictly to the same rules which were observed in Herrnhut. It had daily services. It kept a faithful record of its activities. It kept up a voluminous correspondence and entertained a constant stream of visitors.

Lady Zinzendorf, as head of the common housekeeping, was in charge of finances. Assisting her was Baron Frederick Watteville and later also Jonas Paulus Weiss, a former merchant of Nuremberg who in 1738 placed his generous resources at the disposal of the Brethren. To make ends meet taxed the managerial skill of the countess, despite the Spartan simplicity of food and dress of the Pilgrims. No one received any wages, and the few with private means used their own money. But traveling expenses, rentals, postage, printing costs, and entertaining of guests came high. Sources of income were the Zinzendorf estates, contributions, and loans. The last were at times a source of worry and embarrassment. Such a traveling congregation, or task force, was expensive but very effective in spreading Moravian Pietism on the Continent and in the British Isles.

Concerning that first company in the Ronneburg, Glaubrect in *Zinzendorf in der Wetterau* says:

It was an unusual household that moved into the Ronneburg. The Pilgrim Congregation was made up of persons from all ranks. Among them were some whose background did not make it easy to forego comforts and to discard suddenly the privileges of their rank. A Watteville required more than did a Christian David, with whom it was a matter of indifference whether he slept on straw or feathers. Yet the common purpose erased the differences unbelievably soon. The simple fare, the same for everyone, was prepared in a single kitchen, and all ate with the count at a common table. Conversation and social relationships were unrestrained. Yet the count was the first among equals.[1]

Within six weeks after settling in Wetteravia, Zinzendorf was on the move again, though in this instance he went without the Pilgrim Congregation. In response to urging from Pietist friends there, he set out on July 27 for Livonia, via Jena, Magdeburg, Berlin, and Königsberg. The three months' journey proved to be one of the most rewarding of his career. In Berlin he stayed with his mother and stepfather and

[1] I, 77.

reported finding the former happier than he had seen her in many years. There he was visited by the Lutheran deans Rolof and Karstädt. He and Court Chaplain Jablonsky saw each other daily. Finally, as pre-arranged, he conferred about church matters with several Brethren from Herrnhut.

From Berlin he proceeded to Riga, the Livonian capital, without further business en route. Beyond Königsberg he walked much of the way and wrote to his wife concerning it: "I walked on the shores of the Baltic with a delighted heart. To spend so many days with the Saviour without interruption is a great favor, and almost renders us unfit for any other society."

Arriving at his destination on September 8, Zinzendorf lost no time in contacting key persons, members of the clergy and the nobility, in order to lay the groundwork for an extensive Diaspora program. At Riga he visited Superintendent Fischer of the Lutheran Church in Livonia. At Wolmar he was entertained by one of his most loyal patrons, the widowed Lady von Hallert, who asked him to send her a chaplain and tutors for a teachers' training institute which she had opened at her home. There he met General von Campenhausen and Major von Abedyl. From Wolmar he went to Reval, capital of Estonia, where he had interviews with several of the pastors and where he preached in the cathedral. Before leaving Reval, he organized a society as a unit of the Moravian Brotherhood. Also in the same city he was instrumental in raising money for the formation of a Bible society and the subsequent printing, in 1739, of the Scriptures in the language of the Lettonians. Later he preached again at Orel and Riga. In each case there was a general enthusiastic response to his personality and message.

A month later, while at Memel on his return, Zinzendorf wrote to King Frederick I of Prussia, asking for permission to help build an orphanage for Salzburger refugees in his territory. This letter had far-reaching consequences; for when the count arrived back in Berlin on October 25, he found a personal reply from Frederick, inviting him to his hunting lodge at Wusterhausen, where his court was in session. Having heard so many adverse reports about Zinzendorf, the king was eager to learn firsthand what kind of man he was. The count, realizing that much was at stake, responded to this invitation immediately. It could mean that Frederick would join the ranks of his enemies and banish him from Prussian territory; or it could mean the opposite, the gaining of an influential supporter.

Expecting to meet an odd fanatic, the blunt, pious Frederick was so impressed with his visitor that the audience developed into a three-day conference in the presence of many of the king's attendants. The monarch was completely won over and went so far as to advise Zinzendorf to have himself consecrated as a bishop of the Brethren. He promptly communicated his sentiments to Jablonsky:

Having now seen and spoken with Count Zinzendorf myself, and found him to be an honest and intelligent man, whose only intentions are to promote true and real religion, and the salutary doctrine of the word of God, it is my will, that when you speak with him in Berlin, you discuss those points with him which he has to propose, and afterwards furnish me with your report upon them, according to the letter of this day's date to you on the subject.

Your well-affectioned king,

Fr.W.

The reference to the points he wishes Jablonsky to discuss with Zinzendorf was to the matter of the latter's consecration. Having had Jablonsky's report, Frederick wrote a second note to him in which he said:

From your statement of 30th October, I have seen what has transpired in your conference with Count Zinzendorf. With regard to the examination of his orthodoxy and religious sentiments, I have, for certain reasons, intrusted it to the two deans of Berlin. If their testimony, as I hope, should prove favourable, you can ordain him at his desire, because I am myself of the opinion that the ministerial profession is worthy of all honour, and degrades no one.

Your well-affectioned king,
Fr.W.[2]

With the way clear for his theological examination at a later date, preparatory to his consecration as bishop, Zinzendorf was ready to leave Berlin for home. He left behind him pertinent documents for the Lutheran deans to study in coming to a decision about him. He took with him letters of recommendation from Frederick to the city council of Frankfort, the Counts of Ysenburg, and Count Degenfeld, the Prussian king's ambassador in the upper Rhine region.

[2] Spangenberg, *Leben Zinzendorfs*, tr. Jackson, p. 221.

Affairs had not run smoothly at the Ronneburg during the count's prolonged absence. Not all of the Wetteravian neighbors of the Brethren appreciated their activities. Even before his departure Zinzendorf, because of complaints against him, had to explain his conduct to his landlord. Lady Zinzendorf, alone with the Pilgrim Congregation, found the atmosphere exceedingly uncomfortable. On top of this trouble came family tragedy. Christian Ludwig Theodor, three and a half years old, died of a fever on August 31. The news of his death reached the count in Riga just before his return journey. The boy's illness had been unusually difficult for the mother because no doctor was available at the Ronneburg. When in October the youngest child, Marie Agnes, became ill, the countess felt she could no longer stay at the place, and with the sick child and her four other children went to the Schrautenbach home at Lindheim. Though warmly welcomed, she stayed there only a few days before she moved on to Frankfort, where the count found her upon his return on November 8. Happy to say, Marie Agnes recovered and was one of the four children of the family to grow to maturity.

During the next few weeks the center of activity shifted from the Ronneburg to Frankfort, where a considerable portion of the Pilgrim Congregation joined the Zinzendorfs. It was a period which greatly advanced the cause of the Brethren in the city. New friends were won and old ones strengthened in their attachments. Clergy and city officials were friendly to the count and did not stand in the way of the attendance of state church members and separatists alike at the services conducted by him. This was the beginning of a flourishing Diaspora society, the one which years later meant so much to Susannah von Klettenberg, the intimate of Goethe and whom he immortalized as the *"schöne Seele"* in *Wilhelm Meister*. Goethe's mother was also a member of the society. The poet himself was not a member, but a frequent visitor. Zinzendorf referred to this brief stay in Frankfort as one of the most satisfying experiences of his career.

In the meantime his eyes had turned again to Marienborn; and having taken a lease upon it, he called the leading Brethren there for a conference in early December. This conference, in session from the sixth to the ninth of December, 1736, is looked upon as the first synod of the Renewed Moravian Church. It was succeeded by numerous similar gatherings during the count's lifetime, though strictly speaking the era of synodical government did not begin until after his death.

Not until then did the synods become representative gatherings of elected delegates representing the whole church.

Foremost among the subjects under discussion was the significance of the Moravian episcopate, beginning to be recognized as something which gave to the Brethren's Church a distinct and independent position. Beyond this, business was transacted to further the interests of the various new ventures entered upon: Pilgerruh in Danish Holstein; Heerendyk in Holland; the Diaspora in the Baltic States, France, and Sweden; the missions in Surinam and North America. Specifically, it was agreed to purchase the Ronneburg, to send Watteville on an evangelistic tour to Cevennes, and to send additional catechists to Livonia.

The synod concluded, the count was soon on the move again, to Holland and then to England. Before leaving, he sent his son Christian Renatus, under the care of John Nitschmann, to the academy in Jena. Nitschmann was commissioned not only to act as the boy's governor but also to do religious work among students and townsfolk. The young Countess Benigna was sent to Herrnhut in the company of those Brethren who had been in Marienborn for the synod. On December 18 the Zinzendorfs, Watteville, and others of the Pilgrims arrived in Amsterdam and made it their headquarters. By this time the count was able to conduct services in the Dutch language, as well as in his native German. During his stay in Holland of nearly a month he prepared the *Daily Texts* for 1737, inspected what the Brethren had begun at Heerendyk, and, as usual, contacted individuals in behalf of his church's program.

His going to England had at least a fourfold objective; to consult with the Georgia trustees about the Moravian settlement begun the year before in Savannah; to begin evangelistic work among the considerable number of Germans in London; to discuss the Moravian episcopate with Archbishop Potter of Canterbury; and to seek a revival of the Order of the Grain of Mustard Seed. With him in England, though they came on a different ship, were the countess and Bishop David Nitschmann, the latter having been to Georgia earlier in the year with the second group of Moravian colonists.

A stay of nearly two months in London laid the foundation for the permanent establishment of the Moravians in the English-speaking world. Archbishop Potter became a warm friend and went on record as recognizing the Brethren's Church as "apostolic and episcopal." He saw nothing in its teachings opposed to the Thirty-Nine Articles. He let it be known that his previous high opinion of the Moravians had been strengthened by his meeting with Count Zinzendorf. He urged Zinzendorf to have himself consecrated as a bishop. General Oglethorpe, already an admirer of the Brethren through his experiences with them in Georgia, likewise was favorably impressed when he came to know the count personally. A group interested in mission work among slaves persuaded Zinzendorf to take steps to send a missionary to South Carolina for that purpose. It was this kind of reception in England which made the Brethren breathe easier about the attitude of officials and churchmen toward their missions in English possessions.

In London the devotions of the count's household were attended by many friends, mostly Germans, some of whom had first attended similar services of the Georgia colonists during their stopover in the city. Before returning to the Continent, Zinzendorf organized these friends, at their own request, into a society. This little group formed the background for the more detailed organization, a year later, of the Fetter Lane Society, which in 1742 became the first Moravian congregation in England.

Archbishop Potter's recognition of the validity of the Moravian episcopacy meant much to Zinzendorf. It strengthened his own resolve to become a bishop. It gave him a greater feeling of security with reference to the status of missionaries, though it was not until 1749 that Potter's view was sanctioned by Parliament. Above all it must have eased his mind to have this influential churchman confirm his own conviction that the Herrnhuters were not a new sect but the resuscitation of an old church.

After a brief pause in Amsterdam, where his loyal following, under the leadership of friendly pastors, was taking on the character of a society, he returned to the Frankfort area on March 26. He found the activities of the Brethren flourishing but meeting opposition, since the city council at the instigation of the clergy had forbidden two of his leaders to hold public services. This evoked from him his sixth formal, public declaration of faith since 1729.

The situation at Frankfort hastened his departure for Berlin to meet with his examiners Reinbeck and Rolof. The two clerics were entirely satisfied with his doctrinal views and reported so to Frederick William, but they did raise the question whether his consecration as bishop might not give the appearance of a fourth religion in the Empire. (The Lutheran, Reformed, and Roman Catholic churches were the three recognized by the Treaty of Westphalia of 1648.) The king referred the matter to his court chaplain Jablonsky, asking him to examine the matter carefully. Assured by the civil court that there was no objection, Jablonsky reported back favorably; and Frederick William promptly gave him authority to proceed with the consecration.

The act took place on May 20, 1737, in Jablonsky's home. Bishop Nitschmann assisted, and Bishop Sitkovius of Lissa, Poland, concurred by letter. Present as witnesses were David Nitschmann the syndic and Matthias Schindler. As episcopal consecrations go, it was a highly unusual affair, as had been the consecration of Nitschmann two years earlier. A clergyman of the Reformed Church consecrating a Lutheran to the episcopacy of a third church is hardly conventional. Yet there could have been no more apt symbol of the spirit of both the Bohemian Brethren's Church and of its successor, the latter-day Moravian Church. To Jablonsky his part in the proceedings was a debt he owed to his grandfather Comenius. The latter would have rejoiced to see the centuries-old church order of the Unity take on new life. Comenius, who had worked so hard and spoken so eloquently for the union of the Christian world, would have rejoiced, too, to see the three churches of the Consensus of Sendomir tied together in this one act. Significantly, Jablonsky had written a history of this pioneer attempt at church union of 1570. The renewal of the episcopacy in this manner was prophetic of what the Renewed Moravian Church was to become, both a denomination and a brotherhood of interdenominational status.

Zinzendorf as a bishop was an even more controversial personage than Zinzendorf as an ordinary pastor. On the one hand, Frederick William and Archbishop Potter headed the list of those who sent him congratulations. On the other hand, among the clergy in general his new office was occasion for intensifying opposition. Since Jablonsky belonged to the Reformed Church, some said that the count in being consecrated by him had ceased to be a Lutheran. Others said the act was invalid according to ecclesiastical law. Others, opposed to the bishop's office, said that he was assuming the airs of a Roman Catholic prelate. To be sure, he did sometimes sign himself "Ludovicus Ecclesiae Moravo-Slavicae Episcopus." Still others disparagingly referred to him as a "traveling bishop," without a diocese, serving a motley assortment of scattered dissenters.

Through the intervention of his stepfather a break in the count's exile from Saxony came shortly after his consecration. General von

Natzmer persuaded King Augustus to give Zinzendorf permission to return to Herrnhut. Taking prompt advantage of the amnesty, Zinzendorf was back among the Brethren by the end of June, remaining until almost the end of the year. Having been away for fifteen months, he found much to occupy his attentions by way of an intensive pastoral ministry. Hardly at any other time in his career were he and the countess so long together in one place without travel interruptions. During this stay in Herrnhut the couple's tenth child, Johanna Salome, was born on August 4.

It had looked for a while as if his banishment would be revoked, and well might this have been the case had he been willing to compromise his stand. In August came the long-delayed report of the second royal commission to investigate Herrnhut. Though it left the community free to continue as before, its tone was unfriendly. The object of the report apparently was to impress the residents that they were being tolerated on condition that they abide by the "unaltered doctrine of the Augsburg Confession." Fortunately George Ernest von Gersdorf, prefect of Upper Lusatia, who communicated the edict to the Herrnhuters, was a friend. By tactful diplomacy he staved off resentment and the probable emigration of many of the residents.

Similar toleration was offered Zinzendorf, had he been willing to agree to certain conditions. But the document presented to him was worded in such a way that his signature on it would have been self-incrimination. In short he would have been promising to give up religious irregularities for which he did not admit guilt. A plea for a change in the wording was of no avail, and he resolved to leave soon again. He had already been gone from Herrnhut for some months when the final decree of perpetual banishment against him was issued in March of the following year.

Also during the summer of 1737 Berthelsdorf-Herrnhut lost the services of Pastor Rothe, who had been on the scene exactly fifteen years. One of the original four to enter into the covenant of 1723, he had played an important part in the rise of the community. The fact that his enthusiasm for Herrnhut had cooled during the last few years did not seem to lower Zinzendorf's esteem for him. The count unsuccessfully tried to dissuade him from accepting a call to the parish of Hermansdorf, near Görlitz. Later he even extended Rothe a call to be his chaplain at Marienborn, which offer, however, his friend declined. Replacing Rothe in the Berthelsdorf parish was Caspar Leonard Mukke of Nochten, who assumed his duties in late November.

Despite the continuing uncertainty of Herrnhut's position and the change in pastors, the moral of the community was high. Zinzendorf's presence brought new enthusiasm. Observance of the community's fifteenth anniversary had the effect of a revival, which expressed itself in a deeper prayer life, self-discipline, stepped-up interest in missions. Having overcome the problem of undisciplined enthusiasm early in its existence, namely in 1727, Herrnhut was therefore able to combine enthusiasm with stability, and thus to lend strength to the whole Moravian movement.

Berlin was again to be the center of the count's activities for a few months, but not before he attended briefly to affairs in Wetteravia and Frankfort. At the Ronneburg, on December 15, he performed his first official act as bishop, the ordination of Peter Böhler. Böhler, who had just completed his theological studies at Jena, left the next day to carry out his assignment as a missionary among the slaves in South Carolina. En route to the new world, he first met John Wesley at Oxford the following March 4. His skillful counseling with the discouraged cleric, more than any other factor, helped Wesley to come to his "heart-warming" experience at the Aldersgate meeting, though Böhler was already at sea when the climax came. On this visit to Wetteravia, Zinzendorf also arranged for the purchase of the land near Büdingen, where Herrnhaag was to be built. In Frankfort he took time to draft a reply to a critical article about the Brethren in one of the city's periodicals. Then, by way of Jena, where he visited Christian Renatus and the several Brethren stationed there, he went to the Prussian capital to join the Pilgrim Congregation which had preceded him.

Zinzendorf had chosen to go to Berlin for strategic and personal reasons. It was much nearer Herrnhut than was Wetteravia. It was under a monarch whose favor he enjoyed. Here lived his mother and stepfather, the latter a man of influence with the king of Saxony, with whom the count was not in good standing. Finally, in Berlin, as in Frankfort, he still found the fruits of the ministry of Spener. Concerning this he said: "Everywhere I had found traces of Spener's labors, and especially in Dresden and Frankfort I had attempted to water the seed he had sown. Now I wished to do the same in Berlin by preaching the gospel."

His intention was to keep his daily devotions a private matter for the Pilgrims and to use the churches of the city in speaking to the public. But he soon discovered that no pulpits were open to him; the clergy had united solidly against him. Then reluctantly, but with the written permission of Frederick William, who encouraged him to "preach the pure word of God," he admitted visitors. Almost immediately he found himself preaching to an audience that overflowed into the street. Beginning in one room, the meetings spread to an anteroom; and when these two together became too crowded, the count held forth in the large loft. Even then, no chairs were provided, except for the aged and infirm, in order to make room for a maximum number. Finally he decided to preach to the men and women separately, to the former on Sundays and Wednesdays, and to the latter on Tuesdays and Thursdays. It was a cosmopolitan audience that came to hear him. The upper classes were as well represented as those of the lower strata. Spangenberg reports that on a certain day forty-two carriages were lined up outside the door.

Zinzendorf delivered sixty addresses between January 1 and April 27. The ones to the women were expositions on the Lord's Prayer and those to the men expositions on the second article of Luther's *Catechism*. There were also sermons on miscellaneous biblical texts. He himself summed up his subject matter as follows:

1. The essential, sole, and eternal divinity of him who became man.
2. The essential, real, and complete humanity of God who is in heaven.
3. Grace, the only means of salvation for men, and the pardon of every sin by the merits of the sacrificed Lamb.
4. The precious privilege that Jesus obtained for us by his blood, namely, deliverance from sin, and the power to lead a spiritual life.

About himself he said:

My preparation is the wretchedness and poverty that I feel in the hour before, so that I often go up to speak, hardly knowing where I am. As soon as I begin to speak I feel the coals from the altar. I am sensitive to the varying moods of my hearers. They often shed tears, which is the case even with the soldiers among them. May the Saviour give permanence to what they feel.[3]

Soon after the count had established himself in Berlin, he had his son Christian Renatus come from Jena to join the family. His tutor

[3] Spangenberg, *Leben Zinzendorfs*, p. 1090.

at the time was John Michael Langguth, the son of a Lutheran pastor at Walschleben and a student at the university. This young man was a constant attendant upon Zinzendorf's addresses and on his own initiative wrote them down in a kind of shorthand. So pleased was Zinzendorf with the results that he decided to have the material published, especially upon discovering that distortions of his utterances were being circulated. In early June appeared the addresses to the women, with a dedication to the Prussian queen. Later followed the addresses to the men and after that the third series, which dealt with miscellaneous subjects. The Berlin addresses passed through a large number of editions and rank high among the influential writings of Zinzendorf.

The sequel to Langguth's story is that he became the count's secretary. Seven years later, as the adopted son of Frederick von Watteville, he became Baron von Watteville. In 1746 he married Benigna, the count's oldest daughter. In 1747 he was consecrated a bishop and in this capacity served the Moravian Church for over forty years. All of Count Zinzendorf's descendants who are living today trace their ancestry through Benigna and her husband.

Meanwhile the Brethren's work was continuing to spread under the direction of the Pilgrim Congregation at its Berlin headquarters. At this date there were already missions in the West Indies, Georgia, Surinam, Greenland, and South Africa, while the membership of the Diaspora fellowship at home was in the thousands. Just before leaving the city, Zinzendorf organized a society, which later became a Moravian congregation. In the neighboring village of Rixdorf was a colony of Bohemians, who had the same background as many of the Herrnhuters. This group, too, eventually became a society and then a congregation.

Undoubtedly it was the friendship of Frederick William which enabled Zinzendorf to stay in Berlin as long as he did. This friendship with the monarch was strengthened during the period; and two days before he left the capital, Zinzendorf had an audience with him at Potsdam. The two exchanged letters up to the very last days preceding the king's death in 1740.

Having left Berlin on April 29, the count spent a month on the return trip to Wetteravia. From a letter to his wife we learn the outline of his itinerary. At Cotbus he spent several days in conference with some of the Brethren. At Jena he paused to observe the progress of Christian Renatus at school. In Erfurt he visited members of the clergy. At Gotha he interviewed the counselor of the ecclesiastical court. Outside of Gotha he and Langguth secluded themselves for some hours to pursue literary labors. In observing Zinzendorf en route, we note that his contacts along the way usually became as important as his destination. On the very last leg of this journey, at four in the morning before even returning to the Ronneburg, where were most of the Pilgrims, he went to the plot of ground where Herrnhaag was to be built and prayed over it. The Brethren were divided in their residence between the two castles, with the count establishing himself at Marienborn for the next five months. In early September he managed a secret week's visit to Herrnhut in the course of a trip to Jena. At the latter place the precocious Christian Renatus Zinzendorf in his religious activities among fellow students was to some extent duplicating what his father had done a generation before at Halle. Upon his return the count learned that his wife had given birth to their eleventh child, David, on September 22.

With reference to Zinzendorf and the Brethren, Wetteravia was a beehive of activity during the summer of 1738. A second Herrnhut was arising; and with the experience of fifteen years to draw upon and with the support of a greatly enlarged following, progress was much more rapid in the case of Herrnhaag. Before the year was out, the Brethren's and Sisters' houses had been erected. A boarding school, a house of worship, an orphanage, a residence for the count, and other structures followed in rapid succession. While all this local activity was in progress, the almost daily stream of visitors, the coming and going of itinerant Diaspora workers, and the heavy mail testified to the fact that the Brotherhood was on the march.

Among the visitors was John Wesley, fresh from his Aldersgate experience. With him was the Reverend Benjamin Ingham, popular Yorkshire revival preacher, who was later to turn over his societies in England to the Brethren, though he himself remained a member of the Church of England. Wesley during the course of his two weeks' stay, beginning July 4, in a nearby private home was obviously favorably impressed. He commented in his *Journal*, "O how pleasant a thing for brethren to dwell together in unity." He later referred to the "living proofs of the power of faith" he observed in the Moravian community. A few weeks later he was similarly impressed with what he experienced in Herrnhut and wrote, "I would gladly have spent my life here; but my Master calling me to labour in another part of his vineyard . . . I was constrained to take my leave of this happy place."

Yet from the outset there appeared to be a shadow over the Wesley-Moravian relationship. We note, though he does not record this in his *Journal,* his conspicuous exclusion from the Moravian Communion

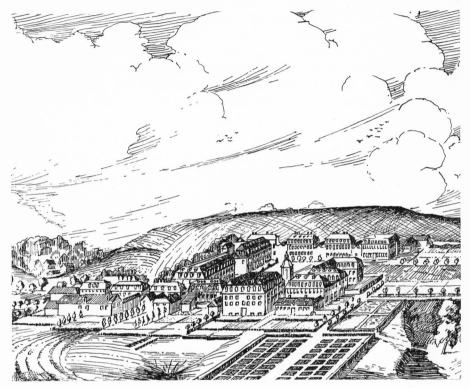

BIRD'S-EYE VIEW OF HERRNHAAG

service in Marienborn. The grounds the Brethren gave for their action was that he was a *homo perturbatus*—that is, a disturbed man. His companion Ingham did partake with the Brethren. At any rate it was not long after Wesley was back in England that he became critical of the count and his followers and began going his separate way. We can only wonder why Spangenberg, who gives us so much detail about the count's life, should have omitted Wesley's name when he refers to the visit of Benjamin Ingham at Marienborn.

Having almost a year before resolved to do so, Zinzendorf finally set out upon a journey to the mission field on October 22, 1738, to observe firsthand what it meant to be a missionary. That he should have undertaken such a visit was, of course, quite in keeping with the whole pattern of his life. But it is also true that his resolve was quickened by the taunts of his enemies. Fifteen missionaries had already succumbed to the tropical climate of the West Indies, and the critics were saying that the count was sending others to places he himself was unwilling to go.

Expecting to sail almost immediately from Amsterdam upon his arrival there on October 27, the count was unexpectedly delayed for two months because of failure to secure passage. He had good reason to regard this as providential, for it was at this very time that there erupted in Holland a wave of hostile criticism against him, spearheaded by a tract entitled *Pastoral Letter*. The affair had its roots in a spirited argument Zinzendorf had had with several ministers on the question of election during his visit to the country two years before. Discussed at synods in both South and North Holland, Zinzendorf's views were referred to the classis of Amsterdam. From this body came the *Pastoral Letter,* warning the public against the unsound teachings of the Brethren. Its accusations were based upon citations from Lelong's history of the Brethren, from letters, and from the Moravian hymnal. The tract declared that Zinzendorf and his followers were not to be identified as the continuation of the Bohemian-Moravian Brethren, but were sentimental mystics, neither Lutherans nor Reformed. It was the beginning of the era of polemic literature against the Moravians. Zinzendorf stated his own side of the case in letters to the classis and to civil authorities. The controversy did not prevent the formation of a society along permanent lines in Amsterdam. At this time also Leonard Dober was making an attempt to evangelize in the Jewish quarter of the city.

The count boarded his ship on December 11 but was kept waiting another ten days while the vessel lay at anchor. In the interval he prepared the watchwords for 1739. Just before his ship entered the open sea from the English Channel, he sent back with the pilot a lengthy document, dated December 27 and addressed to the elders and helpers of the church, under the heading *Eventual Testament*. In this writing he frankly faces the dangers of the St. Thomas' visit and the possibility of his not returning. Though not containing anything different from what he had expressed from time to time, it is an excellent summary of his position on church matters.

The month's journey to the West Indies was unusually swift for that era of sailing vessels. It was Zinzendorf's preference to make this voyage in the winter season, despite the greater danger from storms, because he fared better in cold than in hot weather. Ordinarily he was a poor sailor, but on this occasion he recovered from seasickness after only a day of it before even sailing. He reports his cure in these words: "Since I had so much to do, I talked with the Saviour, saying that it would not be convenient for me to be sick, and so I became well even before we sailed."

Accompanying Zinzendorf were three outbound missionaries, George Weber, Valentine Lohans, and the latter's wife. At the island of St. Eustatia they transferred to a smaller vessel and within twenty-four hours were approaching St. Thomas. It was with deep anxiety that the party stood on deck as they sailed into the harbor at Tappus in late January. Thinking aloud, the count said, "Suppose the Brethren are no longer here; what shall we do in that case?"

"In that case we are here," Weber replied.

"Gens aeterna, diese Mähren!" (an eternal race, these Moravians) exclaimed the the count.

It was an unhappy situation which Zinzendorf encountered. The missionaries Frederick Martin, Matthias Freundlich, and the latter's wife were there, but in prison on trumped-up charges instigated by the resident Dutch pastor Borm. Having failed to get the governor to prohibit Martin from baptizing converts, he had the missionaries summoned to give evidence in a theft case. Because of scruples against taking oaths, which the case necessitated, the Brethren were fined and, failing to pay the fine, were imprisoned. All this had happened some three months before the count's arrival. It was the most serious among many incidents through which planters unfriendly to mission efforts sought to impede the work of the Brethren.

Zinzendorf's immediate vigorous protest to the governor of the island apparently had great weight, for the next day the missionaries were released, and the governor personally apologized to the count. His explanation was that the action against the Brethren had been without his knowledge. He and the count came to an amicable understanding during the latter's stay. However, Zinzendorf must have sensed that the matter had got beyond the governor's control, for upon his return to Europe he interceded directly with the Danish crown on the Negroes' behalf. In response the crown sent a directive to the West India Company ordering freedom of worship for the Negroes of the Moravian mission.

It was a busy three weeks for the count. Besides conducting services almost daily in Dutch for the Negroes, of whom there were some eight hundred actively interested in the mission, he applied himself to the task of organization. He divided the island into four districts, assigning missionaries and native helpers to each. To the extent that he deemed wise, he introduced features of Herrnhut's congregational life. He set up a choir system, suggested the formation of small bands, appointed elders, helpers, overseers, advisors, distributors of alms.

Concerned as the count was with the welfare of underprivileged people, his was a socially conservative point of view. With regard to slavery and class distinctions he was a product of his age and background. This is clearly revealed in a farewell letter he addressed to the Negroes of St. Thomas a few days before his departure. In exhorting the slaves to Christian faithfulness, he stressed, along with other things, obedience to their masters. He reminded them that God made all ranks—kings, masters, servants, and slaves—and of the special punishment resting upon the Negro as a descendant of Ham. He explained that conversion brought them freedom, not from the control of their masters, but from wicked habits and thoughts.

Before leaving the islands, he visited St. John and St. Croix and at the latter paid his respects to the memory of missionaries buried there. The return journey was less comfortable than had been the outbound voyage. Because of adverse winds it took eight days in a crowded vessel to reach St. Eustatia, a distance he had covered in one day in the opposite direction. Later, on the larger ship, the discomfort was of the count's own choosing and in keeping with his character. He took with him from St. Thomas a Danish acquaintance and a Negro convert, whose freedom he had purchased in order to take him back to Germany to visit the Brethren before serving his own people. Upon transferring to the second ship at St. Eustatia, Zinzendorf had difficulty in securing accommodations for his party but at length was assigned to a stateroom and half of the cabin. On the smaller vessel he had met a destitute Portuguese Jew by the name of DaCosta, who wished to go to Amsterdam. The generous count agreed to pay his passage and that of his wife and went further by turning his stateroom over to them, while he himself shared the cabin with other passengers. The captain, however, noting that the count was busily engaged in study and literary labors, had the thoughtfulness to erect a partition to afford him more privacy. Even so, his accommodations were cramped, and the voyage was a strain on him physically. Yet for the seven weeks under these circumstances he sought to work as usual. To his wife he wrote, "I do all that I am wont to do on shore, and even more."

This statement is a true picture of Zinzendorf on board ship, for he was the chaplain of the passengers and crew. On Sundays he conducted services, and during the week he used the personal approach. Conversations between him and DaCosta lasted far into the night. The Jew did not become a convert but listened reverently as the count sang hymns in honor of his Saviour. As he listened, he often wept. The count gave the same reverent attention when DaCosta in turn expressed his views. Spangenberg says, "He loved to philosophize." This friendship deepened Zinzendorf's interest in a mission to the Jews, and upon his return he arranged for the work to continue in Amsterdam, first under Leonard Dober and then for two more years under Samuel Lieberkühn. Though this mission accomplished little, it is to be noted that among the Brethren during the count's lifetime were a few converts from Judaism.

Incessantly writing wherever he happened to be, Zinzendorf produced some of his best-known and -loved hymns during the course of his voyage to St. Thomas. Among them is "The Saviour's Blood and Righteousness," written on the island of St. Eustatia, and perhaps the one hymn most representative of his theology. Especially expressive of his whole life's motivation are these stanzas:

> The Saviour's blood and righteousness
> My beauty is, my glorious dress;
> Thus well arrayed, I need not fear,
> When in His presence I appear.
>
> Thy incarnation, wounds, and death
> I will confess while I have breath;
> Till I shall see Thee face to face,
> Arrayed with Thy righteousness.[4]

Back in England in late April he made short visits to Oxford and London. The revivals in progress there impressed him favorably, but he did have reservations about the open-air preaching by laymen. Also

[4] The Rev. C. Kinshin, tr.

147

he was beginning to object to the emphasis upon the doctrine of sinless perfection as propounded by Wesley and his followers.

In Holland he found that the *Pastoral Letter* had wrought even more harm than he had feared at the time of its issuance. Yet, despite the prevailing opposition to the Brethren, the morale of the society in Amsterdam and in the settlement of Heerendyk was good.

The count rejoined his family at Marienborn on June 1, having made the round trip to the West Indies in such a remarkably short time that some skeptics doubted his having been there. The joy of reunion was marred by the loss of another child, four-year-old Anna Theresa, who died at the time her father was setting sail from Amsterdam. He learned of her death only upon his reaching England on the return voyage. Added to this burden was the run-down condition of the count's health. It took him about two years to recover from the ill effects of the fever-infected tropics, during which time he had several attacks of severe illness, probably malaria. While convalescing from the first of his attacks, in midsummer of 1739, he said in a letter to his friend King Frederick William: "For the last four weeks I have been very ill. I had great hopes of being dismissed from my labours, and being with the Lord; but they are vanished for the present."

His weakened physical condition, however, seemed to have little more than a temporary effect upon his capacity for leadership and work. The two years between his return from St. Thomas and his departure for Pennsylvania were a time of great advance for the Moravians, with the count at the center of it. Even before he had reached home, he sent word to the countess that he would call a synod as soon as possible to report on his trip and after that go on a mission to Württemberg. The synod, largely a review of the current status of the Brethren's work, met at Ebersdorf from June 9 to 16. Zinzendorf's preaching tour of Württemberg occupied the month immediately following. Then same the near fatal illness. Recovered, he threw himself into intensive pastoral work among the residents of the three Wetteravian communities, Marienborn, rapidly growing Herrnhaag, and the Ronneburg.

The Ebersdorf synod was the first of four such gatherings during the formative years between his two visits to the new world. After Ebersdorf the Brethren met once at Gotha and twice at Marienborn to take actions which consolidated and advanced their movement both as a denomination and as a Diaspora within the state churches. These synods gave clear expression to the independence of the Moravian Church as a distinct ecclesiastical body, as evidenced, for instance, in the issuance of a catechism, the first of the Renewed Moravian Church. Two more bishops were consecrated in this period of time, Polycarp Müller and John Nitschmann, bringing the total to four. Müller was placed in charge of the theological seminary founded at Marienborn about the time the count returned from the West Indies. Concurrent with the consecration of bishops was the ordination of other Brethren to fill a growing demand for their services. Yet the influence of Zinzendorf was dominant enough to keep the denominational emphasis in check. Though in use locally and unofficially before this, the word "Diaspora" appeared for the first time in the minutes of a Moravian synod at the Gotha meeting. It was the Diaspora concept to which Zinzendorf clung all his life, though inadvertently he sometimes gave impetus to denominational development. His establishment of a theological seminary at Marienborn, as noted above, would be a case in point.

In these years the Brethren established themselves in several localities in French Switzerland, with the Watteville castle at Montmirail as the base of operations. Two extensive visits by Zinzendorf himself spearheaded the work in this country. The second visit turned out to be a three months' stay with the Pilgrim Congregation in Geneva between February and May of 1741. An important motivating factor behind the Geneva stay was the count's desire to become better acquainted with Calvinism. The attention he and his Pilgrims attracted was parallel to that in Berlin three years earlier. As might be expected, the reactions ranged from enthusiastic acceptance to bitter antagonism.

Behind all this activity lay daring imagination. Illustrative is a stirring letter which Zinzendorf wrote to the Reverend Philip Doddridge in England in December of 1739. In part he said:

Now I seem sufficiently recovered to undertake a journey to the Swiss, by whom I have recently been invited. Bern, Basle, Stetin, Mulhausen, Schaffhausen, have heard the gospel; nay, even Geneva, hitherto so devoted to philosophy, that it scarcely submitted to the ignominy of the Cross. The churches and the Esthonion churches and the Livonian church flourish. The barbarous inhabitants of which pant for Christ. Greenland resounds with the gospel. I however, disapproved of the conduct of the brethren who philosophize rather than *evangelize*. Even of the Caffrarians, thirty have already given their names to the Cross and are baptized; a thousand Moors also in the island of St. Thomas. The people of Savannah, Carolinas, Pennsylvania, Berbice, and Surinam expect fruit. They are preparing to visit from ten to fifteen heathen tribes dwelling in Virginia, speaking different languages. The Ceylonese have not yet written back. Lapland is now visited. In Russia the gospel is preached. Wallachia is succoured. Constantinople is visited. The gospel is declared to a hundred Carthagenian [African] captives. From Guinea there is nothing new. A brother Moor [Negro] who lives there is endeavoring to erect schools for his fellow countrymen. The apostles of the Samoiedes [Tartar tribes] have returned from captivity and are solicitous for re-establishing the preaching of the gospel there. Shortly we shall visit the East Indies, and the savage tribes of New York, and the Magi in Persia. Through the whole of Germany the churches are preparing for Christ, in Lusatia, Saxony, Brandenburg, Alsace, Swabia, Franconia, Württemberg, several imperial cities, Halsatia, the Palatinate, the Netherlands, and several states along the Rhine. Pray for us.[5]

Obviously the Zinzendorf family life had little more than an incidental place, merging with the life of the Brotherhood. Apart from the absorption of both parents in the church's work, the choir system de-emphasized the family unit. The couple's twelfth and last child, Elizabeth, one of the four to grow to maturity, was born at Marienborn on April 25, 1740. The two oldest children early took an active place in the religious life of the Brethren. Benigna became an eldress in the girls' choir before she turned fourteen. Christian Renatus had both brilliant intellect and precocious piety. As the church grew, so did the responsibilities of the countess, who became increasingly indispensable to her husband as his chief financial manager. Outwardly at least she seemed as willing to relegate her family to second place as was the count.

---

[5] Daniel Benham, *Memoirs of James Hutton*, p. 53.

15

PRELUDE TO PENNSYLVANIA

The needs and opportunities in the American colonies had intrigued Zinzendorf from the very beginning of the Brethren's missionary outreach. In 1734 he had sent George Böhnisch, one of his evangelists, to Pennsylvania with the Schwenkfelders. The next year he dispatched Spangenberg to Georgia with the first band of colonists and missionaries. Having finished his assignment in the South, Spangenberg spent the years 1736 to 1739 among the Germans of Pennsylvania. In 1740 Christian Henry Rauch began his mission among the Indians along the New York-Connecticut border, and Andrew Eschenbach continued further work among the Pennsylvania Germans. About the same time that the Georgia settlement was ending in failure, the last of the Brethren were leaving for Pennsylvania. There under Peter Böhler they began the construction of George Whitefield's proposed school for Negroes in the forks of the Delaware, at a place to which he gave the name Nazareth. Meanwhile Bishop David Nitschmann was en route from Europe with a small company to begin a Moravian settlement in Pennsylvania, for it had not taken Spangenberg long to acquaint himself with the religious destitution of his fellow Germans in that commonwealth. His first letter from there so impressed Zinzendorf that he later regarded it as his "first call" to Pennsylvania. It was on the basis of Spangenberg's favorable reports that the Nitschmann contingent was sent from Marienborn. In late December of 1740 this group joined forces in the Forks of the Delaware with the company which had come from Georgia.

Whitefield's plans miscarried because of financial reverses, and he was glad to sell his five-thousand-acre Nazareth tract to the Moravians. But some months before the English evangelist was forced to drop his project, the Brethren had purchased another piece of land, totaling five hundred acres, on the Lehigh River, ten miles south of the Whitefield property. Thus the Moravians in the summer of 1741 found themselves in possession of two promising locations for settlement some fifty miles north of Philadelphia, ideal bases for evangelizing among the Germans and for missionary work among the Indians.

It was at this point that Zinzendorf in Wetteravia decided that the time had come for him to visit the colony himself. Some weeks before he left home, he resigned his episcopal office, a rather unusual step, since consecration as a bishop, like ordination to the ministry, is not something the individual is free to lay aside. What Zinzendorf's action amounted to is that for the time being he turned over his duties to John Nitschmann, whom the synod which dealt with the matter elected to fill his place. The same synod, in session between June 20 and July 3—one of the four referred to above—refused to accept Zinzendorf's resignation as general warden of the church, or Leonard Dober's resignation as chief elder. The count in laying aside the responsibilities of the bishop's office did so in order that he might not be looked upon in Pennsylvania as a Moravian bishop but as a free servant of the church universal, the full import of which was soon to be revealed.

With select members of the Pilgrim Congregation, including his wife and daughter Benigna, he set out for England on August 7. En route, in Heerendyk, Holland, he reiterated publicly his purpose:

I have been commissioned by the Lord God to spread the word of Jesus' blood and death, without concern as to what happens to me as a result. This has been my calling even before I knew of the Moravian Brethren. I have been, and still am, associated with the Moravian Brethren, who have taken our gospel of Jesus Christ into their hearts and called me and other Brethren to serve their fellowship. Yet I do not separate myself thereby from the Lutheran Church, for a witness of Jesus can remain in this church. Meanwhile, I cannot restrict myself as a witness to one church, for all the earth is the Lord's, and all souls are his. I am debtor to all.[1]

An epoch-making synodical conference in London, between Septemtember 11 and 18, was the focus of the count's final preparations before setting sail. Only ten persons were present—Zinzendorf; his wife; Benigna; Leonard Dober; Anna Maria Lawatsch, general eldress; Frederick von Watteville; Rosina, the wife of Bishop David Nitschmann; David Nitschmann the syndic; and Spangenberg and his wife. These, meeting in a house on Red Lion Street instead of in the count's

[1] Verbeek, *Des Grafen von Zinzendorf, Leben und Character*, p. 232.

own apartment in order to avoid undue publicity, sought to arrange for a proper administration of affairs during Zinzendorf's absence. They had expected Dober to remain as chief elder and in addition assume the duties of general warden. He remained firm in his refusal to continue, because he felt that the church had grown beyond the capacity of one person to occupy such a position. The lot confirmed his stand. In several attempts the conference failed to secure the lot's approval of other nominations. Could the church continue without a chief elder? On the sixth day of the conference, September 16, the idea came simultaneously to all present that "the Saviour shall be our Chief Elder." Various passages from the *Daily Texts* seemed to point to this solution to their problem. Finally they put the specific question to the lot, "Whether this signified that the Saviour would himself undertake the office," and found an affirmative answer. The duties hitherto assumed by the chief elder and the general warden were then assigned to a newly created board, the so-called General Conference. Bishops Müller and John Nitschmann and Frederick von Watteville were among the original members of the conference. The countess continued her position as business manager.

When announced to the Moravian Brotherhood at large, on the following November 13, the experience of the London conference had the effect of a spiritual revival. The declaration that Christ was henceforth to be the Chief Elder of the church stirred emotions in Herrnhut almost as deep as those of August 13, 1727. November 13 continues as one of the important festival days of the Moravians. The meaning of what it commemorates is summarized by one Moravian historian as follows:

By this experience the Moravian Church was saved from a spiritual popedom. Personal daily fellowship with the personal Saviour is one of the essentials of the Moravian conception of religious life. The headship of Jesus in the church contains in it truths of first moment for the denomination as such. It finally carries with it the Moravian conception of the ministry, viz., that ministers are absolutely the property of Christ, unreservedly consecrated to His service. All forms of labor done for Him and unto Him are therefore equally honorable.[2]

The records of the London conference may not so indicate, but it seems rather apparent that the concept of the chief eldership of Christ

[2] J. Taylor Hamilton, *History of the Moravian Church*, p. 101.

was the inspiration of Zinzendorf himself. It was not the only occasion at which his presence moved others to think "simultaneously."

Conspicuous among the events of these weeks was a sharp encounter with John Wesley. James Hutton had arranged for Wesley and Zinzendorf to meet at Gray's Inn Gardens, then open to the public as a park. Speaking in Latin, they lost no time in challenging each other's views and parted with each more firmly convinced than before that the other was wrong. Wesley, the activist, put emphasis upon the striving after holiness and perfection. Zinzendorf, the thoroughgoing disciple of Luther, condemned anything suggestive of righteousness by works. More will be said later about the difference between the two. Suffice it to say at this point, that the conversation at Gray's Inn Gardens on September 3, 1741, dramatized that Methodism and Moravianism were embarking on separate ways in England.

There were seven persons sailing with the count from Gravesend on September 28—Benigna; his secretary John Jacob Müller; Rosina Nitschmann, who was joining her husband in America; Abraham and Judith Meinung, a missionary couple; David Bruce, another missionary; and John Henry Miller, a printer, who joined the Moravian Church in Philadelphia a year later. Because of the war between Spain and England there was considerable danger of attack on the high seas, and Zinzendorf was advised to travel by man-of-war rather than by merchant ship. However, he chose the latter, particularly because he was en route to Pennsylvania and did not wish to alienate himself from the Quakers and Mennonites, with whose pacifist position he was well acquainted. Before sailing there was doubt whether a leg injury on Benigna's part would permit her to go through with the journey; but once at sea, despite a rough initial passage through storms, she made a rapid recovery and went on to be a great asset to her father's work in America. It hardly need be said that the count was not idle during the two months on the water. Hymns, letters, and theological treatises came from him copiously before the ship landed in New York on November 29.

Controversy over him had preceded him to the colonies, and immediately upon setting foot on shore he found himself a widely discussed figure. A count was much more of a rarity on the other side of the Atlantic than in Europe, and one who had sacrificed wealth and position to devote himself to preaching was well-nigh a curiosity. Particularly prejudicial to him in New York was the hostility of the

Reformed clergy who were in touch with their fellow religionists in Holland, where feeling over the *Pastoral Letter* still ran high. This made for later serious difficulty in Moravian mission work among the Indians in the New York colony.

Notwithstanding, in conformity with long habit, he made the most of his opportunities during his week's stay in the city. He was the guest of the merchant Thomas Noble, one of the members of the society organized by Peter Böhler early that same year. Zinzendorf reorganized this society, and a few years later it became the first Moravian Church in the city. On Staten Island he visited Captain Nicholas Garrison, whom he had met and won as a friend on the island of St. Thomas. Garrison, as captain of the Moravian ship *Irene,* was soon to play a key role in the transportation of colonists and missionaries across the Atlantic.

Leaving New York on December 6 and proceeding overland, with stops in New Brunswick and other places in New Jersey, the count reached Philadelphia on the tenth. Bishop Nitschmann was on hand to welcome him and see him received as a guest in the home of the well-known Huguenot merchant John Stephen Benezet. After this he established himself in rented apartments on Second Street near Race.

The excitement surrounding his arrival was even greater than in New York, though the more tolerant spirit in Pennsylvania promised him a fairer hearing. He sent a formal notice of his presence to Governor Thomas, announcing himself, however, not as Count Zinzendorf, but as Herr von Thürnstein. Knowing that titles were a handicap in America, he rather naïvely hoped to be able to hide his rank. As in Stralsund when appearing for examination in 1734, he chose one of his family names. Some five months later, on May 26, after his disguise had proved completely ineffective, and even detrimental, he went further and formerly renounced his title. He did so in a Latin oration before Governor Thomas and a score of other leading officials and citizens, among whom was Benjamin Franklin. Besides being called Thürnstein, he was also addressed as Brother Ludwig and Johanan by his Brethren, and Friend Louis by the Quakers.

Spangenberg tells us that Zinzendorf while in Pennsylvania wore the ordinary clothes of the middle class, which in summer were of linen. He sometimes traveled on foot but mostly on horseback, for carriage roads and bridges were practically nonexistent in most of the localities he covered. There was usually a company of Brethren and

Sisters along with him and often a few converted Indians. Inns were scarce, and he frequently found himself forced to travel through the night. Carrying papers and books with him, whenever he stopped, if not engaged in conversation, he devoted himself to study and writing. He suffered from his inability to eat salt pork, the common item of food on the Pennsylvania frontier.

The count's activities in America can best be understood if we first look at religious conditions among the Germans in Pennsylvania. German migration, beginning in 1683, was at this time continuing in flood proportions. The transatlantic crossing had been almost fatal to organized religious life. A few minority groups, like the Mennonites, Dunkers, and Schwenkfelders, had come for the sake of religious freedom. The majority, represented by the Lutherans and the Reformed, had come largely for economic reasons. In the New World the memory of the oppressive formality of the German state churches made the immigrants indifferent or even hostile to organized religion, now that they were free to live without it. Few pastors had accompanied the Germans to America and only a handful of their churches had been organized before the 1740's. Many families had never availed themselves of the rites and sacraments of their denomination. Even the above-mentioned minorities had lost much of their conviction. Poverty and frontier toil had lowered the general cultural level, and the absence of churches was matched by an absence of schools. Conditions were somewhat better among the English-speaking people with their Anglican, Presbyterian, and Quaker churches.

The situation was fertile soil for sectarianism. Among the Lutherans, Reformed, Dunkers, and Schwenkfelders there had arisen splinter groups like New Lights, Inspired, Seventh-Day Baptist monks and nuns who built the Ephrata Cloisters, and even hermits who lived along the Wissahickon Creek.

About the time that Spangenberg arrived in 1736, a handful of thoughtful and devout men of different denominations, but generally of separatist views, were beginning to take steps to improve matters. The presence of a man of Spangenberg's caliber gave impetus to their plans. Sometime the next year they formed what they called "The Associated Brethren of Skippack," and which they continued for about three years. Their real leader was Henry Antes, Reformed lay preacher, whose homestead and mill in Frederick Township were widely known in the region. In the group also was Christopher Wiegner, one of the

Schwenkfelders who had come to Pennsylvania from Berthelsdorf and was thus close to the Moravians. His newly opened farm at Skippack, in present-day Montgomery County, became the monthly meeting place of the Associated Brethren for edification and mapping of strategy for evangelizing the Germans. Some twenty to thirty men from communities as widely separated as Skippack, Fredericktown, Oley, and Germantown comprised the core of the union.

The Associated Brethren may well be regarded as a direct forerunner of the Moravian Church in Pennsylvania. Its influence, at least, was highly formative. George Böhnisch, the first Moravian in the commonwealth, had come with the Schwenkfelders in 1734, helping Wiegner to open his farm and living with him until his return to Europe in 1737. Likewise, the Wiegner farm was Spangenberg's home during his first stay of three years in Pennsylvania, and his evangelistic labors were greatly facilitated by the co-operation which the group meeting there gave them. In early May of 1740 Peter Böhler and George Whitefield jointly conducted services in both the Wiegner and Antes homes. It was on this occasion that they entered into the agreement for Böhler and his followers to work for Whitefield on the Nazareth tract. The influence of the Skippack Association upon Zinzendorf, though it had ceased to function by the time he came on the scene, was significant. Doubtless it was Spangenberg's reports concerning it which inspired the count in Europe to conceive his scheme for an evangelical alliance of German Protestants in Pennsylvania.

It would not have been necessary for Zinzendorf to go to Pennsylvania personally simply to plant a Moravian colony. That he could have delegated completely to competent men like Spangenberg, Nitschmann, or Böhler. But he had in mind for Pennsylvania something greater than the Moravian Church, namely, a "Congregation of God in the Spirit." Of course, the whole Piestist movement was that, and it was further embodied in the Moravian Diaspora. But Pennsylvania seemed the ideal place for it. No ecclesiastical organization had yet arisen to stand in the way of proceeding toward his ideal. In the light of this it is easier to understand why he resigned as a Moravian bishop and what he meant when he said in Holland, "I cannot restrict myself as a witness to one church." Such were the dreams of the man who came to Philadelphia in December of 1741. Unfortunately Pennsylvania was then not yet ready for their fulfillment.

16

IN THE QUAKER COMMONWEALTH

The count needed some time for orientation before acting. Getting acquainted in Philadelphia occupied him for a week. The natural thing for him was to visit his associates in the Forks of the Delaware. There the Brethren were concentrating first on the site at the mouth of the Monocacy Creek, postponing further building on the original Whitefield tract. During the preceding winter they had erected a combination dwelling and stable and in late September had laid the cornerstone of a community house (*Gemein Haus*), to be built also of logs. This latter structure, its logs covered with clapboards, still stands as the oldest building in Bethlehem.

Zinzendorf's itinerary on this first journey in Pennsylvania further reveals the importance to the Moravians of the Associated Brethren of Skippack. Leaving Philadelphia late on December 18, he spent the night in Germantown with John Bechtel, a licensed preacher of the Reformed Church and prominent in the association. A considerable group came to the Bechtel home that night to meet with the count. The journey really began at Germantown, for that is where all those who were to go along with him assembled. The next two overnight stops were at the Wiegner and Antes farms respectively. Antes met with an enthusiastic response as he told his guest of his plan to issue within a few days a circular letter calling for a "conference of religions."

The fourth day brought the travelers to their destination. About three miles down the Lehigh from the infant settlement, still without a name, they passed the mill of Nathaniel Irish at the mouth of the Saucon Creek. Irish was a friend who had helped the Brethren temper their differences with George Whitefield and who, as agent for William Allen, had sold them land at a time when it looked as if they would have to vacate the evangelist's property. Still on the south side of the river, they were greeted next by the Ysselstein family, Hollanders who had settled on a spot today submerged by a steel mill. Then following the trail of the old Indian ford, they crossed the stream to where stood the log-cabin dwelling and stable and the unfinished community house.

Two hastily prepared rooms on the second floor of this community house were the count's accommodations during his stay. There is no record of the events of the next few days, but we can assume that a festive spirit prevailed. Some thirty or more people must have been in the settlement—those who had accompanied the count from Europe, the two companies who had come under Böhler and Nitschmann, and friends picked up on the way from Philadelphia. Perhaps Wiegner and Antes were present.

Sunday, December 24, 1741, stands out, for that was the day on which Bethlehem received its name. Only a Zinzendorf could have christened a community so dramatically. It was Christmas Eve, not for the colony as a whole, which as an English possession was still

FIRST HOUSE IN BETHLEHEM

159

using the old calendar, but for those who were following the calendar used by their Brethren on the Continent. A day of services was climaxed with the Holy Communion. Then, in honor of the Saviour's birthday, they continued with vigils after nine o'clock. Under the same roof with them in their crude sanctuary were their cattle. Surrounding them was the wilderness inhabited by the Indian tribes to whom they hoped soon to be preaching their Saviour. Zinzendorf's impulsive imagination rose to the occasion. Leading the worshipers to that end of the building which sheltered the animals, he began singing a German Epiphany hymn combining Christmas and missionary thoughts:

> Jesus call Thou me
> From the world to flee,
> To Thee hasting;
> Without resting;
> Jesus call Thou me.

> Not Jerusalem,
> Rather Bethlehem
> Gave us that which
> Maketh life rich;
> Not Jerusalem.

> Honored Bethlehem,
> Pleasant I esteem;
> From Thee springeth
> What gain bringeth;
> Honored Bethlehem.

> Thou no more of right
> Art called least in might;
> Unto all men
> Yea the heathen,
> Brings't Thou health and light.

> Point me out the star
> Which my course, afar,
> Guides from pagan
> Ways forsaken;
> Point me out the star.[1]

No extant record tells exactly what happened next. Both the hymn and the occasion suggested to one and all that the place be called

[1] J. M. Levering, *A History of Bethlehem, Pennsylvania,* p. 78.

Bethlehem. It is safe for us to assume that with Zinzendorf there, it was his inspiration.

His program during the next six months illustrates his earlier declaration that as a witness of Christ he could not restrict himself to the Moravian Church. He left Bethlehem on Christmas morning for the home of Jean Bertholet, another of the Skippack members, at Oley, near present-day Reading. In Bertholet's house that night Zinzendorf preached his first sermon in Pennsylvania, his only one on this particular trip. From Oley he went as far west as Ephrata before turning back toward Germantown. He had intended to confer with Conrad Beissel, superintendent of the Cloisters, but changed his mind at the last moment. Ten days after leaving Philadelphia, he was back in Germantown with John Bechtel, having covered in exploratory fashion much of the rural Pennsylvania-German area. He made no secret of his disappointment in the reception given him on his tour. Some weeks later in an open letter to the Germans he said:

I expected to be received with love and confidence, but I encountered a great deal of mistrust and suspicion. Is it to be wondered at, that I felt dejected, and that the lukewarmness of my countrymen in Philadelphia depressed me. But I thought: I will keep silent, and not open my mouth. The Lord will help.

I traveled through Pennsylvania, but could not speak anywhere, except in Oley. Therefore, I can tell you, my countrymen, in a few words, what I have done in these two months: I traveled and prayed, and wept and bore witness, and sought for peace, and seek it still.[2]

This experience did not discourage him from acting a pastor's part in the Philadelphia area, where he lived during the first half of his American visit, in the city itself and in Germantown. Zinzendorf's work in Pennsylvania falls rather neatly into four parts: his pastoral ministry in Philadelphia; his participation in the first seven Pennsylvania synods; his organization of the Moravians in the Forks of the Delaware; and his three missionary tours in Indian country. Each can be depicted best if considered separately, though they are closely interrelated.

The first phase of these activities began the day after his return to Germantown, when he preached in the Reformed Church, of which Bechtel was supply pastor. The response was favorable enough for him

---

[2] Levin Theo. Reichel, *The Early History of the Church of the United Brethren*, p. 96.

to be asked back. In his quarters in Philadelphia he followed the practice he had used with the Pilgrim Congregation in Europe, holding household devotions with visitors in attendance. His Lutheran auditors felt that his interpretation of the Scriptures was in line with their upbringing. Without a pastor and with only a rented barn, on Arch Street, as a place of worship—which the Reformed also rented once a month—they saw in Brother Ludwig, as he wished them to call him, an answer to their search for spiritual leadership. On January 21, on invitation of the church wardens, he began his ministry to them, though not yet as their duly appointed pastor. Not until May 19 was he so installed, at which time John Christopher Pyrlaeus, recent theological student at Leipzig, became his assistant. However, only a month after his installation he left to spend most of his time in Bethlehem and on his mission trips to the Indians. Under the count's pastorate a deep undercurrent of spiritual life began to reveal itself.

Zinzendorf's relations with the Reformed congregation worshiping in the same quarters were quite different. Its pastor, the Reverend John Philip Boehm, who served the charge as one of a circuit of churches, was among his bitter opponents. This is understandable, since the minister was under the supervision of the classis of Amsterdam, whence issued the troublesome *Pastoral Letter*. He did his best to create dissatisfaction with Zinzendorf but took no overt action until the latter's absence on his first trip among the Indians in July. He first had a padlock put on the church door on the pretext of keeping out the cattle; and when the Lutherans came the following Sunday, the man with the key was designedly absent. Only by breaking the lock could the worshipers enter. After the service was under way, a band of ruffians broke in and forcibly dragged the assistant pastor Pyrlaeus from the pulpit. Their accusation was that the congregation had entered the locked church illegally. Zinzendorf, having heard of the incident while at Tulpehocken, returned to the city to lodge a complaint with the authorities. Though of little significance, there was a belated court decision in his favor.

The affair was the end of the count's pastorate in that place of worship and the beginning of a split among the Lutherans, some of whom Boehm had succeeded in alienating from the count. Out of it came the beginning of the Moravian Church in Philadelphia. Zinzendorf later that year erected at his own expense a church for those Lutherans who remained loyal to him. By that time Henry Melchior

Muhlenberg had arrived to head Lutheran work in the colony, and the count's leadership was checkmated. In the meantime, also, the remnant loyal to Zinzendorf had been augmented by more Moravians from Europe, the "First Sea Congregation," which arrived in the city on June 7. Of these fifty-seven new arrivals some went to Bethlehem and Nazareth, and some remained in Philadelphia. Zinzendorf's last public act in the city, in January of 1743, was the preaching of a sermon in the church he had built.

The count's associations with the Reformed in Germantown were happier than with members of their denomination in Philadelphia, and he continued to preach for them on Sunday afternoons during the time he was serving the Lutherans in the latter city. The Germantown group represented a different wing of the Reformed Church, one which had no official connection with Amsterdam but which followed the canons of the Synod of Berne of 1532. It included, moreover, a strong separatist element. Zinzendorf did his best to promote their cause in a number of ways. He had David Nitschmann ordain Bechtel to be pastor of the church he had been serving as a licensed lay preacher and to be superintendent of other churches to be organized. He compiled a catechism based upon the articles of the Synod of Berne, which Bechtel used, in connection with the articles themselves, as a manual for teaching. Bechtel, after editing it, had it published under his own name. About the same time the count published a collection of hymns entitled *Hirten Lieder von Bethlehem* (*Pastoral Hymns of Bethlehem*). Benjamin Franklin was the printer of these and most of Zinzendorf's other works which he wrote in America.

As noted, the compelling reason for the count's coming to America was his interest in church union. Not the initiator of the Pennsylvania synods, he was the dominant personality of the first seven, between January and June of 1742. Six days after talking to the count about it, Henry Antes, on December 26, sent out from his home in Frederick Township a circular letter to all denominations and sects, inviting their representatives to attend a meeting at Germantown on "New Year's Day" (January 12, New Style). His letter, addressed to "Beloved Friend and Brother," included this statement of purpose:

... not to quarrel with one another, but to negotiate in love, concerning the most important articles of faith, in order to see how close together we can get on fundamentals, and on non-essentials, which do not impair salvation, to bear with one another in love.[3]

Though not explicitly stated, it is clear that the intention of the conveners was that there be a series of conferences. At least such was the outcome. Accordingly, the place and time of the seven synods which Zinzendorf attended were as follows: (1) at Germantown in the vacant house of Theobald Endt, January 12-13; (2) in Falkner Swamp at the home of George Hübner, January 25-26; (3) at Oley in the home of John de Turck, February 21-23; (4) at Germantown in the home of John Ashmead, where Zinzendorf had his headquarters for several months, March 21-23; (5) in the Reformed Church of Germantown, April 18-20; (6) at Germantown in the home of Lawrence Sweitzer, May 16-18; and (7) at Philadelphia in the home of Edward Evans on Race Street, June 13-14.

The average attendance at these gatherings was above one hundred, with about half that number participating as accredited delegates. Practically all of the religious groups in Pennsylvania had delegates or visitors at the first three synods. There were Lutherans, Reformed, Mennonites, Schwenkfelders, Seventh-Day Baptists, Separatists (men who had broken with the church and constituted practically a party of their own), Hermits, and Moravians. Though the affair was primarily a German project, Anglicans, Presbyterians, and Quakers were among the visitors.

The position of the Moravians was a peculiar one. Since their church had not yet been organized in the colony, they did not consider themselves one of the denominations of Pennsylvania. Some of them, therefore, were present as individuals, as Bishop David Nitschmann and Anthony Seiffert. Others considered themselves as part of the Moravian Brotherhood but still members of the churches in which they had been brought up. This was the case with Zinzendorf himself, who with Christopher Pyrlaeus and Laurence Nyberg was registered as a Lutheran. Only after the arrival of the Sea Congregation, so-called because of its organization as a congregation on board ship, in time for the seventh synod, were the Moravians officially registered.

The obstacles confronting Christian unity were apparent the moment the first synod opened, with Henry Antes presiding. At this gathering

<hr>

[3] *Büdingische Sammlungen,* **II,** 72.

most of the attention was devoted to efforts to define a Christian position common to all, irrespective of creed. A strongly Christocentric statement was arrived at. In print it was a fine, irenic document. It stressed that the true Church, or communion of saints, was the "Congregation of God in the Spirit," that all who belong to Christ are members of it, and that the diversity of the church, so long as each division of it remains true to Jesus, is her beauty. Clearly the Pennsylvania synods did not aim to submerge the identity of individual denominations.

Little did this published statement reveal the bitterness of discussion preceding it or foresee the sharper bitterness following it. To anyone familiar with the count's theology, it was clear that the synod's statement of the Christian faith and of the membership of the true Church was his creation. That fact alone made the findings unacceptable to many. Some deserted the synods after the first one. Others came back only to re-emphasize their differences. A considerable nucleus remained loyal to the count and continued to elect him moderator for all of the meetings after the first. After the fourth synod the Lutherans, Reformed, and Moravians alone were left; and, of the former two, most of them were in reality Diaspora Moravians, who later joined the Moravian Church outright.

As a union effort the Pennsylvania synods were failures, increasing rather than decreasing religious rivalry. But in a negative sort of way they ushered in a revival by moving the denominations to action. The Lutherans soon united behind Muhlenberg and the Reformed behind Michael Schlatter to effect their church organizations before the end of the decade. Dunkers, Mennonites, Schwenkfelders, and even the Ephrata Cloisters were galvanized into new life.

For the Moravians the synods were both gain and loss with respect to denominational growth, with the long-range result being decisively the latter. Inasmuch as a significant number of the participants—including both Reformed and Lutherans, and an individual here and there of some of the lesser bodies—eventually joined the Moravian Church, the result was an accession of fine leadership for the church. Also, a handful of preaching places under the sponsorship of the synods became Moravian churches. The same applied to the schools, so commonly a part of each parish in those days before the public school. On the other side, the synods delayed Moravian efforts to establish themselves other than as an interdenominational fellowship. Zinzendorf at first even conceived of Bethlehem not as a Moravian community but as the headquarters of the Congregation of God in the Spirit. When Spangenberg returned to America in 1744 to head the economy at Bethlehem, his instructions were that "the Brethren in America should not call themselves Protestant or Lutheran or Moravian, but simply Evangelical Brethren and a Brethren's Church." Illustrative of the outlying places was the situation at Oley, where the Moravian lay preacher Andrew Eschenbach had gathered a congregation of persons of varying denominational background. At the time the third synod met there, the group had reached the point of being ready for formal organization. At Zinzendorf's insistence the synod recognized the Oley congregation as a nondenominational church, with the members being listed as belonging to the denominations of their origin. The synod then had Eschenbach ordained at the hands of Bishop David Nitschmann, assisted by "Brother Ludwig as a theologian from Tübingen" and Anthony Seiffert, a presbyter of the Moravian Church.

Such an ordination, as well as later events, made it clear that the seemingly undenominational projects of the synods were really those of Zinzendorf's Moravian Brotherhood. Along with Eschenbach three other Brethren were ordained: Pyrlaeus, the count's assistant in Philadelphia, and Christian Henry Rauch and Gottlob Büttner, Moravian missionaries to the Indians. Rauch had brought three of his converts with him for baptism. These three were Delawares—Shabash, Seim, and Kiop—were renamed Abraham, Isaac, and Jacob, as "patriarchs" of the Indian church, also as a token of the current belief that their race descended from the "Lost Ten Tribes" of Israel. A school for girls was opened in the Ashmead home in Germantown on May 4, following a decision to that effect at the fourth synod. Countess Benigna and two assistants were the first teachers. Within a few months the girls were transferred to Bethlehem, and the institution eventually became the Moravian Seminary and College for Women.

Of the 124 present at the seventh synod, in Philadelphia, all but about 30 were Moravians, by virtue of the inclusion of the Sea Congregation. One of the sessions was in the form of a love feast on board the *Catherine,* the ship on which the newcomers had arrived. Aware that the first phase of the union effort had ended, the seventh synod attempted to summarize what had been done. The result was a series of observations on the state of nine groups: Quakers, Moravians, Lutherans, Reformed, Mennonites, Schwenkfelders, Dunkers, Seventh-Day Baptists, and Separatists. Though designated as the "unanimous result of the General Synod of Pennsylvania," the conclusions were unmistakably the personal opinion of Zinzendorf. Unfortunately they did not reflect the usual magnanimous spirit of the count but showed all too clearly his disappointment.

Of more immediate consequence was the decision to continue quarterly workers' conferences "to be attended by all who had remained faithful to the decisions of the first Conference, and open to all servants of Christ, who acknowledged his divinity, did not believe in the doctrine of reprobation, and promised not to abuse the confidence of the Synod." The quarterly conferences were called General Synods up to 1745, and in 1746 and 1747 Synods of the Brethren, and in 1748 and thereafter Provincial Synods. In other words it took about six years for the name to catch up to what they really were, synods of the Moravian Church.

Why did this union effort in Pennsylvania fail? Admirers of Zinzendorf are among the first to admit that he was one of the reasons. He did not have a personality that made for peace among theologians. Apart from that, his rank was against him. The free spirit of Pennsylvania disliked titles and grand airs. Whether Zinzendorf called himself Brother Ludwig or Pastor Thürnstein made little difference. He continued to be Count Zinzendorf. Knowledge in America of the controversy surrounding him in Europe put him at a disadvantage from the outset. The timing of the synods was wrong. Twenty to thirty years later would have been better. The immigrant generation, with its first taste of freedom from the restrictions of the Old World, was still suspicious of anything that might hamper its individualism. Finally, the idea was difficult to understand. Zinzendorf's aim was neither organic merger nor simple federal union, but an attempt to make visible the invisible or true Church. Such a task neither theologians nor everyday Christians seemed as yet able to achieve.

In analyzing the forces which opposed Zinzendorf in America, we see further what an impossible task he faced. In general he was attacked by three groups—the strict Calvinists, the Separatists, and the Lutherans who followed Muhlenberg. Most of this opposition was a transfer from the Old World and, as noted, confronted him on arrival. Nor was it confined to the borders of Pennsylvania.

The quarrel with the first group was theological, centering primarily around the doctrine of reprobation, against which the count had strong convictions. It was on this point that the Brethren had quarreled with Whitefield. The same subject brought Zinzendorf into conflict with Gilbert Tennent, a friend of Whitefield, at their one and only meeting in New Brunswick at the time the count was en route to Philadelphia for the first time. Tennent thereafter was one of his bitterest and most unfair opponents, printing vicious attacks against him and the Moravians. He even repeated from a pulpit in New York the lie, printed in various papers, that Benigna was not his daughter but the daughter of a naval officer whom he had taken into his company. Among the Germans, Philip Boehm in Philadelphia was the leader of this group. It was he who published in America the *Pastoral Letter* of the classis of Amsterdam. Boehm had an ally in Christoph Saur, the German printer. The pages of his *Pennsylvania Geschicht Schreiber* were a forum open to Zinzendorf's enemies. Calvinistic Scotch-Irish Presbyterians had settled in the Forks of the Delaware some years before the Brethren and were unfriendly neighbors until after the Revolution.

Equally prompt to attack Zinzendorf were the Separatists. Prominent among them were Adam Gruber, one of the founders of the Skippack Brethren, and John Hildebrand of the Ephrata Cloisters. Being true Separatists, they objected to Zinzendorf's emphasis upon the church. According to him, so it seemed, one had first to be a member of some denomination before one could be part of the Church of God in the Spirit. To them the true Church was unknowable. They resented his reference to them as schismatic. Adding to the misunderstanding on Gruber's part was his close connection, through correspondence, with Rock in Germany, with whom Zinzendorf had parted company some years before. Their attacks, printed by Saur, were couched in strong language, with the use of such epithets as the "beast of the Revelation," and "false prophet." Zinzendorf replied in the *Pennsylvania Gazette,* published by Franklin, as well as by separate pamphlets.

Henry Melchior Muhlenberg came on the scene only a few weeks before Zinzendorf's return to Europe, and there was only one meeting between the two. Actually the Lutheran opposition to the count had begun months before the arrival of Muhlenberg, who was the man sent to America to give it leadership. Muhlenberg's work was undoubtedly the most effective of all the obstacles to Zinzendorf's influence in Pennsylvania. If the latter had any hopes of bringing the Lutherans into the Congregation of God in the Spirit, Muhlenberg dashed those hopes completely. The bulk of the Lutherans in Pennsylvania rallied around the able emissary from Halle, leaving only a handful here and there to stay with the Brethren in the Pennsylvania synods and eventually to become Moravians.

There can be little doubt that Muhlenberg's coming was in direct response to the challenge raised by Zinzendorf's efforts to organize the Lutherans in Pennsylvania. Prior to these efforts the church in Germany had shown little concern for the situation in America. Muhlenberg came armed with credentials from Francke at Halle and from the German court preacher Ziegenhagen in London, also a Halle partisan. There was a personal touch in the Muhlenberg-Zinzendorf feud. The former's last position in Germany had been the superintendency of the orphan house sponsored by Zinzendorf's aunt Henrietta at Hennersdorf. The institution had closed because of financial difficulties early in 1741, and it was at this point that Halle got hold of him and persuaded him to accept the Pennsylvania appointment. Henrietta, it will be recalled, had long before sided with Halle against Zinzendorf. Judging from the sharp exchange of words between Zinzendorf and Muhlenberg at their one meeting in Philadelphia, the latter had absorbed the aunt's low opinion of her nephew. One of Muhlenberg's gibes was, "You are just what your aunt told me you were."

Having named Bethlehem shortly after his arrival in America, Zinzendorf was too occupied otherwise to give it further attention for another six months. Only a handful of colonists under Father Nitschmann (David Nitschmann, uncle of the bishop with the same name) were kept on the job of finishing the community house. When on one occasion Nitschmann asked the count for more assistance, he was told that the spiritual work must be attended to first. The close of the synods and the arrival of the Sea Congregation, in charge of Peter Böhler, meant that the time had come to do something about the settlement in the Forks of the Delaware. To this Zinzendorf devoted most of the second half of his Pennsylvania stay. It proved to be his most worthwhile achievement in the New World, for the phenomenal success of Bethlehem removed all doubts as to the permanence of Moravian work in America.

In the beginning the colony on the Lehigh was a combination of two groups, the remnant of the Georgia mission and the little company sent directly to Pennsylvania in 1741 under Bishop Nitschmann. The third and largest component was the first Sea Congregation, whose coming was the final prelude to organization. The next step was to send the German members of this congregation to Bethlehem, where they arrived on June 21, after a three-and-a-half-day's walk via Skippack and Falkner's Swamp. Zinzendorf had gone ahead on horseback and was on hand to greet them by joining in the songs of thanksgiving which they sang as they crossed the Lehigh. The English members remained temporarily in Philadelphia with Peter Böhler.

Saturday, June 23, was the beginning of three days of services and conferences on the part of some eighty persons. There were seven meetings in all on that first day, including the dedication of the chapel in the community house, addresses by the count on the objects for which Bethlehem was being founded, and the reading of correspondence and reports from missionaries, according to the custom begun long before in Herrnhut of devoting Saturday to this subject.

The worship services on Sunday were followed by a general church council at which preliminary basic policies were outlined. On the surface the procedure may have been democratic; but, to one reading between the lines, it appears that the decisions may well have really been announcements of what the count had worked out beforehand. Bethlehem was to be a dedicated community with a mission to perform. To accomplish this the congregation was divided into two companies, the Pilgrim Congregation and the House Congregation (*Pilgergemeine* and *Hausgemeine*), the one to man the mission outposts, the other to occupy the home base. All of the 120 members in America, not just the 80 present, were assigned to one or the other. For some the assignment was in accordance with an expressed preference; for others it was by lot. This twofold division, with subdivisions and frequent reshuffling, was continued during the early days of Bethlehem. At times a brother or sister might be part of the Pilgrim Congregation and again part of the House Congregation.

Another striking decision of the first council was to set Saturday aside as a day of rest and prayer. In contrast Sunday was to be emphasized as the day for preaching, public worship, and instruction. There was never any doubt among the Moravians that Sunday should be observed in the traditional Christian way, and the Saturday question in no sense meant a minimizing of Sunday. Probably the chief reason for the action was the desire of Zinzendorf to be on friendly terms with the Sabbatarians in the colony, particularly the Seventh-Day Baptists of the Ephrata Cloisters, who were then very vocal on the subject. He felt that it would take away their monopoly on something to which they attached great importance.

At the same time some good reasons, even to Christians already observing Sunday, presented themselves for adding Saturday as a holy

COMMUNITY HOUSE IN BETHLEHEM

day. It conformed to the creation account of God's resting on the seventh day. It called attention to the fact that Christ's body lay in the tomb on Saturday. The Brethren also remembered that the first Christians still kept the seventh day, even after they had already begun to commemorate Sunday as the Lord's day. A final reason, long since dismissed as fanciful, was that if the Indians, as descendants of the lost tribes of Israel, were to be redeemed, it might be a step leading them back to the true God to restore the Sabbath of their ancestral religion. This double holy day was discarded for practical reasons within a few years.

The count, with his daughter Benigna and several others, spent most of Monday visiting Nazareth, where, among other things, he conferred with Captain John, the leader of the Indians at the nearby village of Welagameka who were vainly trying to retain their last foothold in the Forks of the Delaware. In the meantime George Neisser, secretary of the council, was in Bethlehem preparing material for the final session that evening. When that time had arrived Zinzendorf opened the meeting by leading the congregation in a *Singstunde,* long popular among the Brethren in Europe. The division of the members into small bands or classes was announced. There were to be eight divisions for the home group and eleven for the pilgrims. A high light was a sermon by the count on the text for the day, "Strong is thy dwelling-place, and thou puttest thy nest in a rock" (Num. 24:21). Ever since 1752 the day of June 25 has been observed as the anniversary of the Bethlehem congregation.

The following months were ones of elaboration upon the pattern laid down during the initial days. Helping to shape Bethlehem was the experience gained in building Herrnhut and Herrnhaag. But the freedom of Pennsylvania gave room for experimentation on a scale impossible in the Old World. During the half year that Zinzendorf was personally on the scene, he made full use of that freedom. Much as he forced his own ideas upon others, he was quick to make changes when he thought them necessary. No one was at "ease in Zion" during that first year in Bethlehem. There was always some new project on which to work.

There was a full quota of religious services similar to those already described in connection with Herrnhut. Preaching was done by Zinzendorf, Böhler, Bishop Nitschmann, Anthony Seiffert, and others of the few ordained men available. The main Sunday morning service was in German. In the afternoon there were English services, Bible lectures, services for individual choirs, prayer meetings, and so on. At these more informal gatherings the pilgrims, full of experiences from the field, were often the speakers. When in the village, Zinzendorf was regarded as the head pastor, with Böhler next in line. Like Herrnhut, Bethlehem also had its head elder, in effect as much of a spiritual leader as the pastor himself. Anthony Seiffert and then Andrew Eschenbach were the first to fill this position. Assisting the chief elder were vice-elders and eldresses for the different choirs. There were numerous other elected and appointed officers to oversee the various functions of the community's life.

Illustrative of the count's colorful way of doing things was the nomination by the church council, on July 15, of ten brethren as "fishermen." They were to proceed to designated communities and cast out the "gospel net." Five weeks later they returned to report what they had done. Soon they were on the road again with the instructions—not unusual for early Moravians—not to interfere with any servant of Christ and to avoid all disputes. An entry in the November diary says, "Today the wheel ran out," the wheel being two brethren and two sisters on an evangelistic tour. The figure was from Ezekiel. These evangelists were also referred to as the "Pennsylvania Wagon."

The free circulation of letters, diaries, and reports from among Moravians throughout the world made them aware, from the beginning, of the need for postal service. It was natural, therefore, that almost immediately the Brethren set up a weekly mail service to and from Philadelphia, probably the first such arrangement for an inland part of the colony. The carriers, traveling on foot, left Bethlehem on Monday mornings, made overnight stops at the Holstein home in Falkner's Swamp and at Bechtel's in Germantown, and on Wednesday reached Philadelphia, where Zinzendorf's assistant, Pyrlaeus, acted as postmaster. Returning to Germantown the same day, the carriers left for Bethlehem on Thursday morning and reached there the next evening. Later Henry Antes speeded up the service by providing horses.

Father Nitschmann superintended the physical side of the community's development, bringing to his task long experience as a carpenter. It goes without saying that there was no line of demarcation between the "sacred" and the "secular." When the pilgrims happened to be home, during brief intervals between assignments, they cheerfully became part of the House Congregation, applying themselves to burning bricks, building barns, clearing fields, splitting fence rails, or cobbling shoes. The common purpose eased the hard toil, the scant fare, and the physical inconveniences of the first days of Bethlehem. Everyday tasks were performed as if they were sacramental acts.

The community did not have long to wait to witness the full round of rites and ceremonies that are part of a church's life. The first funeral took place on June 27. It was that of John Mueller, a young man from Rhinebeck, New York, who had come to Bethlehem with missionary Rauch, and who died there on June 26. Accompanied by Christian Fröhlich, Zinzendorf went into the woods, about a hundred yards northeast of the community house, and selected a spot at which Fröhlich dug the grave. In conducting the funeral, Zinzendorf consecrated the ground as "God's Acre." A month later Böhler conducted the funeral of their good neighbor Isaac Ysselstein, on the south side of the river.

However, he was buried on his own farm. Zinzendorf officiated also at the second interment in God's Acre, on September 12—that of John Hydecker, who had died two days before on an evangelistic tour.

Again it was the count who, on July 8, performed the first wedding ceremony, that of the missionary couple John Zander and Johanna Mueller. A month later, on August 9, Nitschmann and Zinzendorf ordained Zander to the ministry, the first ordination in Bethlehem. Likewise it was the count who baptized the first child born in Bethlehem, Anna Regina, born on July 16, daughter of Paul and Regina Bryzelius. The baptism was administered on the day of her birth. Another first among baptisms was that of three Indians, on September 16, at which Zinzendorf and the missionaries Büttner and Eschenbach each baptized one of the candidates.

One short-lived experiment deserves special mention. About a month after the German portion of the Sea Congregation had gone to Bethlehem, the fifteen to twenty English members of the group followed, after it had been decided to locate them at Nazareth as the nucleus for a future English congregation. David Bruce, the Scot who had come to America with the count, was to be their elder. It was hoped at the same time that Nazareth would be the base for a program of evangelism among the English population, as Bethlehem was for the German. The venture lasted only during the months of July and August; and most of the folks returned to Philadelphia, except a few who were sent to itinerate in non-German areas. For the next thirty years Bethlehem and Nazareth were operated as twin communities, until in 1772 Nazareth became a settlement congregation on its own. However, Nazareth has had its own separately organized congregation since 1747, the year 1772 applying only to its separation as an independent community. During the months of Zinzendorf's residence in the Forks of the Delaware, Nazareth was only an outpost with the two cabins built by the original company from Georgia two years before and with the foundation laid for the abortive school venture of Whitefield.

With Bethlehem organized and a corps of missionaries on the march, next on Zinzendorf's schedule for personal attention was the mission to the Indians. Between July 24 and November 9 he was absent from Bethlehem on three separate exploratory tours, for a total of more than eleven weeks, on behalf of the project. The personnel of about a dozen, which accompanied him on these ventures, was different for each one; but among those who went along on all three trips was Anna

Nitschmann. The first journey, covering the two weeks between July 24 and August 7, was the shortest and only partly in Indian territory, for it included a roundabout return by way of Philadelphia. The original plans apparently called for a journey of only a few days, the terminus being the Indian village of Meniologameka, immediately north of the Blue Mountain, only a day's direct travel from Bethlehem. But when on the morning of the fifth day the party, after having stopped at a few minor Indian villages, had arrived at Meniologameka, the count was seized with a strange premonition that he should go at once to see Conrad Weiser, the well-known mediator and interpreter between the whites and the Indians, at his home at Tulpehocken. He had become acquainted with Weiser through the Pennsylvania synods. Taking with him only John Zander, John Lischy, and their Indian interpreter, Zinzendorf went to Tulpehocken and sent the others back to Bethlehem.

He said afterward that he went to Weiser's "in strong faith . . . knowing neither why nor wherefore." The impulse turned out to be providential, for at Tulpehocken he met the deputies of the Six Nations (Iroquois Confederacy), who were returning from a conference with Governor Thomas in Philadelphia concerning the delay of the Delawares in leaving the Forks of the Delaware. Zinzendorf's visit with the Indian deputies resulted in a pact of friendship, attested to by their giving him a string of wampum. This pact included permission for the Brethren to travel freely among the Six Nations. One can only speculate about the "premonition" which had such a far-reaching result. But well informed as the count was of affairs in the province, it is more than likely that he was not entirely surprised to find the Indian deputies at Tulpehocken. At any event it was a well-timed decision, making this brief excursion a significant event.

Having gone to Philadelphia from Tulpehocken, Zinzendorf returned to Bethlehem on August 7. Three days later he was on the move again, this time bound for Rauch's mission at Shekomeko, in Duchess County, New York, some twenty miles east of Rhinebeck. This journey involved a week's rough travel each way, over the Blue Mountain, through the Jersey Minisink area, and across the Hudson. During the eight days of his stay at Shekomeko the count baptized converts, organized the first Indian congregation of the Moravian Church, and made plans for an extension of the mission, including evangelization of neighboring whites.

On the return to Bethlehem the party had a taste of the intolerance so widespread against the Brethren. Preferring not to travel on Sunday, the count stopped for the day near Hurley, New York. While composing a poem which his daughter was writing down, he was interrupted by visitors. Preoccupied with his dictating, he left others in the group to carry the burden of the conversation. Obviously annoyed at the lack of attention given him, one of the visitors remarked that the count appeared to be very industrious, and announced himself as a justice of the peace. The next morning he haled the count, Benigna, and Anthony Seiffert into his court and fined them a total of eighteen shillings for Sabbath violation.

The third expedition, into the Wyoming Valley of the upper Susquehanna, occupied the count during the six weeks between September 21 and November 9. At the last moment it was decided that the trip would be too strenuous for Benigna, and she was left behind. Going by way of Tulpehocken, where Conrad Weiser joined it, the company proceeded along the Susquehanna to the Indian town of Shamokin, where now lies the city of Sunbury. Here Zinzendorf met the Indian chief Skikellimy, who was later to be so helpful in promoting mission work. Less profitable was his meeting, at Ostonwakin, with the famous Madame Montour, whose late husband had been a Seneca brave. Hers was a half-Christian, half-pagan religion, but in connection with Moravian missions her influence was an obstacle. At Ostonwakin, Weiser had to return home; and the count, under the guidance of Skikellimy, went on to the Shawnees in the Wyoming Valley.

For the next twenty days he lived a rather precarious existence, during which he clearly demonstrated his ineptness both for getting along with the Indians and for roughing it in the wilderness. He offended his hosts from the first by pitching his tent some hundreds of yards from their village. He spent much time alone in literary labors, especially on a supplement to the Brethren's hymnal. Intrusions upon his privacy annoyed him. He considered the Indians crude and made no effort to hide his feelings. Until the opportune return of Weiser, who understood and loved both the count and the Indians, his life was actually in danger. Among other things they suspected him of being an agent of interests having designs on silver deposits in the region. When on one occasion two puff adders slithered across his papers, it was discovered that he was seated at the mouth of their den. At another time his saddle girth broke, and he was thrown from his horse into a creek, landing on his back with the saddle on top of him. After Martin Mack had extricated him from this predicament, he kissed his rescuer and said: *"Du armer Bruder! Ich plage dich doch was rechtes!"* (My poor brother, I am an endless source of trouble!) Provisions were scarce for man and beast. On the return trip they were hampered by swollen streams. It was a weary count who returned to Bethlehem on November 9.

However, his unpleasant relations with the Indians at Wyoming in no wise diminished his zeal for going ahead with missions among them. Before he left America, he had already nominated twenty brethren for this branch of the service. He had the visions, but it remained for lesser men and women to give them substance.

Moravian developments in Europe, news of which awaited Zinzendorf in Bethlehem, made him anxious to return home as soon as possible; for certain actions of the Brethren during his absence displeased him. But there was still enough to do in Pennsylvania to detain him for another two months. Most of his attention during this final period was devoted to organization. Conferences at Bethlehem between November 13 and 15 arranged for the administration of the Indian mission, the evangelistic work among the whites, and the schools. At this point it had become difficult to distinguish between Moravian projects and those of the Pennsylvania synods, as revealed by the prominent role played in these conferences by Henry Antes and other members of the synods. Bishop Nitschmann was made president, with Anthony Seiffert as his assistant. Peter Böhler was placed in charge of the Indian work.

The count made a final tour of the German settlements, preaching seventeen times, between December 2 and 10, at Maguntsche, Heidelberg, Oley, Tulpehocken, Conestoga, and Lancaster. Because of the scarcity of churches most of his meetings were in houses or barns. Back in Bethlehem again, he held a series of intensive personal interviews with key personnel.

The Christmas Eve Vigils of 1742, between the hours of eleven and one, were almost as memorable as those of the year before when the community received its name. Under the count's personal direction much had been accomplished during the preceding months. All were conscious that he was about to leave. The watchword for the day was, "And the name of the city from that day shall be, The Lord is there." Zinzendorf again rose to the occasion, this time by extemporizing a hymn of thirty-seven stanzas which has come to be known as the "Bethlehem Christmas Hymn." Though not among his best hymns, portions of it have stood the test of time and are still in use.

Following a farewell love feast and Communion service, Zinzendorf left Bethlehem on December 31 in the same style in which he had first arrived. The Brethren escorted him across the river to the singing of chorales. On the south side of the Lehigh where he had stopped the year before to greet the Ysselsteins, he now paused to bid them good-by. The imprint of his personality had been indelibly stamped upon the community which he had set up to be the center of the Brotherhood in America.

Some of the persons who were to accompany him back to Europe went directly to New York from Bethlehem. Others went with him to Philadelphia to help wind up his business. There was a final meeting, on January 8, with officers of the Pennsylvania synods at a place known as the Ridge, about six miles from the city. There were, also, organizational details to be worked out with members of the congregation he had founded. It was to become a Moravian church a few years later, but at this stage it was still under the jurisdiction of the synods. On January 9, at the Benezet home where he had first been welcomed to Philadelphia, he made a valedictory address which he called his *Pennsylvania Testament*. Taken down and later printed, this very lengthy speech was one of the most important of his career, revelatory of his whole philosophy of life. It summarizes specifically his views with reference to the work of the Brethren in America, the Church of God in the Spirit and the Church of the Pilgrims in Bethlehem. His last address was his farewell sermon, on January 11, in the new church on Race Street, which he had built at his own expense. To avoid the emotional strain of personal leave-takings he left during the closing hymn, going immediately to Frankford where he spent the night. Two days later he was in New York waiting to sail.

During the next week there were more conferences, interviews, and last-minute appointments for the churches and missions in the New World. Peter Böhler was to be in charge of affairs until such time as Spangenberg could return from Europe. Assisting Böhler was to be Bishop Nitschmann, with responsibility for the Indian work shifted to him. An important acquisition to the Brotherhood was the previously mentioned Captain Nicholas Garrison of Staten Island, whom the count enlisted to captain the ship he intended to purchase for the use of other "sea congregations" headed for America. Garrison was among the some twenty persons in the count's company which embarked on January 20.

17

BACK TO EUROPE

Captain Garrison's high esteem for the man to whom he had so recently attached himself was immeasurably raised by an episode near the end of the voyage. On February 14 such a severe southern gale overtook the *James* near the Scilly Islands that she was in danger of foundering on the rocks. It was enough to frighten thoroughly all on board, including Garrison, a veteran of the sea. Zinzendorf was undisturbed throughout and after some time calmly informed Garrison that the storm would be over in two hours. At the end of that period he told his friend to go on deck to look at the weather. The amazed Captain Garrison saw the prediction being fulfilled, and the vessel was soon out of danger. Upon his asking the count how he could so accurately forecast the storm's end, he received this answer:

For more than the past twenty years I have had a trusting relationship with my dear Saviour. Therefore, when I find myself in an unusual or dangerous situation, the first thing I do is to analyze carefully whether I am to blame. If I find something with which he is dissatisfied, I fall at his feet to ask forgiveness. Thereupon my Saviour forgives me and generally at the same time lets me know how the affair will end. But if he does not choose to reveal the outcome to me, I remain silent and conclude that it is better for me that I do not know. This time, however, he assured me that the storm would last only two more hours.[1]

Garrison goes on to say that the count's transparent Christian conduct during the whole voyage made it easy to accept his explanation. Without further incident the ship reached Dover on February 17, and from there Zinzendorf went on to London.

Moravian work in England under Spangenberg had prospered greatly during the year and a half since the count had been on the scene.

[1] Spangenberg, *Leben Zinzendorfs*, tr. Jackson, p. 316.

The Brethren were active in many localities but particularly in Yorkshire where Benjamin Ingham had turned over to them his societies with a membership of twelve hundred. Eager to confer with Spangenberg, Zinzendorf went at once to the Yorkshire district, accompanied by Benigna, Anna Nitschmann, and James Hutton. One of the matters weighing upon his mind was the fact that the year before Spangenberg had authorized James Hutton to take out a license for the Fetter Lane Society, on the terms granted to dissenters. It was distasteful to Zinzendorf that his followers be so regarded. Furthermore, he looked upon it as a step in the direction of denominationalism at a time when he was still standing firm on keeping the Moravians only a society. Already in Pennsylvania he had drafted a vigorous protest to be deposited in the archives of the Archbishop of Canterbury. The Yorkshire visit to some extent disarmed him, for there he found many who were not of the Established Church. He conceded that the time had come to plan for a settlement congregation in England.

En route back to London, Zinzendorf called on some of the professors at Cambridge. Another stop was at Broadoaks, a castle in Essex, where the Brethren had located their schools for children in preference to London. Benigna stayed temporarily at Broadoaks, or Lamb's Inn as it was renamed, to assist in the schoolwork.

Between March 11 and 25 Zinzendorf spent most of his time with the Fetter Lane congregation in London, where he delivered a series of daily sermons. English translations of these sermons were read in the church the following day to those who did not understand German. The day before he concluded the series, he learned that there were some Frenchmen present who understood neither German nor English; whereupon for the first time in his life he preached a sermon in French. Also occupying some of his attention were the affairs of the Society for the Furtherance of the Gospel Among the Heathen, which James Hutton and others had organized to serve Moravian missionaries en route to and from the field. It was to become the mission arm of the British Moravian Church, which is still at work at the present time.

During this London stay Zinzendorf met for the first time the zealous John Cennick, revival preacher associated first with Whitefield and Wesley and after 1745 with the Brethren. When Zinzendorf talked with him in London, he was worshiping with the Fetter Lane congregation but was not yet fully identified with the Moravians. During his brief career, ending with his death at age thirty-seven in 1755,

Cennick was the outstanding Moravian preacher in the British Isles. Also on this occasion the count renewed his acquaintance with Archbishop Potter of Canterbury. Another noteworthy contact was with James Erskine, member of Parliament from Scotland. He extended an invitation to the Brethren to evangelize in Scotland, which matter was followed up within the year. Erskine revealed his interest in the Moravians by telling Zinzendorf that he had found in the library at Aberdeen the original document recording the protest of fifty-three Bohemian nobles against the execution of John Hus.

Differences with Whitefield came to the fore during this London visit, with the outcome the same as in the case of the clash with Wesley in September of 1741. Having talked with Whitefield and having heard him preach on the subject of reprobation, Zinzendorf publicly renounced all connection with him soon after he returned to Germany, "on account of this abominable doctrine so contrary to sound reason." In a letter to Whitefield he said:

You must first formally recant, and preach openly *free grace* in the blood of the Lamb, and an *election of grace* as taught in the Scriptures, which is quite different from the doctrine of predestination which you teach; and if not, our church must necessarily be opposed to you.[2]

Zinzendorf was not always consistent in his opinion of Whitefield. At a synod in 1744, for instance, he said: "Whitefield is an instrument of our Saviour; he belongs to the same household of faith; his foundation is like yours." A year later he said of the evangelist:

He desired to enjoy *for himself,* and not *with us,* what he had learned of Böhler in 1738; he did not fully understand our doctrine of the atonement; this led him to the doctrine of predestination, when, in the same year, he went to America and separated from us.[3]

On the Continent the church had not stood still while the count was in America. But the direction in which it had moved displeased him greatly. Even more than in England steps had been taken to make of the Moravian Church a separate denomination. Zinzendorf came home determined to undo the damage. It was too late. His absence had enabled the denominational impulse to gain a momentum which even

[2] Benham, *Memoirs of James Hutton*, p. 112.
[3] *Ibid.*

he could not stop. However, it is open to question whether he could have changed the course of events even if he had been in Germany in 1742.

The Moravian refugee element in the General Conference, the board delegated to administer the church during the count's absence, was quick to take advantage of certain opportunities which presented themselves during this period. In December of 1741, just about the time Zinzendorf arrived in Philadelphia, other Bohemian refugees in Saxony expressed a desire to organize themselves into a community like Herrnhut. Under the patronage of Sigismund Augustus von Gersdorf, lord of Trebus, they founded Niesky the following August. While these negotiations were still in progress, the Brethren were approached by Frederick the Great. Like his father, he was their champion; but for a different reason. The devout Frederick William had been attracted to Zinzendorf's Christian faith, while his religiously indifferent son was impressed by the thrift and industry of the Herrnhuters. When in July of 1742 Silesia came into his possession, he invited the Moravians to found communities in this new domain. Among the concessions held out to them was the recognition of their church as an independent body with an episcopal form of government and freedom of conscience for its members. Acceptance of this offer was made possible when another patron stepped forward in the person of Ernest Julius von Seidlitz, a Pietist of long standing, who had suffered for his convictions when Silesia was still under Austria. The two settlements of Gnadenfrei and Gnadenberg were started on his estates in rapid succession in March and May of 1743.

A similar opportunity for another settlement arose in central Germany through the patronage of Balthasar von Promnitz, another Silesian noble and a recent convert to the Brotherhood. No sooner was he in the church than he took an active part in its affairs and was among the representatives who carried on the negotiations with Frederick. Early in 1742 Promnitz purchased from Count Gotter the abandoned village of Neudietendorf near Gotha in Thuringia. The place had been built for an industrial enterprise which failed, and its houses had been standing empty for some time. Moravian families lost no time in occupying these homes, and the General Conference started proceedings to secure concessions like those granted to the settlements in Silesia.

Still another step the Conference took, with Abraham von Gersdorf as representative, was to secure ecclesiastical liberty in Holland, primarily to facilitate missions where Dutch influence prevailed. This too involved overtures to the States-General in a way which emphasized the independence of the church. In Wetteravia a new contract involving refinancing had been entered into with the count of Ysenburg-Büdingen. In this Herrnhaag was conceded to be a Moravian Church under the rule of its bishops.

These were the things which so disturbed Zinzendorf when he heard of them in Pennsylvania. He had registered his protest immediately and again in England and sent them in advance of his return to the Continent.

Affairs in Holland occupied him about two weeks, during which time he was in Rotterdam, The Hague, Amsterdam, and the Brethren's settlement of Herrendyk. At Amsterdam he met with the General Conference in early April and reiterated his position. It was the latter part of the month before Zinzendorf returned to his headquarters in Wetteravia, where he found the Brotherhood so flourishing as to tax the combined capacity of Herrnhaag, Marienborn, and the Ronnenburg. Paradoxically this very prosperity seemed to heighten his previously expressed uneasiness over the course of developments. In his *Natural Reflections* he said: "I cannot deny, but I felt more inclined at that time to preach repentance to my people than to share in their glory."

In the meantime the countess had been almost as active as her husband in traveling for the church. When he came home, she was still absent from Marienborn on her eight months' stay in the Baltic provinces on behalf of the Moravian Diaspora. She did not rejoin him until May 22, a month later. When he left for America in September of 1741, she had gone back to Wetteravia for the remainder of the year. The first two months after that saw her in Ebersdorf and Gotha. In the former she tried to effect a reconciliation between the little church there and the Brethren. But not until five years later did Ebersdorf rejoin the Brotherhood. Then came four months of residence in Herrnhut, followed by a journey to Denmark via Berlin. The Danish visit included a stopover with the Brethren at Pilgerruh and an audience with the queen at Copenhagen.

The stay of the countess in Livonia extended from late August of 1742 to the following May. Object of her visit was to play the part of a diplomat in bettering relations between the Diaspora workers and the

Lutheran state church. (Among the Germans of this region the Lutheran was the established church.) Her efforts took her to St. Petersburg for two months, though most of her time was spent at Wolmar, the chief center of Moravian work at the time. Unfortunately the situation had got out of hand before her arrival, and her efforts were fruitless. Nor did the count have better success on his visit a year later.

Death struck twice among the Zinzendorf children during the absence of their parents. While at Herrnhut, in the weeks before her departure for Copenhagen, the countess received word from Marienborn that four-year-old David had died on June 6. With her when the news came was Johanna Salome, one year older than her brother. In her grief the mother composed a few hymn stanzas on the death of her child. Noting the tears fall, Johanna Salome said: "Mama, will you cry for me also? When one goes to the Lamb, one sings verses. If you should have neither a David nor a Salome, we shall be with the Lamb. There it is much better than here." The child's words were prophetic. A little more than a half year later, on December 21, she followed David. Again the countess could not be at the deathbed of her child, for she was still on her mission in Livonia.

18

VINDICATION IN SAXONY
RECOGNITION IN BRITAIN

The 1740's were in some respects as critical and formative for the Brotherhood as had been the 1720's. There was no longer any question as to its continued existence. That was assured. The issue centered around what was to be its role in the religious life of Europe and the nations under European influence. The group had grown beyond the capacity of one man to dominate, and the failure of the count and his followers to see this aggravated the problems of the growing Moravian Church. Zinzendorf continued his fight for the purely Diaspora and missionary objective. His colleagues did little to resist him, and the Moravians indelibly took on the nature of an interchurch society. At the same time circumstances beyond the count's control also gave the Brethren the status of a denomination. Opposition continued from many quarters, but this was far outweighed by growing recognition and acceptance from other quarters, especially on the part of civil authorities. An expression of theological sentimentalism on the part of the Moravians was fortunately checked before it had permanently damaged their church.

Pastoral and administrative work in Wetteravia occupied Zinzendorf for two months after his return and postponed his attempted reversal of what the General Conference had done during his absence. Then at a synod convened between July 1 and 12 of 1743, at the castle of Hirschberg, belonging to Count Reuss of Ebersdorf, he acted vigorously. Expressing his disapproval of their recent conduct of affairs, he announced to the assembled leaders that the General Conference was dissolved. In its place were set up offices vague in their functions. The synod capitulated completely, going so far as to agree to have the count seek a reversal of the concessions in Silesia. He still hoped to have the

Moravians there placed under the supervision of the Lutheran consistory.

Soon after the synod, accompanied by the countess and Christian Renatus and followed later by others of the Pilgrim Congregation, he went to Berlin to consult with the minister of state concerning the matter. His efforts were fruitless. The Lutheran authorities preferred not to have the Brethren with special privileges under their supervision. Nor would Frederick grant the holding of an examination into their doctrinal status, for which Zinzendorf was pressing. The count's aim, of course, was to have the Lutheran orthodoxy of his church a matter of official record as insurance against future difficulties. Frederick, indifferent to theological hairsplitting, did not wish to give his theologians the opportunity of throwing roadblocks in the way of such valuable prospective citizens. Zinzendorf was reminded that the examination he had passed in connection with his consecration as bishop in Berlin was valid for his followers also. Not only did the count lose out in his attempt to prevent the independent development of the Moravian Church in Silesia, but out of the discussion came plans for yet another community, Neusalz on the Oder. Only in the case of Neudietendorf in Thuringia did he effect a reversal of plans. Ever since, this congregation has occupied an anomalous legal position.

Thwarted in his resistance to the course of events, the count nevertheless went along with the program of settlement building. He spent most of the late summer and early fall of 1743 in Silesia and adjacent territory, personally lending his encouragement to the beginnings in Gnadenfrei, Gnadenberg, Neusalz, and Niesky. His principal headquarters during this time was the castle at Burau belonging to Count Promnitz. At Burau, which he called Gnadeck, it was possible to have with him the Pilgrim Congregation; and it was close enough to enable him to keep his finger on the pulse of affairs in Herrnhut. So many of the Herrnhuters visited him that he arranged for a regular schedule for them. In this he made provision for purely personal counseling and for conferences on behalf of church administration. Here, assisted by Bishop Polycarp Müller, he consecrated his long-time associate Frederick von Watteville as bishop. To Burau, also, came Spangenberg to consult with him about the Second Sea Congregation soon to leave for America. A similar headquarters for Zinzendorf in Silesia was at Peilau, the home of von Seidlitz.

The difficulties confronting the Diaspora in Livonia moved Zinzendorf to plan a visit there as soon as he had finished his business in Silesia. The prospect of a lengthy absence again presented the problem of administrative responsibility. Part of the misunderstanding arising during his stay in America had been due to the fact that two synods had previously refused to accept his resignation as general warden. Yet the General Conference in subsequent important decisions had proceeded as if there were no general warden and had acted without consulting him. In order to avoid a possible repetition of such a situation, he insisted on a clarification of his authority, asking that either it be confirmed or taken from him completely. He reminded the church that he had asked for the latter in his original resignation.

Still in the mood of the synod of Hirschberg, his colleagues at Peilau gave him all the authority he asked for; the alternative was not even considered. It seems rather obvious that this is exactly what he expected. In a document handed to him on November 21 at Breslau he was asked to serve as *Advocatus et Ordinarius Fratrum*—that is, the head of the Brethren, invested with full power. Expressing gratitude for his service to their church up to date, the Brethren assured him that nothing of importance would be undertaken without his consent. The paper concluded with the request that he nominate a successor to his office to assure the continuance of their cause in the event of his death or resignation. Accepting this appointment tentatively, the count delayed a full year before giving his formal acceptance, probably because he himself at this point was unclear in his thinking as to what the Moravian Church should be—society or denomination. In the course of the ensuing year he developed his "tropus" scheme combining the two concepts.

He was now ready to leave for Russia. On November 26, at Lissa, Poland, the former important center of the Bohemian Brethren and home of the great Comenius, he parted from the countess, who had accompanied him that far. Then with Christian Renatus, Jonas Paulus Weiss, Anna Nitschmann, and others, he set out for Riga via Königsberg. Almost a month later, on December 23, after long miles over rugged roads in raw weather, he was in the Livonian capital.

The situation in Russia with respect to the Herrnhuters seemed hopeless. The visit of the countess earlier in the year seemed to have added fuel to the fire. So it would appear from an edict which Empress Elizabeth had issued before the countess had left the country:

It has been brought to the attention of her royal majesty that a new sect called the Herrnhuters has arisen in Livonia, whose founder is a certain Countess Zinzendorf. The sect has so multiplied that already large buildings have been erected, especially in the vicinity of Dorpat, for the gatherings of those who follow it in Livonia, and meetings are held in secret. Among the members of the sect are a group of Livonian nobility, pastors, and especially peasants. Therefore be it ordered that the Livonians, be they who they may, be forbidden to continue to adhere to the teachings of the Herrnhuters; that their buildings be closed; and that gatherings, whether in such buildings or elsewhere, be forbidden.[1]

This edict had gone into effect about the time that Zinzendorf was leaving Germany. Not only were the prayer halls closed, but also those Diaspora workers, some forty or fifty in number, who had come from Germany, were ordered to leave the country. Diaspora members were forbidden to communicate with their banished leaders.

Zinzendorf was unwilling to admit defeat. Part of his plan in going to Russia was to offer himself for examination before a commission both in Riga and St. Petersburg. To prepare the way he had some months before sent ahead his experienced envoy, Arvid Gradin. Gradin was promptly arrested and was to remain in custody in the Russian capital for the next four years. It is also to be noted that three other brethren—Conrad Lange, Zacharias Hirschel, and Michael Kind—seeking passports for missionary work among the Calmucks had already been imprisoned the year before. They too had to wait until 1747 for their release. The count was fully aware that for him to go to Russia was to enter unfriendly, to say nothing of dangerous, territory. But the Baltic Diaspora meant much to him. He had personally laid the foundations for it seven years earlier. Now, with seven thousand persons already in active fellowship with the Brethren, this field comprised about one third of all his followers.

He got no farther than Riga and was fortunate in escaping the fate of Gradin and the others in St. Petersburg. His request for a pass to St. Petersburg was refused by Governor-General Laski who, while awaiting orders from higher authorities, confiscated his papers and kept him and his party under arrest in the city's fortress, the Citadel. On January 9 word came from the empress that he was to quit Russian soil immediately. Three days later the Zinzendorf party, escorted by

[1] Th. Harnack, *Die Lutherische Kirche Livlands und die Herrnhutische Brüdergemeine*, p. 82.

soldiers, left Riga for the Prussian border and on January 21 was back in Königsberg.

The count had been treated firmly, but kindly, during his three weeks' detention between December 23 and January 12. En route home, Christian Renatus wrote to his mother: "We had our song and prayer services every day in the Citadel, so that I often wondered whether I really was under arrest." In customary fashion Zinzendorf accepted this experience as the Saviour's will. Through this venture he had accomplished nothing. Yet the Russian Diaspora, under ban until the time of Catherine the Great, continued to prosper, so firmly had it taken root among the people.

The desire to have his Moravians recognized as a legitimate part of the Lutheran Church, adhering to the Augsburg Confession, had become almost an obsession with Zinzendorf. He spent two weeks in Königsberg in a fruitless effort to persuade the university faculty and ranking clergy of the city to meet with him in a colloquy aimed toward clarification of his and the Brethren's status. In view of the ceaseless attacks aimed at him, his insistence is quite understandable. He made another futile try in Berlin before returning to Burau.

The next two-and-a-half months in Burau and Peilau, between February 11 and April 22 of 1744, were much like the time prior to his Baltic trip. The countess and Benigna joined him there. The brethren and sisters from Herrnhut again came to him in large numbers. Progress in the new Silesian settlements and in Niesky in Saxony, a half-day's carriage ride from Herrnhut, went on apace. Apparently the Saxon government was already relenting somewhat in its attitude toward him, for he made two short visits to Herrnhut, one on March 26 and the other on April 22 just before he set out for Marienborn. Though the visits were illegal, he made no effort to conceal his presence while there. On one occasion he preached, and on the other he partook of Communion in the church at Berthelsdorf. He spent much time in consultation with the officers of the congregation and with the choir leaders. He also repeated a visit he had made months before at Niesky.

Over twenty years had elapsed since the beginning of Herrnhut. In addition to the missions and widely scattered fellowship groups on the home front, seven other settlements had meanwhile come into being—four in Germany and one each in Holland, Denmark, and America. Their promise of growth induced Zinzendorf to pay close attention to standards of admission. In this he had come to the conviction that only those who felt a "call" should be admitted to the settlements with their strict discipline. As highest administrative officer of the Brotherhood, he put this policy into effect. Moravian communities were remarkably successful in maintaining this exclusiveness for about a century.

But unlike most exclusive groups, the Moravians retained a remarkable closeness to the established church. This fact, too, was in large measure the fruit of Zinzendorf's thinking. Back in Wetteravia, he concentrated on the problem of incorporating the Brotherhood into the framework of the existing state churches. He made this one of the major items on the agenda of a series of synods at Marienborn, in May and October of 1744 and in January and July of 1745. Here he expounded and put into operation his tropus plan (from the Greek *tropoi peideias*—methods of training). He contended that all of the churches were essentially one, with each having some unique contribution to make in imparting the Christian message. For Germany, Zinzendorf conceived the Brotherhood to be composed of three tropuses, Lutheran, Reformed, and Moravian. Each division was to keep its identity, for he held further that one who was brought up a Lutheran, Reformed, or according to the discipline of the old Moravian Church could be a better Christian if he remained faithful to the pattern of his training. For many years the Brethren were entered in the membership lists according to the church of their background.

The plan was more clearly defined by the appointment of bishops for each of the three divisions. The first of these were Polycarp Müller for the Moravians, Frederick von Watteville for the Reformed, and Zinzendorf himself for the Lutherans (after the Reverend George John Conradi of Schleswig-Holstein had declined because of age). The practice of appointing heads for the respective tropuses continued until 1789, when the synod of that year appointed these officers for the last time.

What existed at the time of the formulation of the tropus principle was theoretically four entities. There were Lutherans, Reformed, Moravians, and the composite body of all three—the last designated simply as Brethren. Actually, however, the Moravian tropus was practically synonymous with the over-all association of Brethren. It was the Moravians who were especially set apart to be the "pilgrim" laborers in gathering the ideal community of awakened Christians. What soon happened was that the Moravian tropus became the Renew Moravian Church. Step by step the reviving denomination asserted its ecclesiastical individuality. Before Zinzendorf's life had run its course the Unity of Brethren and the Moravian Church could be considered almost identical. Herrnhut and the other settlements had become the symbols and the rallying points for a body of Christians in which a denomination and an interchurch fellowship were merged.

The foundation of all this was the count's basic concept of Christianity and the church. Central was his "heart religion" (*Herzens-religion*), the personal relationship of the believer to Christ, the common bond of Christians everywhere. Beyond that the intellectual formulations of faith might differ and should differ. He retained his own deep preference for the Augsburg Confession but departed from most of his fellow adherents of that confession by his insistence that other confessions served their adherents equally well. Christian fellowship, according to the count, should not be on the intellectual level or in the realm of polity, but on the experiential level. He conceived the chief role of himself and his Brethren to be apostles of experiential Christian fellowship.

Concurrent with the formulation of the tropus concept and contributing to the side of denominational development was the revival of the ministerial orders of the Bohemian Brethren. Henceforth the Renewed Church, like its predecessor, was to have bishops, presbyters, and deacons. Also revived was the office of acolyte for those serving the church in a special way but not in the administration of Sacraments. Thus the Moravians in this formative decade acquired the orders which they retain to this day. The working out of a church constitution, however, was a matter for the count's successors to deal with. As long as he was on the scene, he was the book of order.

The Marienborn castle was Zinzendorf's headquarters during the middle 1740's and, of course, that meant also the headquarters of the church. Here the Pilgrim Congregation again held forth. As noted, the count had been appointed *Advocatus et Ordinarius Fratrum* in November of 1743. Upon his formal acceptance of this title about a year later, he began to call himself the "Ordinary of the Brethren," a designation which he retained the rest of his life. Popularly he was called simply the "ordinary." His prodigious capacity for work continued. Expanding administrative duties saw no lessening of his attention to pastoral work of a personal nature or of the activity of his ever-busy pen.

To say that the count's home was at Marienborn is a relative statement, for the lifelong pattern of travel prevailed. There was a trip to Holland covering two and a half months between mid-February and late April of 1745. The following October and November saw him in Berlin, among the new settlements in Silesia, and very briefly in Herrnhut. In Holland, through wealthy friends in Amsterdam, he arranged for the purchase of the barony of Zeist near Utrecht. The property included a beautifully landscaped village and a castle which had once been the home of Louis XIV of France. The next year Zeist became a Moravian settlement. In Berlin he ironed out some differences that had arisen between the Brethren and the authorities in Silesia. There, too, he persuaded the court chaplain John Christian Cochius to accept the presidency of the Reformed tropus in place of von Watteville.

During 1746 he was away a total of seven months, about equally divided between Holland and England. The castle at Zeist was the scene of a synod during several weeks of May and June. It was here in the presence of a large representative gathering of the Brotherhood that the count officiated at the wedding of Benigna and Baron John von Watteville. His new son-in-law had for some years been his close assistant, and Benigna had been a capable leader of the Single Sisters' Choir. Zinzendorf himself had suggested the match.

In July he crossed the channel to England, where shadows were threatening the flourishing work of the Moravians. Many of the Brethren were opposed to taking an oath, and this put them in an awkward position, since the rebellion in Scotland against the crown made all nonjurors suspect. Moravians were accused of being papists in disguise and adherents of the Stuart Pretender to the throne. This, added to the opposition stirred up against them by the followers of Wesley and Whitefield, made for a highly disagreeable situation. The trouble had spread to America where the New York assembly had passed an act in 1744 declaring that "all vagrant preachers, Moravians and disguised Papists" should not be allowed to preach to the Indians without first taking oaths of allegiance and abjuration. The next year missionaries Zeisberger and Sensemann had suffered a seven weeks' imprisonment in New York City for refusing to comply. In the face of all this the Brethren, at the instigation of James Hutton, had sent their senior civilis (a secular bishop whose special function was to negotiate with governments), Abraham Gersdorf, to England to clarify the difficulties before the Board of Trade and Plantations. The most he had been able to accomplish was to get a promise that the New York authorities would be advised to leave the missionaries alone.

Zinzendorf went to England determined to arrive at some explicit understanding concerning the relationship of the Moravians to the Established Church. His approach was the same as in Germany. After some weeks in the country he called the Brethren together at a synod in London and tried to persuade them to apply the tropus scheme to England. He suggested that in due course they find some bishop to act as superintendent of an Anglican tropus. Meanwhile he would serve in that capacity. He persuaded the synod to accept a plan for the use of the Book of Common Prayer in Moravian worship and for the joint ordination of Moravian clergymen by Anglican and Moravian bishops. His friend Archbishop Potter rejected the proposal, at least for the time being. Before it could be brought up again, within the year, Potter died, and Zinzendorf lost thereby the one person who conceivably might later have been willing and in a position to put such a plan into effect.

The count had to content himself with a lesser accomplishment. Upon the advice of the Archbishop, Oglethorpe, Thomas Penn, and others, he appealed to Parliament to broaden the Naturalization Act of 1740. This had granted exemption to Quakers from taking oaths, and in Pennsylvania to "foreign Protestants" as well. Oglethorpe, himself a member of Commons, introduced the clause which extended the provisions in force in Pennsylvania to all the colonies. On December 27, 1747, the bill was passed in Parliament.

An intriguing side light on General Oglethorpe is that he was in serious trouble during part of the time that Zinzendorf was in England. Having helped to put down the Jacobites, as the Scottish rebels were called, he was court-martialed for failing to capture a contingent of them which his soldiers had defeated. Zinzendorf and other brethren visited him in his London prison where he was awaiting trial. Spangenberg's account of the affair makes it clear that the count and the general were spiritually akin:

He asserted his innocence, but at the same time acknowledged that he was not sure of making it appear in court. Meanwhile he would resign himself to God; and if he thought fit that he should lose his life upon an unjust accusation, he would not murmur, but think he had deserved it by his other sins; for he had experienced many drawings of the grace of God in his heart, but had been disobedient to them. But if his innocence should be made manifest, he would heartily thank God for it. The latter took place before the Count left London; and he was not only declared innocent, but reinstated in all his offices. Meanwhile the Count visited him in prison, and the General never forgot this proof of his friendship.[2]

To the growing array of imposing structures at Herrnhaag the community had added a home for their ordinary. Early in 1747, six weeks after his return from England and Holland, he and the Pilgrim Congregation took possession. With its spacious quarters and chapel, this new residence was specifically designed to accommodate the Pilgrims. Herrnhaag, with a thousand inhabitants, was then at the zenith of its brief existence. From its beginning it had the character of an international community. Of seven persons received into membership in a single day early in the life of the settlement, each had been from a different country—Poland, Hungary, Switzerland, England, Livonia, Germany, and Sweden. Coincidental of course, but indicative of what the community became and what it was when the count made it his home. Visitors there were from far and wide. Here outgoing missionaries received their instructions and returning ones were furloughed. In the course of the year 1747 two hundred brethren and sisters went from here to their posts of duty. In the Single Brethren's Choir alone there were 162 applications for admission, of which only 50 were approved—the others were advised to return to their homes. Thirty brethren and sisters were ordained as deacons and deaconesses, and four brethren as presbyters. Leonard Dober and John von Watteville were consecrated as bishops. One hundred persons were initiated as acolytes in the service of their Lord and their church. This was the count's answer to the challenge, "What hast thou done for me?"

Vindication in Saxony came at last. Herrnhut's thriving industry, fertile fields, and orderly community life—the fruits of a practical piety—were testimony too eloquent to be ignored. With other heads of state, notably Frederick of Prussia, wooing the Brethren, the authorities in Dresden began to reappraise the banished count. Their interest was heightened when in 1746 he purchased his boyhood home, the estate of Grosshennersdorf, for his daughter Benigna. The negotiations prompted the king's ministers at Dresden to re-examine the

[2] Spangenberg, *Leben Zinzendorfs*, tr. Jackson, p. 363.

circumstances of the count's exile. In perspective the reasons for it lost much of their validity. The king himself sometime in 1747 visited Herrnhut and like most others was impressed by what he saw. The result was an unofficial letter to Zinzendorf from one of the king's ministers, informing him that a friendly reception was awaiting him, should he choose to return to Saxony. These overtures were coupled with a request that Zinzendorf help procure a loan for the electoral treasury from friends in Holland.

He was quick to take advantage of this amnesty and arrived at Herrnhut on September 16, waiting, however, to make a ceremony of his homecoming until it received official sanction a month later. He went on immediately to visit the Silesian congregations and after that to Leipzig, where he conferred with Count Hennicke, the Saxon minister who informed him that his exile was at an end. The royal decree revoking his banishment and restoring his privileges was dated October 11, 1747. The decree invited him to make additional settlements in Saxony.

In high spirits he came back to Herrnhut at four o'clock on the morning of October 14. That afternoon two hundred persons joined him in a love feast. Among those present were two Greenland Eskimos, who gave the count occasion to remind his followers that the first missionaries to Greenland had left Herrnhut at the time of his first exile. (He left Herrnhut in 1733 thinking he was exiled.) The watchword for the day of his return was, "The Lord turned the captivity of Job, when he prayed for his friends" (Job 42:10) .

There followed six weeks of intensive pastoral work, during which he took quarters in Hennersdorf for greater privacy. In the room where forty years before he had first felt the touch of the Saviour's power, he counseled and prayed with those allied with him in that contagious faith which never lost its glow. If the Herrnhuters came to him, he also went to them. In the close fellowship of the choirs, in love feasts, *Singstunden,* the Communion service, in the larger church services, he made Herrnhut and Berthelsdorf feel anew the impact of his personality. Herrnhut was different from Herrnhaag—older, more disciplined, of more dignity. His homecoming was not only good for Herrnhut; it was good for the count too.

Yet Herrnhut, though Zinzendorf was now free to make it his permanent home, was so only symbolically. The end of the banishment had its emotional overtones. In reality it meant little to one who was by nature a pilgrim. The church's business took him back to Herrnhaag by early December and kept him there through March of 1748. Trouble was brewing for the settlement in the growing estrangement between the Brethren and the house of Büdingen. Zinzendorf succeeded in easing the situation temporarily. Besides carrying on his regular program of preaching and pastoral work, he lectured on the Augsburg Confession in the Brethren's theological seminary at Lindheim and published more issues of *Natural Reflections,* a periodical which he had begun a year earlier in defense of his case. This periodical, published later in book form, remains an important primary source for the study of his thought.

What concerned him most at this time was still further definition of the Brethren's position in Saxony. Certain of the outcome, he pressed for and won another royal inquiry of Herrnhut, in preparation for which he returned to Upper Lusatia in April. The commission, composed of five laymen and three clergymen, was in session between July 29 and August 12. Theirs was a thorough procedure, based upon a study of voluminous documents and long interviews with the count and other representatives of the community. The result was all that could be hoped for. The Moravians were recognized in Saxony as adherents of the Augsburg Confession and, as such, granted complete freedom of conscience and worship. The royal decree to that effect followed on September 20, 1749. Even before the decree was issued, Zinzendorf, in November of 1748, leased from the government the royal estate and castle of Barby, on the Elbe, for the establishment of the third settlement congregation of the Brethren in Saxony. The authorities were as happy over the matter as were the Moravians themselves.

The count wanted similar recognition in England, and in December of 1748 we find him again crossing the channel. He had left Herrnhut immediately following the inquiry and had devoted the late summer and fall to the churches in Wetteravia and Holland. It was an impressive company of Brethren that landed in England in January. With Zinzendorf to help him with legal details were Abraham von Gersdorf, Louis von Schrautenbach, Charles von Schachtmann, Henry Cossart, and David Nitschmann the syndic. They promptly took London quarters at Northampton House on Bloomsbury Square and set themselves to the task in hand. Swelling the number of Moravians shortly thereafter were the 150 brethren and sisters en route from Holland to Pennsylvania on the brand new ship *Irene.* This ship had been built for the Brethren at a Staten Island shipyard, and Captain Garrison had just brought it to Europe to pick up its westbound cargo. The presence of these enthusiastic colonists convinced the Londoners that the Moravians meant business and helped the count sell their cause to Parliament.

Though there was much maligning of the Brethren in England at the time, there really was no serious opposition on the part of the English lawmakers to what he wanted from them. Oglethorpe again played the part of a warm friend, advising on procedure and personally championing the Moravians in Commons. Thomas Penn, too, was helpful. They advised a petition to Parliament, asking for certain concrete things—a petition which later could be embodied in a bill which if passed would become an act. Accordingly Zinzendorf and his associates petitioned for exemption from oaths and bearing arms. Accompanying the petition was a full doctrinal and historical survey of the Moravian Church, going back to the rise of the Bohemian Brethren. In all, 135 documents were studied by the Parliamentary committee of investigation. Oglethorpe first presented the matter before the Lower House on February 20. Commons finally passed the bill on April 16, and the House of Lords on May 12. The royal signature was affixed on June 6, 1749, and on June 24 "An Act for Encouraging the People Known by the Name of Unitas Fratrum, or United Brethren, to Settle in His Majesties Colonies in America" became the law of the land.

Members of the Unitas Fratrum—the name upon which the count insisted rather than Moravian—were henceforth exempt from taking oaths and bearing arms. The significance of the act was, however, not in these provisions but in the preamble which acknowledged the United Brethren as an "ancient Protestant Episcopal Church," the legitimate successor of the Bohemian Brethren. The Moravians henceforth had status in Britain and her dependencies.

19

COSTLY ENTHUSIASM

Middle age was for Zinzendorf the height of his career. A visionary with a mission, he had thrived on opposition. Now some twenty thousand of the most dynamic Christians of Protestantism were his followers. More than could be accepted were seeking admittance to his settlements. Yet it must be said that Zinzendorf at his best was also Zinzendorf at his worst. At the very time when he was winning recognition in Saxony, Silesia, Britain, and beyond the seas, he was behaving in a manner of which his admirers never cease to be ashamed. The Moravian historian Hutton writes: "As the Count advanced toward middle age, he grew more domineering in tone, more noble in his dreams, and more foolish in his conduct. He was soon to shine in each of these three lights." The last of these observations refers to that strange period in the life of the count and of the Moravian Church from about 1743 to 1750, known as the "Sifting Period." Centered in Herrnhaag, it affected the whole denomination.

The Sifting Period was a distortion of a basically sound emphasis upon the atoning death of Christ. Its outward manifestation was a morbid concentration and wordplay upon the blood and wounds of the crucified Christ and a simulated irresponsibility of behavior supposed to be a demonstration of childlike faith. With the impact of a conversion experience, insight into the significance of the Saviour's death had come to Zinzendorf before his ordination in the year 1734. Thereafter the preaching of "Christ and him crucified" was the core of his message. In the hands of enthusiasts, such as the Brethren were, it was as dangerous as it was effective. The fertile imagination and bent toward extravagant imagery on the part of their leader were invitations to fanaticism.

There is a grand dignity about a hymn like Zinzendorf's "The Saviour's Blood and Righteousness." It is but a short step from there to less worthy expression. The Moravians took that step. As early as 1740, on the eve of her departure for America, Anna Nitschmann, in her capacity as eldress, addressed a circular letter to the congregation, in which she said: "Like a poor little worm, I desire to withdraw myself into his wounds and nailprints. . . . Let it be your element to bathe and swim in the sea of grace, that is in the blood of Jesus." Two years later she wrote from America: "It is well with me in Jesus' side hole." The count himself at that time could already be quoted as referring to the Brethren as "little blood worms in the sea of grace." There are but samples of what was beginning to happen.

If one were to name a precise date for the actual outbreak of the Sifting Period, one might well pick the time of Zinzendorf's return to Marienborn from America in April of 1743. It was about then that he formed the Order of the Little Fools with some of his close associates. Spangenberg, without naming the society, has this to say about it:

Considering the many difficulties which presented themselves within and without, the count thought it requisite to act with much boldness and cheerfulness. With this view, he made a particular covenant with the brethren and sisters who were the most like him, which had reference solely to a simple and childlike deportment. They agreed to expect every blessing from the love of Jesus, believingly adhere to his word, filially cast all care upon him, and heartily rejoice in him.[1]

Again we may say that it was a short step from this basically sound idea to a distortion of it. Within a few years the Herrnhaag congregation had gone beyond childlikeness to childishness. The count encouraged his Order of Little Fools to behave like children, since God had revealed himself "not to the wise and prudent, but to babes." Therefore, the more childlike they acted, the more they would attain spiritual wisdom. They took him at his word, not only acting, but even talking like children. They addressed the count as "Papa" and the countess as "Mama," or, worse still, as "Little Papa" and "Little Mama." The diminutive form of address was even applied to Christ, spoken of as "Brother Lambkin." For themselves the brethren and sisters had a whole catalog of diminutive terms, in repulsive combination with reference to the wounds of Christ. Thus they spoke of themselves as "little doves flying about in the atmosphere of the cross," "little fish swimming in the bed of blood," or as "little bees who suck

[1] Spangenberg, *Leben Zinzendorfs*, tr. Jackson, p. 328.

on the wounds of Christ, who feel at home in the side hole and crawl in deep." Again they would call themselves "bloodthirsty beasts," "blood leeches," "wound worms," and "side-hole hearts."

During his visit to Gnadenberg early in 1744 Zinzendorf had composed a litany entitled "The Litany of the Life, Suffering, and Wounds of Our Lord Jesus Christ." This order of service, and especially the count's thirty-four sermons on it at Herrnhaag three years later, furnished much of the imagery for the Sifting Period. So did his hymns, for this was a time of prolific hymn writing, both for Zinzendorf and for the Moravian community in general. These were one of the chief means by which the phenomenon was spread throughout the Brotherhood and by which it was advertised to the world. Particularly offensive was the notorious *Twelfth Supplement* to the hymnal, issued in 1748. Today these hymns, fortunately relegated to dusty archives, remain as evidence that the Moravians experienced what has been called "a bad dream."

The longer the extravagance persisted, the more sensual it became; though there is no evidence that Herrnhaag fell into immorality. The expression of love for Christ took on strong sexual connotations. There was an undue exaltation of marriage as the symbol of the marriage between Christ and the soul of the believer, and in this exaltation sexual terminology was freely employed. Earthly marriages were looked upon as proxies in anticipation of the final union of Christ and the believer. The marriage relationship was idealized in long discourses and hymns.

In his sermons on the "Litany of the Wounds" the count compared the Trinity to a family—adding to the traditional designation of Father and Son the term "Mother," for the Holy Spirit. He spoke of the Church, Christ's bride, as being born in his side wound. Since the Church was the bride, he referred to it as the daughter-in-law of the Father and of the Holy Ghost Mother.

In its endless round of services the congregation for a time departed from the usual Moravian simplicity. Gaudy biblical scenes decorated their ordinarily plain chapels. They used tableaux and transparencies to make more real the suffering of the Christ on the cross. They called their church the "visible wound-church." They multiplied their festivals, so that in one year they observed as many as forty. There were elaborate celebrations of the birthdays of the Zinzendorf family. Individuals who expressed a concern for the consequent neglect of practical tasks, and even missionaries on the field were looked upon by the extremists as inferior Christians because they had not yet reached the stage of casting concern aside and entering wholeheartedly into the child's play around the Cross. It goes without saying that the lot was used more recklessly than ever.

In the forefront in Herrnhaag was Christian Renatus Zinzendorf, so much like his father in temperament. At seventeen he was made leader of the Single Brethren's choir. At twenty-one he was ordained a presbyter and appointed pastor in place of his brother-in-law, Bishop Watteville, when the latter went on his American tour of inspection in 1748. Of an attractive personality which spontaneously won friends, Christian Renatus had a warm following. But he had also the weakness of his father and was soon under the spell of Herrnhaag's excesses, carrying his associates along with him. His appointment as pastor extended his influence to the whole congregation.

The effect of the Wetteravian spirit upon the other settlements was of varying degree. Herrnhut suffered least. Bethlehem in Pennsylvania suffered most. Herrnhut escaped because a generation of community discipline had given it stability. The watchful eyes of the Saxon authorities made the Brethren there more careful. Finally, the homogeneous Lutheran environs of Herrnhut were not a good breeding ground for fanciful religious expression. Bethlehem was affected because it was on the receiving end of emigration from Europe, and Herrnhaag was at that time the chief processing center for the emigrants.

Of the Second Sea Congregation, which came to America in 1743, 78 were from Wetteravia, 26 from Herrnhut, and 13 from England. The majority of the 120 of the Third Sea Congregation, in 1749, were Herrnhaagers. There were lesser companies from time to time, among them 19 Single Brethren from Herrnhaag, who arrived in 1748. Bishop Nitschmann, in charge of the Third Sea Congregation, was one of the leading offenders of the Sifting Period. Also infecting Bethlehem was the brilliant young Bishop John Frederick Camerhof, who became Spangenberg's assistant in 1747. Spangenberg from the first objected to the instruction which Camerhof brought with him, and in November of 1748 resigned in protest. After a few months in Philadelphia he returned to Europe. During the two years of Bishop John Nitschmann's regime the flourishing economy built up by Spangenberg was almost wrecked. By that time the count had come to his senses, and Spangenberg was recalled to America to restore the Bethlehem-Nazareth community to a sound basis.

In Sweden these years of sentimental excesses almost spelled the doom of the flourishing Diaspora. In the Baltic States the already awkward position of the Brethren worsened. Old friends like the faculty at Tübingen repudiated the Moravians. The renowned Bengel said that this was no longer the old Moravian Church. Everywhere the enemies of the count were accumulating material for attack. Nothing was so damaging to the Moravians as their own literature and hymns flung back at them long after they had emerged from this time of humiliation.

How shall we assess the Sifting Period? Without trying to exonerate the count for his part in it, we do need to judge it in the light of its context. In the first place the Moravians were not alone in their offense of good taste. The age in which they lived produced the Berleberg Bible with its strange symbolical interpretations of the Scriptures. Older contemporaries of the Brethren, like Rock, Dippel, and Hochmann, had brought to the Pietism of southwestern Germany an extremely mystical emphasis at the expense of the more practical element. In Switzerland there was a piety with a sentimental terminology introduced by Lutz early in the century. The use of endearing diminutives in connection with religious matters was a weakness of Pietism in general. Both the French and German literature of the time reeked with sentimentality. Herrnhaag's location made it especially vulnerable to the spirit of the age. Many who settled in the community were already in the grip of an emotional, sensuous Christianity at the time of their arrival.

It is also to be noted that the period in question coincided with certain experiences of the count which made him less heedful of the extravagances than he ordinarily would have been. He had got his fill of the sectarians in Pennsylvania and was blaming their inability to get along with one another on the undue emphasis which many of them were placing upon sanctification. This distaste for a Christianity centered in a striving after holiness had been deepened by his personal feuds with Whitefield and Wesley. The bitter attacks of Calvinists in both Holland and the American colonies had a similar effect. His reaction was to draw closer than ever to the Lutheran emphasis upon salvation by faith alone, a faith whose chief object was the physical person of Christ, especially his sufferings. Thus Cranz, the earliest of the Moravian historians, depicts his frame of mind:

The ordinary had, during his abode among the various sects in Pennsylvania, acquired a further insight, than he had before into the emptiness and pernicious tendencies of all the methods of sanctification, which are not, solely and alone deduced from the merits of Jesus. On his return to Europe, finding many new inhabitants in the congregations, of several persuasions and forms; he was apprehensive of a similar evil; and therefore labored against it in his discourses and hymns, endeavoring fully to enthrone the merits and wounds of Jesus; and showing that not only the forgiveness of sins and salvation were to be deduced from thence, but that the cleansing from sin, and our true sanctification and preservation, flowed solely from this fountain.[2]

It is understandable that in his reaction against "legalism" a man of his volatile temperament should have gone to excess. To attribute the Sifting Period to an emotional breakdown, as some have done, and to say that he suffered from a pathological condition is going too far. His growing fondness for solitary meditation was no marked departure from his usual pattern of behavior. There was no lessening of attention to the program of his church. There was as yet no letdown in work. What can be said is that the success of his enterprises in the face of steady opposition had made Zinzendorf more heedless than usual of sound criticism. Spangenberg was not alone in raising a warning voice. The countess, the elder Watteville, Peter Böhler, Christian David, Godfrey Clemens, the Neissers, and others of the older, more sober element in the Brotherhood—all had called for a halt to what was going on. Zinzendorf was slow to take heed. Actually he was not aware of the full gravity of the situation. In his presence there was a certain amount of restraint. He was reluctant to believe reports of all that occurred in his absence. Or if he did accept such reports on their face value, he reasoned that the affair would run its course. Spangenberg says in this connection: "He resolved, therefore, to let the matter take its course, until it arrived at maturity; and felt assured that the Lord would grant him grace to repel and extirpate the evil."

Finally, on the crossing to England in December of 1748, one of the Brethren caught his ear. He was the ex-soldier Karl von Peistel, faithful church official at Herrnhut. Attracted to the count in the first place by the orderly lives of his followers, he had become increasingly disgusted by what Herrnhaag's influence was doing to the morale of the Brotherhood. The soldier in him had been impressed by the fact that

___
[2] La Trobe's translation of Cranz, p. 368.

for the Herrnhuters the daily watchword was the equivalent of a command. It pained him to see degeneration set in. He spoke strongly to the count as they traveled together, reinforcing his rebuke with a letter he had received from Pastor Beza of Herrnhut. Beza shared Peistel's concern. Upon Zinzendorf's arrival in England disquieting news both from the Continent and from America further opened his eyes to the true state of affairs.

He acted promptly by drafting a stern letter and dispatching copies of it, under date of February 10, 1749, to all the churches. The conclusion of the letter read: "He that is on the Lord's side, let him join me; and he that is disobedient shall bear his own judgment, whoever he be." At the same time he wrote to Christian Renatus, ordering him to join him in London and to step down as pastor of Herrnhaag. Some of the other offenders were also dismissed from positions of responsibility, some put on probation, and all made to feel deeply that the church had departed from the proper path. First Bishop David Nitschmann and then Leonard Dober were sent to visit the churches on the Continent to help straighten out matters. Bishop John Watteville and Spangenberg, having returned from America in November of 1749, were later sent on similar missions. Zinzendorf also promptly suppressed the *Twelfth Supplement* to the hymnal and ordered many offensive passages deleted from his own addresses and writings. The synods of the Brethren during the next two years also took corrective measures.

Spangenberg tells us that Zinzendorf was very sensitive about the whole affair and refused to listen to details which might have helped him to get to the root of the evil. It was a sore point between the two leaders, as the former frankly states: "I myself was much displeased with him at the time, and he no less with me, because he knew my sentiments; and this went so far, on both sides, that it could not remain concealed from the church, though we both loved each other dearly." Spangenberg goes on to surmise that the count refused to avail himself of all the facts "for fear of himself," for he realized that if he knew the story completely he might in his anger deal too harshly with those to whom he was closely attached. He could not afford to allow himself to become upset over an internal crisis in the church, in view of the attention demanded of him by the impending act of Parliament.

The painfulness of this experience was heightened by Zinzendorf's awareness of his own part in it. In admitting his error he also gives his own version of what happened:

The test we have gone through has been brief but fearful. I probably occasioned it by giving utterance to an idea which I have never been able to lay aside, and which I still hold, namely, that in order to enjoy all the blessings purchased by the death of Jesus, we must become children in the bottom of our hearts. I have been powerfully impressed by this idea, and when I came back from America I sought to inculcate it in my brethren. It found acceptance and was immediately carried into effect. But what was at first a small circle of men, who really had the spirit of children, soon grew into a large society and in a few years greatly degenerated.[3]

A jolt from the outside was the best remedy of all for the Moravians. Count Casimir of Büdingen died in October of 1749 and was succeeded by his son Gustav Frederick, who was unfriendly to them. Advised by Councilor Brauer, the new ruler of Wetteravia, early in the following year, he demanded an oath of allegiance from the Brethren, coupled with a renunciation of Zinzendorf and the Moravian Church. It was a clear violation of the spirit, if not the letter, of the terms on which they had been received into the territory in 1738; for at that time they had been accorded full toleration. It must be admitted, however, that the excesses of the Sifting Period, added to considerable friction otherwise between the rulers and the Moravians, had provided some justification for the reversal in policy. The alternative to the oath of allegiance and attachment to one of the established churches of the realm, Reformed or Lutheran, was emigration within three years. This was undoubtedly only a threat, for little did Count Büdingen think that a community of a thousand people would abandon such a thriving village into which they had put so much labor and money.

The true spirit of the church asserted itself. To a man the Herrnhaag community declared itself ready to move. In March came the final order to vacate. Three days later ninety Single Brethren left for Pennsylvania. Within a year five hundred persons in all had found new homes. Besides the many who went to America, some went to Barby, others to Zeist, and the French-speaking Moravians hailing from Switzerland were transferred to Neuwied on the Rhine. Before the allotted three years had passed, Herrnhaag was deserted. A handful of Diaspora workers remained at Marienborn until 1783. No permanent settlers ever reoccupied Herrnhaag. Only three buildings survived to the twentieth century—the community house, Zinzendorf's residence, and the Single Sisters' house. Even God's Acre, to which the Moravians kept

[3] Bovet, *Le Comte de Zinzendorf*, translation by John Gill, *The Banished Count*, p. 251.

title, was pilfered of its stones. On the spot today there stands a marker, erected in 1871 by the congregation at Neuwied:

Here rest the remains of 429 members of the Church of the Brethren, who were buried between 1736-1772 in the God's Acre of the former Brethren's congregation at Herrnhaag; among them—Count Henry XXIX Reuss-Ebersdorf, brother-in-law of Count Zinzendorf, died 1747; Martin Dober, potter and especially blessed leader of the congregation at Herrnhut, died 1748; Christian Mamutha, an Armenian; Christiane Zedmann, a Persian; two Negresses, Anna Marie and Maria; three children of Count Zinzendorf, Christian Ludwig, died 1736; Anna, died 1738; and David, died 1742; and three Negro children, David, Anna Gratia and John.

Lo, a great multitude, which no man can number, of all nations, and kindreds, and people, and tongues, stood before the throne, and before the Lamb, clothed with white robes, and palms in their hands; and cried with a loud voice, saying, Salvation to our God which sitteth upon the throne, and unto the Lamb. Rev. 7:9-10.[4]

The evacuation of Herrnhaag was major surgery. The courage it took to go through with it paid off. The operation restored the Brotherhood to health. Said the count: "I shall always class this event among the special favors shown to us."

⁴ Uttendörfer and Schmitt, *Die Brüder*, p. 145.

20

CRISIS IN ENGLAND

The count's activities in behalf of the act of Parliament, the growth of the work in Pennsylvania and the New World mission in general, to say nothing of the successes in Britain itself, shifted the focus of Moravian administration to London. There it was to remain for most of the time between January of 1749 to March of 1755. During all but thirteen months of this period Zinzendorf and his immediate associates had their headquarters in the British capital. The exception was the time between July of 1750 and August of 1751, when he gave his personal attention to the churches on the Continent, concentrating particularly upon their schoolwork. Eight of these months were spent in Herrnhut and Hennersdorf. Another two were taken up with an extensive preaching tour of western Germany, Switzerland, and France, just before the return to England. Zinzendorf saw that the congregations in Silesia and Saxony, under government favor, were beginning to stand on their own feet.

England must have appealed to the count for another reason besides its strategic location, namely, its recognition of the Moravians as an "ancient Protestant Episcopal Church." This definitely removed his Brethren from the class of sectarians. Somehow he fared better with English churchmen than with German theologians. From the beginning of his friendship with the late Archbishop Potter he had been made to feel that the episcopacy was a bond of union between the English Church and the Moravians. Leading prelates continued to be his friends, among them the bishops of London, Sodor and Man, Lincoln, and Worcester. The current flood of hostile literature was not representative of the Church of England. Moravians had a place in English church life that pleased Zinzendorf more than their status in Germany. The esteem from the side of the church was matched by that from public figures like Lord Chesterfield, Lord Granville, the Duke of Argyle, Sir Luke Schaub, and, of course, Oglethorpe.

The count did his best to lend dignity to the Moravians by the style in which he lived. Prior to the act of Parliament, and for the year following, he occupied spacious rented quarters in Bloomsbury Square. When he returned from the Continent in 1751, these accommodations were no longer available; and Zinzendorf with his Pilgrims moved to a location close by Westminster Abbey. He lived in what was formerly Hutton's house on College Street, opposite the Abbey. In an adjoining house, overlooking the Abbey gardens, lived Christian Renatus and other Single Brethren. In a third adjoining house lived Abraham von Gersdorf and David Nitschmann the syndic. But in the meantime more pretentious headquarters were in process of preparation.

On the Thames, a few miles above London Bridge, in pleasant, suburban Chelsea, was Lindsey House, a historic mansion of the ducal family of Ancaster and which once belonged to Sir Thomas More. It had been Zinzendorf's headquarters for six weeks during his visit to London in 1737. On this and the adjoining Beaumont grounds he took a ninety-nine-year lease, in June of 1750, for a payment of 750 pounds. The crisis at Herrnhaag and his absence on the Continent delayed his plans for a year, after which he put his architect, Sigisimund von Gersdorf, to work on the estate. Lindsey House was rebuilt in conformity with the style of the age; a clergy house and chapel were erected; a printing press installed; the grounds landscaped; a God's Acre laid out; and for the future a row of houses in hollow squares projected. By the spring of 1753, after an expenditure of 11,500 pounds—nearly twice the original estimate—he was able to take full possession.

Lindsey House was impressive. From its imposing elevation a graceful terrace led down to the steps of the private dock at the river's edge. In these surroundings the count and his retinue lived for two years, making it the nerve center of Moravian affairs. It was shortly before this time that the Brethren began calling Zinzendorf "the disciple," and before long it was as common as the title "the ordinary." Already his house at Westminster was the "Disciple House," and after the move to Chelsea this was the name for Lindsey House. However, not until the count returned permanently to Herrnhut did the daily record of events, previously entitled *Pilgrim Diary,* become *Disciple House Diary.*

To the count, and especially to the countess, who remained in Germany, Lindsey House was more than just another Moravian center. Among the first of the Brethren to be buried in its God's Acre, called Sharon, was Christian Renatus. He was laid to rest there following his death from tuberculosis, on May 28, 1752, at Westminster, a few months short of his twenty-fifth birthday. Of delicate health all his days, he enter the final stage of illness with a hemorrhage in late February. His end came more suddenly than expected, and his father, who was unusually close to him in his last weeks, was absent preaching at Mile End. With the dying son was his old tutor, Bishop John Nitschmann. Three days later the body of Christian Renatus was taken by boat up the Thames for temporary interment at Lindsey House. Late that year, in the course of a synod of the Single Brethren's choir, final burial services were held in charge of Bishop John Watteville.

His mother, informed of his illness, set out from Herrnhut to be with him. En route, at Zeist, she received the news of his death. She finished her journey to see his grave. Just before leaving London again, she wrote to a nephew:

I must return with empty hand and leave behind my precious Christelein. O how deeply it cuts. . . . I have been to Chelsea three times. Tears are not few while one is there. On no day have I been without them. To Papa [Zinzendorf] I have had to put on a brave front.[1]

She bore her loss in true Christian spirit, but the emotional strain was too much. Thereafter she was never herself, withdrawing more and from public; and only four years later she followed her son.

The count's relationship with Christ, as we have seen consistently, was such as to enable him to accept death as wholeheartedly as life. A few weeks after his loss he told his colleagues of the covenant he had long since made with the Saviour concerning his children—"from the moment of their birth never to regard them as his own, but to resign them wholly to the Saviour as his property." Yet his grief was profound. In a letter to the congregations he said: "I do not understand it. . . . He himself will make it clear to all hearts." Revealing are Spangenberg's observations:

I cannot describe how his father felt, who was at Mile End, when the news was brought to him; but I can say this much, that when he afterward reflected what his son had been to him (and this was often the case), his eyes overflowed with grief and thankfulness: but his tears flowed still more freely, on looking over his son's papers, when he found what he had noted down of his daily intercourse with the Saviour. He saw from this, how filially,

---

[1] Wilhelm Jannasch, *Erdmuth Dorothea Gräfin von Zinzendorf,* p. 480.

fervently and tenderly, he had loved the Saviour, and how intimate had been the intercourse he maintained with him. Innumerable tears were shed for the departed Christian Renatus, not only by his father, but by other members of the church; for he was generally much beloved.[2]

Christian Renatus' part in the Herrnhaag extravagances had evoked a temporary coolness on his father's part. But when the count saw how broken in spirit his son was, he gave way to overwhelming affection.

CHRISTIAN RENATUS ZINZENDORF

During the last two years they were very close to each other, Christian Renatus being his father's personal assistant. The sensitive young man never ceased brooding over what he felt had been his betrayal of a trust. His frail body could not long stand the strain of a self-reproach which took the form of a feverish activity by day and nights of study and prayer. He is remembered in the church for several of its finest hymns, among them, "My Redeemer, Overwhelmed with Anguish, Went to Olivet for Me" and " 'Tis the Most Blest and Needful Part to Have in Christ a Share."

However Zinzendorf may have felt, church affairs came first. His son's death came in the midst of a financial crisis which almost wrecked the Brotherhood and at a time when the transfer of the residents of Herrnhaag to other settlements and the relocation of its schools was still in process. The crisis had been long in coming and had been largely of the count's own making. But once in it the Brethren needed the count's credit and financial resources to get out of it. Even he had begun to see the weakness of one-man rule, at least in administrative matters; and by mid-century was sincerely trying to restore the collegiate form of

[2] Spangenberg, *Leben Zinzendorfs,* tr. Jackson, p. 420.

government which he had so abruptly ended when he returned to America. The fifty-year-old count, in contrast to the forty-year-old count, was willing, and even eager, to restrict his leadership to the more purely spiritual realm. This desire lay behind his assuming the name "disciple." He had had the conviction that as a disciple of Christ he had a special call to preaching and pastoral work. As evidence of his sincerity he had for some months at Westminster withdrawn from his usual active administrative work. But his colleagues, appalled by their church's debts, persuaded him that to retire from leadership at that point was like leaving a sinking ship. Thus one-man rule was prolonged; but in the process of solving its problem the church called upon practical men to do the real work, while the count became more of a figurehead. Therefore, out of the crisis did come the beginning of permanent conferential government.

It could hardly have been otherwise that a man with his head in the clouds and his feet so frequently off the ground should have led his church to the brink of financial ruin. The count was a person of means, but also one who through his generosity was continuously in debt. From the time of his purchase of Berthelsdorf estate, with one quarter of it mortgaged, he was never without a lien against his or his wife's property. Moravian settlements invariably prospered and with their cutlery, pottery, linen weaving, farming, and other sources of income would more than have repaid what it cost to build them. But the needs of the cause to which they were committed were always a step ahead of the growing revenue. The continual travel by land and sea, the deputations to courts, universities, and persons of rank, the building of churches and schools, the steady production of printed matter, were expensive. This was so despite the fact that the members of the Brotherhood were under discipline and without pay, frequently earning their own way en route to the mission field or as they itinerated at home.

Fortunately, or perhaps unfortunately, the enthusiasm which the count aroused in others gave him easy credit. There were always friends to contribute means outright or to lend him money on the security of his estates to meet the deficits. All the while there was no distinction between the accounts of the church and those of the Zinzendorf family. In a general sort of way financial matters were in charge of a committee called the General Diaconate, of which the countess was for many years a member; but its lack of defined authority resulted in a most unsystematic procedure. Expenditures were unusually heavy in the late

1740's. Then came the sacrifice of Herrnhaag. When the count returned to England in 1751, the leaders there warned him that the creditors in Britain and Holland were becoming uneasy. Zinzendorf was not alarmed and even managed to borrow some more money. He went ahead with his elaborate plans for Lindsey House.

The worst strain came in 1753, with the bankruptcy of Jacob Gomez, a Portuguese Jew with whom the church's finances had become involved. Overnight the English Brethren, already hard pressed by their creditors, found their debt increased by 67,000 pounds to a total of 130,000. Some of their directors faced imprisonment. The count, with still some credit left on his estates, promptly offered security for 10,000 pounds to meet the most immediate of the obligations. Three times that amount was needed. For a particular note, toward which he had assumed responsibility to save one of the Brethren, he was himself within hours of the debtor's prison. March 3, the deadline for payment, came without money in hand. Zinzendorf himself records what happened:

Ordering my papers to be packed up, I prepared everything as though I were going to the gaol that afternoon, after which I enjoyed a quiet siesta. In the very hour when payment was due and no delay admissible, for London seemed to be made of iron, Hockel entered my room with tears of anguish in his eyes. There was a strange conflict going on in my mind. Our Saviour had assured me by means of the lot, that I should be able to pay this day and in this very hour. It was one peculiar feature of my course not to be able to foresee everything, but to consign certain things entirely to his wise government; and I had promised him to do so, as confidingly as if the desired help were in my own house. Yet the exercise of this kind of faith, just then, was far from being agreeable. At this moment Jonas (Weiss) entered the room with a letter from Cornelius deLaer, enclosing a draft for 1,000 pounds; upon seeing which Hockel's tears of anguish were changed to those of joy.[3]

Hockel was the man for whom the count was prepared to go to prison. It was learned afterward that the Dutch mail, owing to favorable winds, had arrived earlier than usual. Furthermore, deLaer's remittance was unexpected, since he had previously sent a generous amount for emergencies, which had already been used. The daily watchword for that morning had been: "Say to them that are of a

---

[3] Benham, *Memoirs of James Hutton,* p. 276.

fearful heart, Be strong, fear not: behold, your God will come with vengeance, even God with a recompence; he will come and save you" (Isa. 35:4).

By such close margins the Moravians pulled through. Within the next few years the situation eased—first in England and then in Holland—though heavy debts hampered their church for a generation after the count's departure. While it was Zinzendorf's visionary outlook that brought them so close to the brink, it was this same quality that saved them. Had he become cautious—so unlike him—in the midst of trouble, his creditors would have become even more alarmed. As it turned out, the boundless faith of the man saved the day. James Hutton, who was one of the principals in the whole affair, was of the opinion that the count's decision not to abandon Lindsey House preserved the credit of the Moravians in London. In that same dark year of 1753 they went ahead with the purchase of the 100,000-acre Wachovia tract in North Carolina, site of present-day Winston-Salem. The following year they launched their mission on the island of Jamaica. In Pennsylvania brethren from Bethlehem began converting the preaching station at Warwick into the settlement congregation of Lititz. Some deserted the Brethren in their hour of need, but new friends filled the vacancies. The count's own generosity was contagious.

The time of financial distress coincided with a heightened tempo of attack from religious opponents. Hutton, in his history of the Moravians, aptly refers to the years 1749-55 as the "battle of the books." Some of it originated in England itself; some of it was imported from the Continent and translated. The fight began shortly after Zinzendorf's victory in Parliament, when he issued in book form a collection of the documentary evidence he had presented to the Parliamentary committee. This *Acta Fratrum Unitatis in Anglia* was a thoroughgoing manifesto of who the Moravians were, what they believed, and how they worshiped. It touched off a reply from John Wesley—a pamphlet which he called *Contents of a Folio History* and signed "A Lover of the Light." He argued that the Brethren were heretics and deceivers, called attention to their recent extravagant emphasis upon Christ's side wound, and urged all who had been fooled into joining the Brethren to desert them. A milder attack on the same *Acta Fratrum* was that of an anonymous writer who concluded that the Moravians were papists and that their doctrine of the Lord's Supper was little short of transubstantiation.

Another writer lumped Moravians and Methodists together in his pamphlet *Serious Objections to the Pernicious Doctrine of the Moravians and Methodists.* A more kindly man, a country curate, while paying tribute to the high moral quality of the Moravians, accused them of emptying his church and preaching unscriptural doctrines. The title ot his attack was *A Kindly and Friendly Letter to the People Called Moravians in Derbyshire.* In Dublin, in 1751, John Roche published *Moravian Heresy,* a treatise which called the Brethren antinomians. George Whitefield in his onslaught, entitled *An Expostulatory Letter to Count Zinzendorf,* took full advantage of the Moravians' financial predicament of 1753 by adding accusations of robbery and fraud to those of theological error.

Most vicious of all the attacks in that year was made by Henry Rimius in *A Candid Narrative of the Rise and Progress of the Herrnhuters,* first published in German and translated into several languages. Rimius, a former royal councilor in Prussia but then living in London, kept up his barrage for some years, with at least four other books; though he had left little unsaid in the *Candid Narrative.* Also in 1753 came forth *The True and Authentic Account of Andrew Frey,* a translation of a German autobiographical account of a former Moravian who had lived at Marienborn during the worst of the Sifting Period. The bishop of Exeter, having denounced the Methodists, in 1754 turned his guns on the Moravians in a book entitled *The Moravians Compared and Detected.* In the preface he said: "The filthy dreamers have been so evidently detected, their immoralities and impieties so manifested unto all men that their shame is sufficiently conspicuous, and no serious and good person, no sincere Christian especially can look upon them in a favorable light."

True to his long-standing policy, Zinzendorf was reluctant to reply. Frequently he answered public attacks by a personal, private letter to the author. When he did answer publicly, it was usually not in the form of direct reply but in the form of information, prepared either by himself or by his colleagues, to acquaint the general public with the Moravians. Of course, all during his career he had been forced to explain his position, and his apologetic writings were already extensive.

Spangenberg, soon after his return from America in 1749, was assigned the task of clarifying some of the distortions concerning the Brethren. In 1751 appeared, in German, his *Correct Answers to More than Three Hundred Accusations Against the Ordinary of the Breth-*

ren; and in the following year, a sequel in two volumes, *Answers to a Thousand Accusations Against the Brethren's Church and Its Ordinary.* Among statements which the Brethren aimed directly at the English public, during the count's residence in the country, were the following: *The Ordinary of the Brethren's Churches, Short and Pre-emptory Remarks on the Way and Manner wherein he has been hitherto treated in Controversies; The Plain Case of the Representatives of the Unitas Fratrum; An Exposition, or True State of the Matters objected in England to the People known by the name of Unitas Fratrum*—all three by Zinzendorf himself; *A Letter from a Minister of the Moravian Branch of the Unitas Fratrum to the Author of the* "Moravians Compared and Detected," by Frederick Neisser; *An Essay Toward Giving Some Just Ideas of the Personal Character of Count Zinzendorf,* by James Hutton; and the anonymous writings—*A Modest Plea for the Church of the Brethren* and *A Short Answer to Mr. Rimius' Long Uncandid Narrative.*

There was material other than controversial to keep the press at Lindsey House busy. A new edition of the German hymnal, with 2,368 hymns, hundreds of them by the count himself, appeared in 1753. It was followed by a thousand-hymn supplement the next year. Also in 1754 the Moravians published their first official English hymnbook, *A Collection of Hymns of the Children of God in all Ages from the Beginning till now, in two Parts.* Though most of the hymns were of German origin, there were some original English hymns in the book. Concerning the smaller number of the latter, it must be borne in mind that English hymnody was still in the stages of freeing itself from the narrow range of psalmody. Zinzendorf himself did much of the translation for this English hymnal.

During his last year in the country Zinzendorf, upon the request of his colleagues, prepared a sort of book of order entitled *Statutes or the General Principle of Practical Christianity, Extracted out of the New Testament,* designed specifically for the English congregations. At the same time he got ready for publication his London sermons, printed in 1756 in two volumes.

It is not to be concluded from the account of the financial crisis and the "battle of the books" that the Moravians were only on the defensive in England at that time. Quite the contrary. It was the time of John Cennick's meteoric career of evangelism in both England and Ireland. Fulneck in Yorkshire was developing into an English Herrnhut. On a lesser scale Ockbrock in the Midlands and Bedford in Bed-fordshire were centers from which radiated scores of societies. Mora-vians were in the thick of the evangelical revival of the eighteenth century. Not until some years after the count's death did they move to the side lines in Britain.

Yet it was Zinzendorf who, at the height of Moravian successes, set the stage for this later decline. As elsewhere, the Brethren in England were to him, even after the act of Parliament of 1749, a church within a church. The societies which his influence kept from being organized into congregations fell by the wayside; their members went into more aggressive free churches or back into the Establishment. The Moravian creative impact on the foreign-mission movement lasted longer, well into the nineteenth century.

Zinzendorf and Wesley appear to be about equally responsible for the separation between Moravians and Methodists. Though the two were together only twice, the clash between their personalities was un-doubtedly the chief factor behind their two churches going along separate courses. Each was born to rule. As one observer has put it: "Both men were aristocrats by temperament, and both were quick to detect and to resent aristocracy in others." [4] This antipathy aggravated theological differences and was conveyed to their followers.

Their first meeting was a few months after Wesley's Aldersgate ex-perience, when, full of enthusiasm for the Brethren, he visited Marien-born. His expressed admiration for what he saw conspicuously ex-cluded the count, on whom at this stage he is noncommittal. Wesley merely reports hearing Zinzendorf preach and of accompanying him to visit a neighboring German nobleman. Considering the fact that he spent ten days at Marienborn, we may conclude that the abbreviated reference to the count is deliberate.

The story has come down that the count just before the above-mentioned visit put Wesley to work in one of the Marienborn gardens. After his guest had worked up a good sweat, he summoned him to step into his carriage and accompany him on a visit to a neighbor. When Wesley asked for time to wash his hands and put on a coat, Zinzendorf is supposed to have said: "You must be simple, my brother." This unlikely story is probably a distorted interpretation of the kind of invitation the impulsive count might have extended to his guest. That such a tale is one of the items of Methodist tradition reveals

[4] Arnold Lunn, *John Wesley.*

something of the impression early Methodists had of Zinzendorf's egotism.

The other occasion when they were together, previously spoken of in connection with Zinzendorf's departure for America, was their debate at Gray's Inn Gardens in London, on September 3, 1741. By that time their differences had crystallized to the point where agreement was out of the question. It was shortly thereafter that Wesley made an entry in his journal concerning his visit to Germany three years before. From Marienborn he had gone on to Herrnhut and again was favorably impressed, expressing his desire to remain there permanently. Not until the time of the second meeting does he record the critical letter he wrote to the Herrnhuters in 1738, but which he never sent. Among the questions he asked of them is this: "Is not the count all in all? Are not the rest mere shadows; calling him Rabbi; almost implicitly both believing and obeying him?"

It had not taken that long for the fact to become evident that the Moravian Brotherhood was not roomy enough for both a Wesley and a Zinzendorf. Already in July of 1740 the former, with eighteen other members, had withdrawn from the Fetter Lane Society and joined with another society meeting in the Foundry, near Moorfields. To be sure, the count was not directly responsible for this break, but the young Philip Henry Molther, whose exaggerated emphasis upon "stillness" as an expression of salvation by faith disgusted the activist Englishman. But the shadow of the count was in the background, since Molther came to England directly from his time of conditioning at Marienborn.

Apart from the incompatibility between their leaders, it is unlikely that Moravianism and Methodism could have remained together. The one was shaped by its German background. The other, though kindled by the spark from Germany, was thoroughly English in its orientation. Traditional freedom of speech and assembly had prepared the people of the British Isles for mass revival techniques. The Methodists were ready to capitalize on it. The Moravians were not. Revivalism of that kind did not come to Germany until the rise of free churches in the mid-nineteenth century. Of the Moravians, only the English-born Cennick followed this pattern; and his career was cut short in its prime. Zinzendorf actually called the Methodist revival meetings "mobs." He cautioned his evangelists not to approach people aggressively but to let the Holy Spirit have his own way.

Both Moravianism and Methodism began as societies within the

Establishment. Moravians in a halfhearted way soon formed a denomination but still retained their status as a society. Methodism made the break later, but, when it did so, made it without reservations. The German temperament never did feel comfortable in leaving the state church. The English temperament, religiously awakened, rejoiced in vigorous nonconformity. With such difference in character an independent line of development was inevitable for each.

21

THE PILGRIM RETURNS HOME

For nearly two decades Herrnhut had been in the background, with the spotlight elsewhere on the count and his Pilgrim Congregation. But in those years its development had been steady and solid. With industries of international reputation, it was one of the bright spots in the decade of financial troubles. Nor did prosperity keep Herrnhut from its emphasis upon godliness. More than any of the Moravian settlements, Herrnhut typified what was best in Moravianism. That this should be true of the mother community of the Brotherhood must have been a source of deep satisfaction to the count.

Herrnhut, with nearby Gross-Hennersdorf and Berthelsdorf, was also home. It was a double pull which drew Zinzendorf back to Upper Lusatia, after four years of absence. However, he was still planning to travel. Only a year before he had directed Spangenberg to build a home for him in Pennsylvania. In the very weeks when he was on his way to Herrnhut, on May 3, 1755, there was the cornerstone laying of his intended manor house at Nazareth. It turned out otherwise. The count remained in Germany, and the manor house in America became Nazareth Hall, the academy. It was a combination of things which intervened. The illness and early death of the countess, his own declining health, his withdrawal from administrative affairs, the Seven Years' War—each would have been reason enough.

He did not go to Herrnhut directly after leaving London on March 22. His return took the form of a two months' tour of congregations. There was a prolonged stay at Zeist. At Neuwied he found the displaced French colony from Herrnhaag making a fine adjustment to its new home. He visited Neudietendorf and Ebersdorf. In Saxony he was pleased to see continuing results of previous awakenings among the Wends, a colony of Slavic neighbors at Kleinwelke. When he came to Niesky, he was almost home, and there the countess had gone to greet him. Together they entered Herrnhut quietly on the evening of June 2.

Had the arrival been announced in advance, his would have been a triumphal entry, judging by the joyous festivity that took place when word got around that the ordinary had come home. The men regaled him with instrumental music. The girls' choirs, dressed in white, sang hymns of welcome as he came to the evening *Singstunde*. There was a belated birthday celebration in his honor. There were love feasts among the choirs. Life quickened its tempo in Herrnhut for the joy and the awe of his presence. The count rose to the occasion. Hymns, addresses, prayers, tears, so much a part of him, were his spontaneous response.

If Zinzendorf had changed since the Herrnhuters had last seen him, it was in a way that endeared him to them. He came back, as it turned out, less the lord of the manor and more the pastor, less the ordinary and more the beloved disciple. He seemed to have learned finally that for administrative details there were men more qualified than he. At the various synods and conferences of his last years he encouraged the delegation of authority. The synod at Taubenheim, near Herrnhut, in the month after his return particularly helped matters by separating the Zinzendorf accounts from those of the church. He was more content than formerly to leave legal matters in the hands of his civil bishops, the seniores civiles, and financial matters in the hands of an administrative board. Outstanding in money matters was Frederick Köber, who in these years, and following, led the Moravian Church into a sounder system of finance. He was representative of the leaders who arose to supplement the count where he was deficient. As a result, in the area where he excelled, in the things of the spirit, Zinzendorf was at the peak of his influence during the final years allotted to him. Always kindly, he was even more so. His genius with children grew, as did his genius for heart to heart talks with individuals. In short, the count had mellowed.

Adding to the serenity of the last five years were improved relations with neighboring communities. The nobility of Upper Lusatia had overcome their resentment of Herrnhut when they experienced that Herrnhut religion, instead of making subversives of their subjects, made them into better citizens. The same nobility were now encouraging Moravian Diaspora meetings in their villages, in contrast to their former policy of forbidding all contacts. The case of Baron Huldenberg of Neukirch is a dramatic illustration of the change. It was Huldenberg's formal complaints to Dresden which had precipitated Zinzendorf's banishment in 1736. A year before that, the latter had written a friendly letter urging the baron to see for himself before judging Herrnhut. Enclosed with the letter was one of the count's religious tracts, *Concerning Christian Conversation*. The tract was returned unread, together with a sharp reply.

Came the year 1751 and a fire which destroyed all the buildings on the Huldenberg estate, except the main dwelling house, which, however, was badly damaged. Days later, salvaging among the ruins, the baron came upon Zinzendorf's letter of 1735, charred on the edges but legible. He read:

It pains me that you are suspicious of me and my dear Herrnhut. . . . Had I the honor to meet you personally, you would see that I am no lover of disorder. If you knew Herrnhut, you might even wish that your village were like it. . . . Your father and I had such a satisfactory conversation together in Prague, that it distresses me to have a misunderstanding with his son. . . . I assure you further that I am faithfully yours, Zinzendorf.[1]

This letter, which originally had only aroused Huldenberg to greater anger, under these different circumstances opened the man's eyes to the injustice he had done to his neighbor. From that moment he longed for the opportunity to make amends. Two months after Zinzendorf's return he came with his pastor to ask for the count's forgiveness. As a memento he turned over to him the charred letter. Thereafter Neukirch became a rallying point for Diaspora work, and Huldenberg one of the count's admirers.

More of the clergy than formerly were friendly, and in this period there came into being that remarkable annual gathering, the Herrnhut Ministers' Conference. Zinzendorf was not its founder, but he was a motivating force in its formative stages. It began in a very modest way at Berthelsdorf, where seven Lutheran pastors met together, on Whitsunday of 1754, "jointly to converse with each other on attending to the duties of the gospel ministry entrusted to their care in a dignified and conscientious manner." The men were the pastors Groh of Berthelsdorf, Rudolf Reichel of Neukirch, John Reichel of Taubenheim, Benade of Milkel, Michaelis of Hermsdorf, Löwe of Lower Hermsdorf, and Franz of Klix. Present also were Frederick and John von Watteville to represent the Brethren, for it was the purpose of the conference to

[1] C. W. Cröger, *Geschichte der Erneuerten Brüderkirche*, II, 223.

work with the Moravian Diaspora. Zinzendorf attended the second gathering, a year later, and two others before his death.

For 117 years, with a single interruption—in the year 1813, during the Napoleonic Wars—the Herrnhut Ministers' Conference was the rallying point for an interdenominational fellowship. Besides those in attendance, sometimes over a hundred, the conference had many corresponding members, and the reading of their letters became an important part of the proceedings. Lutherans, Reformed, Anglican, and Free Churchmen from a dozen European countries and various mission fields were thus united in a common faith. It helped to inspire the formation of such groups as the London Missionary Society in 1795, the British and Foreign Bible Society in 1804, and other local and regional societies originating in the missionary awakening of the late eighteenth and early nineteenth centuries. The tie binding these evangelicals together was the heart religion of Zinzendorf. In a sense the Herrnhut Ministers' Conference was an expression of his Congregation of God in the Spirit.

Immediately following his return to Herrnhut, Zinzendorf lived in the *Herrschaftshaus* which he and his family had first occupied upon his arrival from Dresden in 1727. While here, he gave much attention to the many visitors who attended services in the village. For this he used the choir system to advantage by having the visitors under the counsel of the particular group to which they would belong if they lived in Herrnhut. Thus the Married Brethren entertained the married men, the Single Brethren took charge of the unmarried male visitors, and so on down the line. The visits of the Wends gave the count special satisfaction, for they had been among the earliest objects of his evangelistic interest when Herrnhut began. The community also had at this time some ninety persons who understood English, a few of them from the British Isles but most of them Germans who had been with the count in England or who had been in Moravian service in America. These he invited to his home for weekly services in English, a practice which continued for about a year.

In trying to be a pastor to his people, Zinzendorf more than ever met with them in their choir groupings. The memory of Christian Renatus and his work with the Single Brethren's choir drew him closer to this group than to any of the others. The children were objects of his attention through his *Discourses to the Children, Daily Watchwords* chosen specifically for them, and a *Hymnbook for the Children*. The schools, such a prominent feature of every Moravian community, also felt the stimulation of his interest. The academy at Barby, growing in importance as a training school for ministers and missionaries, took him away from Herrnhut during October of 1755.

Returning from Barby the count transferred his residence to the manor house (Bethel) at Berthelsdorf; and in line with the terminology introduced in England, Bethel became the "Disciple House." The Pilgrim Congregation had run its course. With the beginning of 1756, the *Diarium der Hütten* (Pilgrim Diary) became the *Jüngerhaus Diarium* (Disciple House Diary). The countess was not part of the Disciple House, but remained in the *Herrshaftshaus*.

Bethel had been the place where the young count, thirty years earlier, first held forth with discourses to supplement the fervent preaching of Pastor Rothe. Just as enthusiastically, the new generation responded to the elderly count's invitation to his house services in the same place. The Herrnhuters came mostly by choirs during the week. Sunday evenings were set aside for the residents of Berthelsdorf itself. The sermons for them were later printed as *The Berthelsdorf Discourses* and had a wide circulation in Germany.

On the wider scene there was cause for anxiety. Zinzendorf's last years were lived against the background of the Seven Years' War, with the Moravian villages in Saxony and Silesia in the thick of the trouble. Herrnhut itself was the headquarters of a Prussian division. But those were not yet the days of total war, and the Brethren came through the fighting all around them remarkably well. Except for Neusalz, burned by Russian soldiers in 1759, their property for the most part remained intact. The homeless inhabitants of Neusalz found refuge in neighboring Gnadenberg. In the long run the war helped the Moravians, for the soldiers, officers, and statesmen whom it brought to their communities were impressed by these oases of peace. They were something to write home about and sights to recommend to their friends. The count went about his self-assumed duties as always, visiting freely among the congregations.

Sad news came from Pennsylvania. There at Gnadenhütten on the Mahony, twenty miles up the Lehigh from Bethlehem, the mission had been burned and ten missionaries and one child murdered by hostile Indians stirred up by whites in the intrigues of the American phase of the war. This tragedy of the evening of November 24, 1755, was announced by Zinzendorf personally to the people in Herrnhut on the following February 6. His way of turning the other cheek was to express the hope that none of the murderers would die before hearing and accepting the gospel of Jesus Christ. Shortly thereafter he sent fifteen volunteers to Pennsylvania as replacements for the martyred missionaries.

Bereavement more personal came a half year later when the countess, on June 19, 1756, finished her earthly course. Only in her fifty-sixth year, she passed on as one too weary to stay longer. On her previous birthday in November she had expressed her premonition that it would be her last. Each year since her son's death she had been able to continue her church activities only with special effort. The diary of her sister-in-law Theodora records that the anniversary of Christel's death, May 28, found her "inordinately quiet, dejected, and in deep thought." She attended the opening sessions of a synod at Berthelsdorf on June 9, though it was with obvious difficulty that she followed the proceedings. Her will power sufficed for only part of the next day, and toward evening, out of sheer exhaustion, she took to her bed in Herrnhut. In no apparent pain she lay there for ten days, sleeping most of the time. Her daughters and women of the church went in and out. There were occasional bright responses. She tried hard to effect such a mood for her husband, who visited her on June 14. She was unaware of his one other visit to her. Finally, on the early morning of June 19 she slept away.

John von Watteville carried the word to the Disciple House. The count took the news hard. There was more than grief in his sorrow, for it was an open secret that all had not been well between him and Erdmuth for the past fifteen years. Beginning with his journey to Pennsylvania in 1741, he had been away from her far more than he had been with her. They had continued to be indispensable partners in church affairs, complementing each other in a way without which the Brethren's Church could not have come into being. It was otherwise with their relationship as husband and wife. In that area their differing temperaments, instead of complementing, had erected a barrier which had grown with the years.

Frederick von Watteville, her "oldest and truest friend," announced her passing in these words to the Herrnhut congregation at morning worship in the Saal: "Our praiseworthy sister and most beloved Mama, the faithful servant and nursing mother of the congregation, has gone over into the arms of her Bridegroom." Recovering his composure, the

count two days later eulogized his helpmate before the synodal delegates in Berthelsdorf. But in this, as in previous and later tributes to
her, the emphasis was upon her place in the church rather than upon
what she had meant to him as a comrade.

Erdmuth was laid to rest on the Hutberg at eight o'clock in the
evening of June 25 in the presence of a large congregation, with Bishop
John Nitschmann, pastor of Herrnhut, in charge of the interment.
Her husband was not present, having gone to be alone at Gross-
Hennersdorf. To Spangenberg in America he wrote later:

She lies there on the Hutberg, just where the pastor stands on Easter
morning. During her burial I was at the Catherine Manor House in Hennersdorf and in my room, overlooking the God's Acre [at Hennersdorf not
the Hutberg], facing a glorious sunset, I could in spirit help bury her.[2]

Whatever may have been his emotions concerning Erdmuth, Zinzendorf went through a year of strain following her death. He moved about
considerably, spending only about half his time, during broken intervals, at Berthelsdorf, Hennersdorf, and Herrnhut. Between times he
visited the nearby congregations, especially Barby, and the more distant Ebersdorf in central Germany. Yet it was a year of much seclu-
sion, for he withdrew to the privacy of his room wherever he happened
to be. One of his retreats was an attic room in the Diaspora House at
Herrnhut, and "not twenty of the thousand residents were aware of
it," as he wrote to Spangenberg. Unlike formerly, his was no longer
creative solitude. There were periods of listless inaction followed by
whole nights of exhausting efforts to catch up on unfinished tasks.

The blunt truth is that the count's sorrow was aggravated by re-
morse. He had not been fair to Erdmuth. Cynics to the contrary, he
had not been unfaithful to her during their long periods of separation; but he had been extremely thoughtless. He had forgotten that she
was a woman, a wife, and a mother. Anna Nitschmann, eldress of the
Brotherhood, had long usurped Erdmuth's rightful place as his companion. He had been so naïve and so blind as to believe that Erdmuth
approved. He had even placed on her the burden of the decision that
Anna become his second wife, should Erdmuth precede him in death,
claiming that she had suggested it in London as he was leaving for

[2] *Ibid.*, p. 239.

Pennsylvania in 1741. Now that she was gone, what he saw in retrospect hurt. This is probably what Spangenberg means when he says:

The Count now reflected, how he might best profit by the circumstances in which God had placed him by calling away his consort. He set apart a certain time to survey, in the presence of the Saviour, the thirty-four years which he had spent in the marriage-state. The Divine favor which he had experienced during this period caused him deep abasement. But he was still more grieved by the faults which he detected in himself: for although he felt conscious of having lived in the marriage-state with all fidelity, yet he was not, on that account, satisfied with himself, because he thought he had not attained to many things, which might reasonably be expected from one who conforms himself in this state of life to the mind of Chirst. He lamented over this with many tears, in the presence of the Saviour, and requested his full forgiveness.[3]

Yet Anna attracted him as strongly as ever, and he was determined to marry her, despite his underlying feeling of guilt. His uneasiness with respect to Anna and himself came from another direction also. He was a count, and all of his religious activities had not erased that fact. Anna was a peasant woman. His aged mother was still living. There were other titled relatives. The nobility had been his patrons. It had been one thing to defy convention by entering the ministry. It was quite another thing to do so in order to marry a peasant. What would be the effect of such a move upon his supporters? Within the Brotherhood itself?

The decision to carry out a plan conceived fifteen years before was made easier by having someone else take the responsibility. On May 10, 1757, John von Watteville called together in special session at Herrnhut the inner circle of the church family. Present were Watteville; his wife, Benigna; Henry von Reuss; the widowed Agnes von Promnitz; Abraham von Gersdorf; John Nitschmann, Jr. (Anna's brother); David Nitschmann the syndic; Pastor Layritz of Herrnhut; Leonard Dober; Carl von Peistel; and Jonas Paulus Weiss. Watteville went on to explain how much the Married People's choir needed the count. Said he: "Almost a year has passed since our blessed Mama's homegoing. We all wish that Papa might again become part of our choir. Things would be better. And we can think of no one else than

[3] Spangenberg, *Leben Zinzendorfs*, tr. Jackson, p. 462.

the *Jüngerin* [Anna]." The others echoed the sentiment, and Watteville was delegated to inform the count of the conference's "unanimous" decision.

A week after the expiration of the year of mourning, on June 27, 1757, the count and Anna were married in the Disciple House at Berthelsdorf in a simple late-afternoon ceremony. The eleven witnesses seated themselves around a red table to await the bridal pair. When the two entered, the count began with an address, explaining that the countess and he, in the best interests of the church, had agreed upon this marriage in 1741. Abraham von Gersdorf, as chancellor, then executed the legal contract. They exchanged rings. Bishop Leonard Dober joined their right hands and pronounced them man and wife. The count was fifty-seven, Anna forty-two.

ANNA NITSCHMANN

All were pledged to secrecy. The one excuse was personal. John Nitschmann in his diary said, "because his mother was still living and he did not know what she would say." Only the day before the ceremony, Benigna, with Weiss and his wife, had been sent to visit Lady Natzmer in Berlin, "so that if she asked any questions, they would not have any information." The other excuse was that Anna had unfinished duties with the Single Sisters' choir.

It was a secret amazingly well kept, leaking to few outside the inner circle during the year and a half before the count announced the marriage from Zeist, in a lengthy letter of explanation to the churches, on November 10, 1758. That he and Anna should have been able to live undetected as man and wife for so long reveals how far removed from the rank and file of the Brethren was the count's private life, even when he was close to them as spiritual adviser. It reveals even more how much family life took second place among eighteenth-century Moravians, from their leader on down.

Also, the secret was easy to keep because much of the couple's time was spent in making the rounds of the congregations, something they had been doing for years before they were man and wife. Two months after their marriage they were on their way, assuming again the role of pilgrims. In September, with John von Watteville and Benigna, daughter Elizabeth, and others, they set out upon a tour of western Germany and Switzerland in the familiar Zinzendorf style. One of the first stops was at Marienborn, where a nucleus of Brethren still remained at their posts. Here the count preached to those who had gathered from the surrounding area, a task which could not have been easy amid reminders of Wetteravia's brief period of success and disaster.

He drew large audiences in Basel, Montmirail, Geneva, and Lausanne. Among the French-speaking Swiss he preached either in German or directly in French, depending upon whether a competent interpreter was available. Though facile in either language, he preferred his native tongue for religious subjects. His reception in Switzerland was friendlier than at any time in his tours through the area, but less so in Württemberg. Only after his death did the theologians in the latter state come to appreciate him and his Brethren.

The strain of travel in the raw weather of late fall was too much for the count, and a month's illness delayed him at Ebersdorf on the return home. However, as Spangenberg commented concerning one of his other illnesses, he did more work when indisposed than most men do when they are well. His pen was active, and even before his recovery he was preaching again. He returned to Herrnhut at the end of January, the tour having stretched out to five months.

Despite continuing ill health Zinzendorf was not content to confine his work to the Upper Lusatia area for long. In mid-July of 1758 he and Anna left Herrnhut again, this time to be gone a year and a half. Kleinwelke, Barby, Zeist, Neuwied, and especially Herrendyk were their principal quarters during this time. Herrendyk had been superseded by Zeist as the center of the Brethren's work in Holland and was practically deserted. Close enough to Zeist for him to meet with his followers frequently, it still afforded the ailing count the kind of privacy he needed. In this way he managed to continue his prodigious labors.

Missions were the special object of his attention. At Herrendyk he briefed many of the Brethren in their duties as ambassadors of Christ as they left from there or from Zeist for Greenland, the American colonies, the West Indies, Surinam, Tranquebar, Abyssinia, the Near East. It was in these months that he gave expression to some of his finest mission theory. It was simple enough: "A missionary seeks nothing else day and night that the heathen find joy in their Saviour, and that the Saviour find joy in the heathen." During the count's residence in the area, Samuel Lieberkühn, former Moravian evangelist to the Jews in Amsterdam, was the pastor at Zeist. The affection which many of the Jews had for him drew them in large numbers to the settlement to hear his preaching. It was a mission project close to the count's heart, though no permanent fruit seems to have come of it.

There were reminders of younger, more vigorous days, when for part of the time Zinzendorf held three daily services at Herrendyk for his house congregation. The first service consisted of a New Testament study; the second was a song service; and the third was centered around the thought of the daily watchword. The year in Holland was one worthy of the count's career.

His time was running out, and he seemed to sense that his final summons was not far off. When in November of 1759 he turned his feet in the direction of Upper Lusatia again, was he thinking of what he had said to his son-in-law upon the death of Erdmuth? "No one departs before the Lord wills it, and when the loss can be endured. I shall also depart—and there will be improvement. . . ." But whether the count was aware of it or not, Providence was taking him to the one most fitting place to finish his course. He and Herrnhut belonged to each other. Its environs lent dignity to his actions. He, in turn, by his presence there during his last years and by dying there, restored the community of his first love to its deserved place of pre-eminence in Moravian affairs.

Christmas Eve was a good time to come home. It meant singing with the children at their vigils in the new church and sharing with them the bright warmth of their beeswax candles. Verses in praise of the Christ child poured spontaneously from the man whose heart was still that of a child.

During the following months the count, from his home in the *Herrschaftshaus,* lived with his people as a pastor seeking to set his congregation in order before taking leave. There were almost daily conferences with elders, choir leaders, teachers, missionaries. He had the Brethren in for Wednesday and Saturday love feasts in his own household chapel. There he presented his verses to those who had birthdays. He read letters from their colleagues in scattered places. He reminisced of God's dealings with the Brotherhood, but in his visions and plans for the future he was still the dreamer.

On Good Friday, April 5, he partook of Communion with the Herrnhut members. On Easter Monday he preached to a congregation of visitors from neighboring communities. That same week he conferred with a delegation of Lutheran pastors. Meanwhile he was working on what was to be his last task, the *Daily Watchwords and Doctrinal Texts* for the year 1761. Toward the end of the month he began showing symptoms of catarrhal fever. He pushed himself that much harder to finish his assignment.

Anna's time was also running out. Months before, she had been stricken with a painful illness, probably cancer. Bedridden much of the time, she had with difficulty attended the festival service of the Single Sisters' choir along with the count, on Sunday, May 4. It was their final appearance together, for she was unable to leave her bed thereafter. The day following was his last out of bed. Monday was the time of the week which he had set aside for the revision of his discourses, and he occupied himself with that during the forenoon. He went to the table for luncheon but ate little, complaining of thirst. That afternoon he composed an ode of thirty-six stanzas for the Single Sisters and attended their love feast. Then he visited Anna and retired.

In bed he continued working and receiving visitors until the very end, four days later. Speech was difficult, but there were moments of intimate conversation between him and his old schoolmate Frederick von Watteville, who had stood with him through the years. There was fatherly advice for his daughters. To all of the considerable company which had access to the sickroom he conveyed the peace which a man of God was experiencing in his final hours. Anna lay dying in another room.

The day before the end was his brightest. With his secretary he made the final corrections of the *Watchwords*. To David Nitschmann, who had been among his earliest associates, he said:

Did you suppose, in the beginning, that the Saviour would do as much as we now really see, in the various Moravians settlements, amongst the chil-

Des

Seligen ORDINARII
FRATRUM

Valet-Segen

enthaltend
der extrahirten Samlung
der

Loosungen

der

Brüder-Gemeinen
Tom. II.

Der zum Schluß dieser seiner
drey und dreißig jährigen Arbeit

Von Ihm selbst
noch ausgefertiget worden ist

auf das Jahr

1 7 6 1.

Gedrukt zu Barby 1760.

TITLE PAGE OF MORAVIAN DAILY TEXTS FOR 1761

"The valedictory of the blessed Ordinary of the Brethren, comprising the extracted Watchwords of the Brethren's congregations. Vol.
II, which at the conclusion of this his thirty-three-year task he was
yet able to complete himself for the year 1761. Printed at Barby 1760."

dren of God of other denominations, and amongst the heathen? I only en-
treated of him a few of the firstfruits of the latter, but there are now thousands of them. Nitschmann, what a formidable caravan from our church
already stands around the Lamb! [4]

Well into the night he continued reviewing the affairs of the Brethren. At midnight a coughing spasm deprived him of speech. Toward
nine o'clock in the morning he could talk again and he asked for his
son-in-law. Watteville came and strained to hear: "My dear John, I am
about to go to the Saviour. I am ready. I am resigned to his will, and
he is satisfied with me. If he does not want to use me I am ready to go
to him. Nothing more stands in my way."

The words became unintelligible. He motioned to Nitschmann for
pencil and paper. It was no use. The power to communicate had gone.
Not quite. There was still a benediction in his eyes for those in the
room. It was ten o'clock when he closed his eyes and laid his head back
on the pillow. Watteville began praying: "Lord, now lettest thou thy
servant depart in peace. The Lord bless thee, and keep thee: the Lord
make his face shine upon thee, and be gracious unto thee: the Lord
lift up his countenance upon thee, and give thee peace." At the word
"peace" Count Zinzendorf breathed his last. It was his finest hour. The
day was May 9, 1760.

The mist enshrouding Herrnhut that morning had changed to rain
by the time the trombones announced the death an hour later. Watteville took the news to Anna and found her sustained by her own illness.
"I have the happiest prospect of you all," said she. "I will soon be
going to him." The next day they carried her to see him and allowed
her time to weep alone beside him. All that day his body, clad in the
white surplice worn in administering the Sacraments, lay in state in its
purple coffin in the salon of the *Herrschaftshaus*. The villagers did their
viewing by choirs. Toward evening the casket was closed and remained
so during the week before the funeral. Meanwhile the Brethren continued their day-and-night vigil beside it.

All during the day of the burial there was a second viewing in the
church. While the organ played and other instruments accompanied
from time to time, men and women from all walks, the mighty and
lowly, took a final look at the count. At five o'clock the body was

[4] *Ibid.*, p. 502.

taken from the church to the square, and Pastor Nitschmann led in singing of chorales. The trombones announced the start of the procession to the Hutberg. Following the old custom of the Bohemian Brethren, singing school children walked ahead. Then followed the musicians playing antiphonally with another group previously stationed on God's Acre. Behind the musicians were more children. Next were the daughters Benigna, Agnes, and Elizabeth, escorted by members of the women's choirs. Nitschmann and the two Wattevilles, both of them bishops, walked just ahead of the coffin. Thirty-two other ministers were pallbearers, alternating in two groups of sixteen. Two thousand of the brethren and sisters from Herrnhut and nearby congregations followed in their choir groupings. There were another two thousand friends and curious from outside the Brotherhood in the background. A detachment of imperial grenadiers from Zittau was on hand to maintain order if necessary. Anna followed the ceremony from a window in the Sisters' house.

They buried him beside the countess, the minister saying: "With tears we sow this seed in the earth; but he, in his own good time, will bring it to life, and will gather in his harvest with thanks and praise! Let all who wish for this say, Amen."

ZINZENDORF BURIAL PLOT ON THE HUTBERG

The congregation made it response. There were more chorales, the remainder of the liturgy, the benediction. Reverently they returned to the village. It was the closing scene of a great chapter in the story of the Renewed Moravian Church.

Anna survived her husband only thirteen days. There are eight graves in the Zinzendorf family plot in the center of the Hutberg. Over the count's grave, between those of Erdmuth and Anna, are these words:

Here lie the remains of that unforgettable man of God, Nicolaus Ludwig Count and Lord of Zinzendorf and Pottendorf. Through God's grace and his own faithful and untiring service he became the honored Ordinary of the Brethren's Unity, renewed in this eighteenth century. He was born at Dresden on May 26, 1700, and entered into the joy of his Lord on May 9, 1760. He was destined to bring forth fruit, fruit that should remain.

INDEX